Pro SQL Server 2008 Mirroring

Robert L. Davis, Ken Simmons

Pro SQL Server 2008 Mirroring

ISBN-13 (pbk): 978-1-4302-2423-5

ISBN-13 (electronic): 978-1-4302-2424-2

Lead Editor: Jonathan Gennick
Technical Reviewer: Glenn Berry
Editorial Board: Clay Andres, Steve Anglin, Mark Beckner, Ewan Buckingham, Tony Campbell, Gary Cornell, Jonathan Gennick, Jonathan Hassell, Michelle Lowman, Matthew Moodie, Jeffrey Pepper, Frank Pohlmann, Douglas Pundick, Ben Renow-Clarke, Dominic Shakeshaft, Matt Wade, Tom Welsh
Project Manager: Kylie Johnston
Copy Editor: Hastings Hart
Compositor: Mary Sudul
Indexer: Julie Grady
Artist: April Milne

Distributed to the book trade worldwide by Springer-Verlag New York, Inc., 233 Spring Street, 6th Floor, New York, NY 10013. Phone 1-800-SPRINGER, fax 201-348-4505, e-mail orders-ny@springer-sbm.com, or visit http://www.springeronline.com.

For information on translations, please contact Apress directly at 233 Spring Street, New York, NY 10013. E-mail info@apress.com, or visit http://www.apress.com.

Apress and friends of ED books may be purchased in bulk for academic, corporate, or promotional use. eBook versions and licenses are also available for most titles. For more information, reference our Special Bulk Sales–eBook Licensing web page at http://www.apress.com/info/bulksales.

The source code for this book is available to readers at http://www.apress.com.

Contents at a Glance

Contents

About the Authors

 **Ken Simmons** is a database administrator and developer specializing in SQL Server and .NET. He is a co-author of *Pro SQL Server 2008 Administration* (Apress, 2009). He has been working in the IT industry since 2000 and currently holds certifications for MCP, MCAD, MCSD, MCDBA, and MCTS for SQL 2005.

Ken is active in the online community and often participates in the SQL forums on MSDN and SQLServerCentral.com. He enjoys sharing tips by writing articles for SQLServerCentral.com and MSSQLTips.com. When he is not working, Ken enjoys traveling with his wife Susan and son Nathan, and he can often be found on a cruise ship, at a Disney resort, or at the beach in his hometown of Pensacola, Florida.

Robert L. Davis is a database administrator and data architect consulting at Microsoft who has worked extensively in setting up and creating automated processes to manage database mirroring for many internal Microsoft applications. He additionally consults with various internal Microsoft IT groups to assist them with their database mirroring needs. Robert is currently working on the Architecture & Performance Engineering team of the CAP application program group. CAP is the internal software used by support personnel for all of Microsoft's customer-facing products such as Xbox, Zune, MSN, Windows Live, and Hotmail. He has over eight years of SQL Server administration experience, much of that in high-availability environments. Rob writes frequently about mirroring and related topics in his blog at `http://www.sqlservercentral.com/blogs/robert_davis/default.aspx`.

About the Technical Reviewer

 **Glenn Berry** works as a Database Architect at NewsGator Technologies in Denver, CO. He is a SQL Server MVP, and he has a whole collection of Microsoft certifications, including MCITP, MCDBA, MCSE, MCSD, MCAD, and MCTS, which proves that he likes to take tests. He is also an Adjunct Faculty member at University of Denver University College, where he has been teaching since 2000.

Introduction

Pro SQL Server 2008 Mirroring is your complete guide to planning, using, deploying, and maintaining database mirroring as a high-availability option. Mirroring protects you by maintaining one or more duplicate copies of your database for use in the event the primary copy is damaged. It is a key component of any production-level, high-availability solution. This book covers the full spectrum of database mirroring, taking you from the planning phase through the implementation to the maintenance phase and beyond.

Who This Book Is For

Pro SQL Server 2008 Mirroring is aimed at SQL Server 2008 database administrators and especially at those who desire to mirror their databases in support of high availability. System administrators and operational engineers who manage Windows Server systems that support mirrored database environments will also find much of interest in the book.

How This Book Is Structured

This book walks you through the basic configuration of database mirroring to the advanced topics you should know after it is implemented.

- Chapter 1 compares database mirroring with other high-availability techniques and even provides a sample plan that combines multiple high-availability techniques.
- Chapter 2 provides you an overview of database mirroring, including the different types of implementation and the new features offered in SQL Server 2008.
- Chapter 3 gives you the knowledge you need during the planning phase of database mirroring, providing you with some best-practice techniques you should know before deploying database mirroring.
- Chapter 4 covers the basic setup of database mirroring using the database mirroring wizard and also provides step-by-step instructions to set up database mirroring using T-SQL.
- Chapter 5 provides you the scripts you need in order to quickly automate database mirroring setup for several databases at once in order to avoid the time-consuming process of configuring database mirroring on a single database at a time.
- Chapter 6 provides you the maintenance scripts you need to run on your database mirroring servers in order to keep them running smoothly.
- Chapter 7 covers the various techniques you need to know in order to monitor database mirroring and to alert you when certain unwanted conditions arise.
- Chapter 8 walks you through the steps to perform a successful database mirroring upgrade including pre- and post-upgrade considerations.

- Chapter 9 covers the various reporting options you have with database mirroring by taking advantage of database snapshots, log shipping, and replication.
- Chapter 10 stresses the importance of knowing how your database mirroring configuration will react to different types of failures and what you should do to be prepared for them.

Prerequisites

Database mirroring was introduced in SQL Server 2005 but wasn't officially supported until Service Pack 1. You can run database mirroring in the original release, but you will need to set a trace flag. In order to run the samples in this book however, we recommend running SQL Server 2005 Service Pack 1 or greater, and if at all possible Service Pack 3. However, in order to take advantage of all of the latest features, you will need to be running SQL Server 2008.

Downloading the Code

You can download the source code for the book on the Apress web site in the Source Code section at http://www.apress.com/book/sourcecode. All of the T-SQL code will be in .sql files prefaced with the name of the stored procedures used in the book. There will be one PowerShell script with a .ps1 extension.

The sample databases are no longer provided as a part of the SQL Server 2008 installation. If you want to download a set of sample databases you can use for testing purposes, they can be found on the CodePlex website at http://www.codeplex.com/MSFTDBProdSamples. You will want to download the SQL Server 2008 Product Sample Databases from this web site and follow the installation instructions.

Contacting the Authors

You can contact Ken Simmons by e-mailing him at cyberjunkyks@yahoo.com, or you can visit his blog at http://cybersql.blogspot.com. There will be a tag on his blog called "Pro SQL Server 2008 Mirroring" you can use to filter posts that are directly related to the book. Please include the book title in any e-mails to help identify questions or comments about the book.

CHAPTER 1

High-Availability Options

Database mirroring is one of several high-availability practices or solutions that you can apply in your SQL Server environment. The term *high availability* refers to the building of fault-tolerant systems to maximize uptime. System failures are going to happen. High availability enables a system to recover from these failures and cover them up from the outside world.

The first step in choosing a high-availability solution for your system is to understand the options available to you. The four options generally employed for high availability are:

- Database mirroring
- Failover clustering
- Log shipping
- Replication

While this book is about mirroring specifically, you should have some idea of the other options. And you should know when to choose mirroring, which is to say that you should be aware of what requirements trigger mirroring as a solution. In addition, you will see that database mirroring works well with other high-availability options to provide even more fault tolerance, leading to maximum uptime for your applications.

High Availability vs. Disaster Recovery

Before we discuss the different high-availability solutions, it is important to understand the difference between high availability and disaster recovery. The terms *high availability* and *disaster recovery* are often confused or thought of as the same thing. Just because you have implemented a high-availability solution does not mean that you are prepared for a disaster. High availability generally covers hardware- or system-related failures, while disaster recovery (DR) covers you in the event of a catastrophic failure due to environmental factors. In many cases, database mirroring provides both high availability and disaster recovery by offering a second copy of the database that can be available to your users in a matter of seconds. While some of the high-availability options may help you when designing your DR strategy, there is not one single solution that works for everyone.

The goal of high availability is to provide an uninterrupted user experience with zero data loss, but high availability can have many different meanings depending on who you ask. According to Microsoft, "A high-availability solution masks the effects of a hardware or software failure and maintains the availability of applications so that the perceived downtime for users is minimized."[1] Many times users will say they need 100 percent availability, but what does 100 percent availability actually mean to the user? Does being 100 percent available mean that the data is 100 percent available during business hours or does it mean the data is available 24x7 Monday through Friday? High availability is about setting expectations and then living up to them. That's why one of the most important things to do when dealing with high availability is to define the expectations in a service level agreement (SLA) that can be agreed upon and signed by all parties involved.

---

[1] http://msdn.microsoft.com/en-us/library/bb522583.aspx

Some of the things you should cover in the SLA are maintenance windows, the amount of recovery time allowed to bring the system back online due to a catastrophic failure, and the amount of acceptable data loss, if any. Defining a maintenance window allows you to apply service packs, patches, and upgrades to the system to ensure optimal performance and maintain compliance. Having a maintenance window allows you to do this in a tested and planned fashion. A drop-dead time should be determined so that a back-out plan can be executed if problems are encountered, ensuring system availability by the end of the maintenance window.

Defining the amount of time allowed to recover from a disaster along with the maximum allowed data loss will help you determine what techniques you may need to use to ensure that your SLAs are met. Every organization wants 100 percent availability 100 percent of the time, but when presented with the cost of a system that would even come close to achieving this goal, they are usually willing to negotiate attainable terms. It is important to have an understanding of what it means for a system to be unavailable. Is it a minor inconvenience because users within your organization will not be able to log their time, or are you losing thousands of dollars in revenue every hour the system is down? Answering these kinds of questions will allow you to justify the cost of an appropriate solution. Each high-availability method brings unique characteristics to the table, and unfortunately there is no cookie-cutter solution. In the next few sections, we will discuss the individual techniques used to meet your high-availability needs.

Database Mirroring

Database mirroring protects at the database level. You maintain a mirror, or copy, of the live database on a separate instance of SQL Server (preferably on a separate machine). As transactions occur on the live database, the primary instance copies those transactions to the mirror database. The live database will fail over to the mirror if the live database becomes unavailable due to failure of the server, the live instance, or the database itself.

You are required to keep the mirror database in a restoring state, which means it is not available for incoming requests. However, you can create a database snapshot of the mirror database, which provides a point-in-time, read-only view of the database.

Database mirroring offers the following advantages and benefits:

- Protection against database failures
- Automatic failure detection and failover
- Support of easy manual failover
- Automatic client redirection
- Multiple operating modes
- No special hardware requirements
- Minimized chance of data loss
- No single point of failure
- Relatively ease of set up and configuration

Database mirroring is highly configurable and easy to work with. It can operate in synchronous or asynchronous modes, sometimes called high-safety and high-performance modes, respectively. It can operate with or without a witness server, and it can be configured for automatic or manual-only failover. We will provide a more detailed overview of the mechanics of database mirroring in Chapter 2.

Failover Clustering

Failover clustering protects an entire instance of SQL Server, whereas database mirroring only protects an individual database. You can cluster two or more identical SQL Server instances together using Microsoft Cluster Service (MSCS). The SQL Server instances share common resources such as a connected disk subsystem, usually a SAN (storage area network.) This cluster of servers presents itself as a single machine on the network. In a failover cluster, one server acts as the active node, or owner of the resources, while the other nodes are waiting to take ownership of those resources. If a non-disk failure occurs on the active node, another node takes over as the active node. The failover occurs behind the scene, and clients that get disconnected are able to reconnect to the new active node almost immediately. Figure 1-1 shows a typical two-node active/passive cluster configuration.

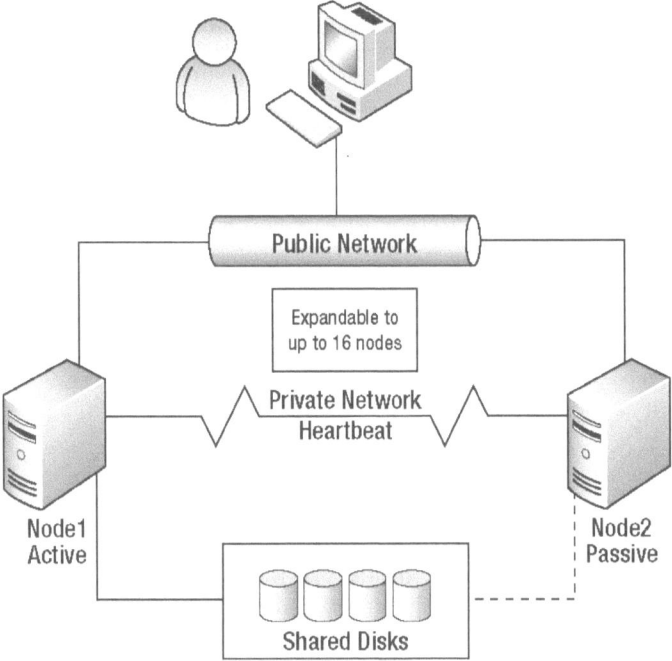

Figure 1-1. Typical two-node active/passive cluster configuration

Clustering offers the following benefits:

- Automatic failure detection and failover
- Easy manual failover
- Automatic client redirection
- Support for more than two nodes
- Protection against failures of the entire SQL Server instance

Database mirroring is a less expensive high-availability solution compared to clustering from a hardware perspective. It has less stringent hardware requirements than failover clustering has. You can implement mirroring with any hardware that fulfills your requirements. Failover clustering requires identical hardware for all nodes and must be certified for Windows clustering and purchased together as a cluster group. You do however incur the cost of the additional disk space required to store two copies of the database when using database mirroring. If your database is small, the additional disk space is not really an issue, but if you are storing terabytes of data, storing an extra copy of the database could get rather expensive. If disk space is not an issue, having a duplicate copy of the database makes database mirroring a far better solution than failover clustering when you are worried about disaster recovery and disk failure. SQL Server 2008 even includes a new feature in database mirroring that will repair corrupt data pages by copying them from the partner once the corruption has been detected.

Database mirroring is easier to set up and maintain. Failover clustering requires in-depth knowledge of Windows Server as well as of SQL Server. Mirroring requires no special knowledge of Windows Server. You can set up a mirrored database by simply following a single wizard.

Clustering has a big weak spot. It requires that all nodes share a single copy of the database files. Only having a single copy of the database files presents a single point of failure for a clustered solution. If the database is lost or corrupted, usually due to disk failure, the entire cluster is down. Database mirroring maintains a synchronized copy of the database on the mirror server. If you lose one database, the other database can take over handling requests. One of the downsides of database mirroring compared to failover clustering is that since you are only mirroring a single database, you must make sure that any external data needed by the mirror database is also copied to the mirror server. For example, you need to copy logins from the `master` database to the `master` database on the mirror server and make sure you have any jobs on the mirror server that are needed by the mirror database.

With database mirroring, you can create database snapshots of the mirror partner for read-only queries. This gives you the ability to offload ad hoc queries; extract, transform, and load (ETL) processes; and reporting queries to the mirror server. The databases are unavailable for any purposes on the inactive nodes of a clustered server.

Failover clustering requires Enterprise or Standard editions of SQL Server and Enterprise, Datacenter, or Itanium editions of Windows Server. Database mirroring operates on Enterprise or Standard editions of SQL Server and on any Windows operating system that supports SQL Server.

Log Shipping

Log shipping is similar to database mirroring in the respect that it applies transactions from the live server instance to a copy of the database on another server instance. Log shipping applies the transactions in batches in regularly scheduled intervals, whereas database mirroring applies the transactions in near real time. Early on, we often referred to database mirroring as real-time log shipping. Log shipping falls under the category of a warm failover solution. Log shipping does not support automatic failover, and there are several steps required to complete a switch to the standby server. You can see a typical log-shipping configuration in Figure 1-2.

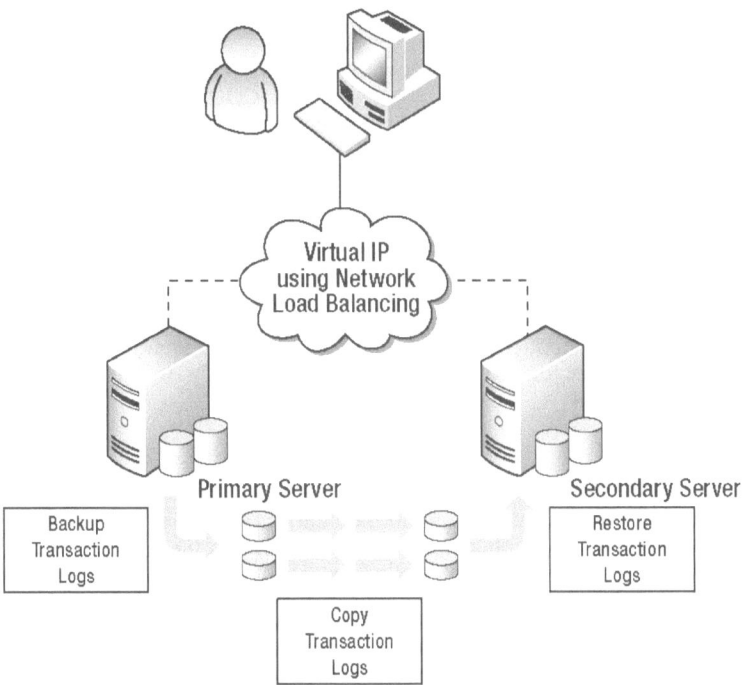

Figure 1-2. Typical log-shipping configuration

Benefits of log shipping include:

- Is simple to set up and maintain
- Supports multiple standby databases
- Supports bulk-logged and full recovery models
- Allows a defined delay for added protection against user error
- Allows use of standby databases for read-only queries
- Is available in Standard or Workgroup editions

Log shipping operates on a schedule. The most common configuration for log shipping is to run the log backup, copy, and restore jobs every 15 or 30 minutes. Another common frequency for the log-shipping jobs is every five minutes. Even if you set the minimum schedule to run every minute, you will still be at least a few minutes behind. For many production systems a few minutes of data loss may not be acceptable. With database mirroring, data transfers to the mirror database continuously. Data propagates on a per-transaction basis in near real time. If you run mirroring in high-safety mode, the principal server does not commit a transaction until it receives confirmation that the transaction was committed on the mirror database.

Due to the near real-time processing of transactions, database mirroring has a much lower chance of data loss in the event of a complete failure. With database mirroring and log shipping, data loss occurs when you force service on the mirror or standby partner without it being in a synchronized state. Log shipping has a much higher degree of data loss because it updates the standby database in batches at set intervals. However, there is an advantage log shipping provides by being able to set the intervals in which to apply the logs. For example, if you set a log delay for two hours, if someone drops a table on the primary server, you have two hours to find out and get the data from the secondary server before the changes are applied.

The standby database in a log-shipping partnership remains offline in a recovering state until you manually break log shipping and bring the database online. Failing over to the standby database is a multistep manual operation. Database mirroring supports automatic and manual failover. You can fail over a mirrored database by issuing a single T-SQL command on either partner. When running in full-safety mode with a witness server, mirroring will automatically respond to a failure and fail over to the mirror partner.

Database mirroring supports role switching between the partners. Whether the failover was automatic or manual, the mirror partner becomes the principal and the principal becomes the mirror. After failover completes, the new principal synchronizes its transactions to the new mirror. When a log-shipped database fails over, log shipping is broken, and the new live database does not synchronize to the old live database.

The failover partner connection string attribute enables client connections to automatically redirect to the defined failover partner if the defined principal partner is offline or unavailable. The failover partner attribute only works if the databases are in a mirroring partnership. It will not redirect to a standby database of a log-shipped database.

Replication

You will most often elect to use replication for workload distribution and for scalability purposes; however, it is a viable availability resource. With replication, you can temporarily point your client applications to another server that continues to serve data while you take another server offline for maintenance. In the event of unscheduled downtime, replication allows some users to stay online.

Replication is a publisher/subscriber model and has multiple topologies. Replication maintains copies of the publisher in one or more subscribers. All subscribers are online and able to process requests. The most common form of replication used for high availability is transactional replication. You can see a typical transactional replication configuration in Figure 1-3.

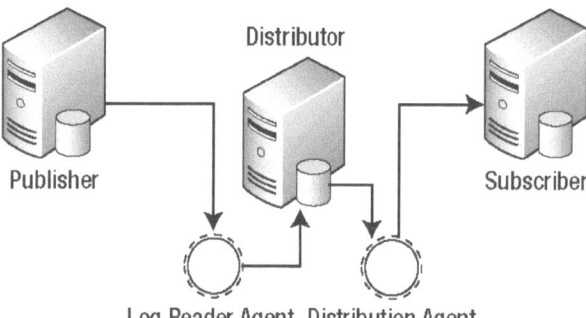

Figure 1-3. *Typical transactional replication configuration*

Here are some of the key benefits of replication:

- Supports multiple subscribers
- Allows subscribers to be read-only or read-write
- Allows data synchronization to be one-directional or bi-directional
- Supports non-SQL Server partners
- Allows for synchronization at the object level
- Is available with all editions of SQL Server

Database mirroring has much lower management overhead than replication. You can consume a considerable amount of resources maintaining the data processes to manage replication. You should consider using replication if you need it for workload distribution or scalability. The management overhead of replication is too great to consider using it for just high availability.

Comparing High-Availability Features

You can use Table 3-1 as a quick reference guide when choosing a high-availability solution. Once you have gathered all of the requirements for your system, choosing the right solution should be easy. You will see that database mirroring turns up as the best choice more times than not. This is because database mirroring provides the best of both worlds when it comes to high availability and disaster recovery. For example, let's say your requirements call for zero data loss. Well, that narrows your options down to failover clustering and high-safety mirroring. Now, if your requirements call for protection against disk failure, your only option is high-safety mirroring.

Sometimes the best solution is a combination of high-availability techniques. You can find out more about combining high-availability techniques in the SQL Server Books Online web site under "high availability: interoperability and coexistence."

Table 1-1. High-Availability Feature Comparison

Feature	Failover Clustering	Mirroring (High Safety)	Mirroring (High Performance)	Log Shipping	Replication
Instance-level protection	Yes	No	No	No	No
Duplicate copy of database	No	Yes	Yes	Yes	Yes
User error protection	No	No	No	Yes	No
Reporting capabilities	No	Yes	Yes	Yes	Yes
Automatic failover	Yes	Yes	No	No	No
Zero data loss	Yes	Yes	No	No	No
Distance limitations	Yes	No	No	No	No
Requires special hardware	Yes	No	No	No	No
Protects against disk failure	No	Yes	Yes	Yes	Yes

Designing a Complete High-Availability Solution

The elements of disaster recovery and high availability overlap in many areas. When you design your high-availability solution, you may want to consider your disaster recovery plan at the same time. High availability does not have to be limited to a single method, and disaster recovery should not be limited to database backups alone.

Database mirroring has built-in compatibility with other availability solutions. You can combine mirroring with all of the other availability solutions. You can configure mirroring to account for cluster failovers so that a mirror failover only occurs in the event the entire cluster fails. Replication and mirroring can combine to add failover support to the replication publisher. If a mirrored publisher fails, the mirror automatically takes over serving as the replication publisher.

If you are designing a solution for a mission-critical database system, your solution should include the following levels:

1. Primary high-availability solutions
    a. Failover clustering
    b. Database mirroring
2. Secondary high-availability or primary disaster recovery solutions
    a. Log shipping
    b. Replication
3. Fail-safe disaster recovery solutions
    a. Backup
    b. Restore

Following is an example of a complete data mitigation plan.

Primary High Availability: Our first-line availability option will be a two-node failover cluster. If the active node of the cluster fails, the inactive node will take over. Secondary to clustering will be database mirroring. We will configure mirroring with a 30-second partner timeout to allow time for a cluster failover to occur. If the cluster has not failed over within the partner timeout or if the entire cluster fails, mirroring will fail over to the mirror partner. You should make sure to set your database mirroring timeout high enough so you feel comfortable that you will allow your cluster time to failover before database mirroring begins to failover. You can see how this configuration would look in Figure 1-4.

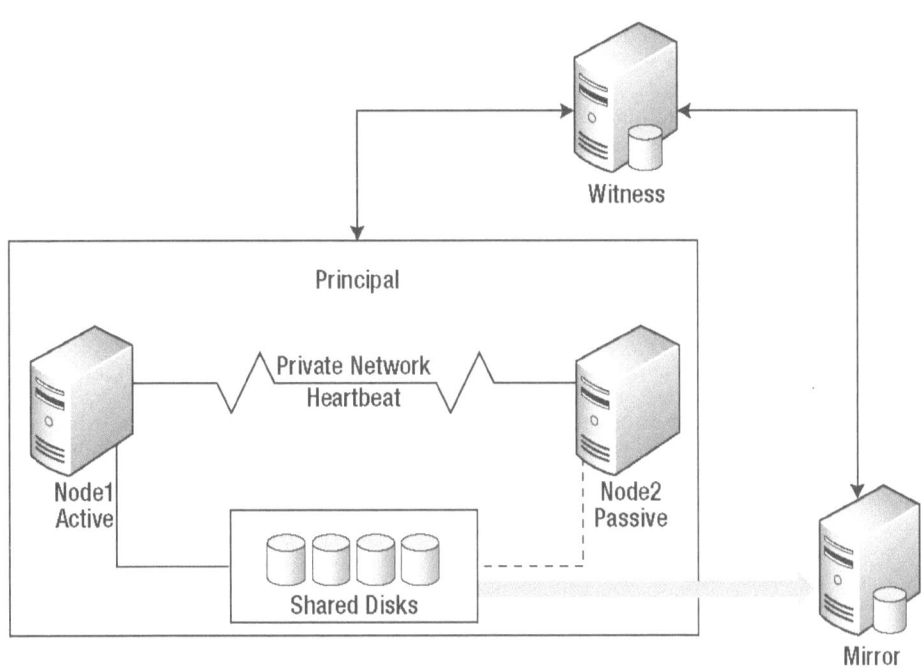

Figure 1-4. *High-availability configuration with failover clustering and database mirroring*

Secondary High Availability: Our tertiary availability options will be log shipping and transactional replication. The replica subscribers and log-shipping partners will service reporting and ad hoc query users. The replica or log-shipping servers will only function as availability options in case of a failure of all nodes of the cluster and database mirroring. These servers would preferably be in another data center in case a major environmental disaster occurs.

Primary Disaster Recovery: In the event that the database is completely lost in the cluster and in the mirror, we will make a determination as to whether the replica database or the log-shipped database has the most up-to-date data for recovery of the database. There will be two log-shipped servers in different locations.

The main server will create log backups for log shipping every five minutes. Log shipping will copy the log backups to the log-shipped servers every 15 minutes. One log-shipped server will restore the log backups immediately after the copy job completes. The other log-shipped server will delay restore of the log backups and restore at a frequency of once per hour. In the event of an accidental severe data loss, this will give us one hour to discover the loss and disable the restore job on the delayed server so that we can recover the lost data quickly.

Failsafe Disaster Recovery: Our failsafe disaster plan will be backup and recovery. We will not be maintaining log backups for recovery purposes at this time. We will be creating a full backup of the main database once per week on Saturday night due to its size and duration. We will create a differential backup of the main database nightly. We will perform a full backup of all other production databases every night.

We will copy backups to tape daily and move them to an offsite location weekly. Backups will remain on the local server for 30 days.

As you can see from the preceding list, designing a highly available redundant system can be very complicated and costly. You should determine the acceptable amount of data loss and downtime you can incur for your applications. I'm sure the availability requirements may change when you present the actual solution it takes to maintain the level of availability everyone would like to have. You tend to hear comments like "Well, I guess we could rekey an hour of data," or "I guess it wouldn't hurt if we can't log in for an hour or so." No matter what solution you use, it's best to set the proper expectations and flush out the real requirements up front.

Summary

This chapter has introduced many of the high-availability techniques available in SQL Server 2008. You should have a good understanding when to use database mirroring instead of other high-availability and disaster recovery options. You have also seen that database mirroring can work with these other techniques to provide an even higher level of availability that you could get by any one technique alone. The next chapter will provide you with a good understanding of the architecture of database mirroring before we move on to configuring and managing a successful database mirroring environment.

CHAPTER 2

Database Mirroring Overview

Database mirroring was introduced in SQL Server 2005 and provides multiple levels of protection depending on the configuration you choose for your environment. Database mirroring is the practice of keeping two copies of your database synchronized with each other so that if you lose one copy, you can continue work with the other. If you have ever worked with log shipping, you should be familiar with many of the concepts in database mirroring. In fact, database mirroring in its early stages was referred to as real-time log shipping or dynamic log shipping. You will see however, that database mirroring is a far more robust and enterprise-level solution than is log shipping. For example, prior to database mirroring, if you had wanted a solution that ensured zero data loss, your only option would have been failover clustering. This chapter will cover all the components that make database mirroring tick. Sure, you can set up database mirroring using a wizard and move on with life. But, since you are reading an entire book dedicated to database mirroring, something tells me you want to know what is going on under the hood.

Defining Key Terms

Database mirroring has its own naming conventions that you need to be familiar with. Using the correct terminology will help make sure everyone has the same understanding when discussing database mirroring. Since many terms in the IT industry have the same meanings with a slightly different twist, using the correct terminology will help you avoid confusion in the long run. Following are some key terms you should be familiar with when discussing database mirroring.

- *Principal*: Source server containing the functionally active database in the mirrored pair
- *Mirror*: Target server containing the destination database in the mirrored pair
- *Witness*: Optional server that monitors the principal and mirror servers to provide a quorum that allows for automatic failover
- *Partner*: Opposite server when referring to the principal and mirror servers
- Endpoint: Object that is bound to a network protocol that allows SQL servers to communicate across the network
- *Session*: Active relationship between the servers involved in database mirroring that allows them to maintain server state information about one another
- *Operating mode*: Safety level you have configured for database mirroring. Database mirroring can operate in one of three modes: high safety with automatic failover (synchronous with a witness), high safety without automatic failover (synchronous without a witness), and high performance (asynchronous without a witness).
- *Role*: Function that a specific server in database mirroring is performing. A server is either performing the "role" of the principal, mirror, or witness.

Choosing an Operating Mode

You can configure database mirroring to run in one of three operating modes. You should be aware of the pros and cons that come along with each operating mode when choosing which mode is best for your environment. Figure 2-1 shows each of these modes as they appear on the Mirroring page of the Database Properties dialog box. Notice that since there is no value in the Witness field, the "High safety with automatic failover" mode is unavailable.

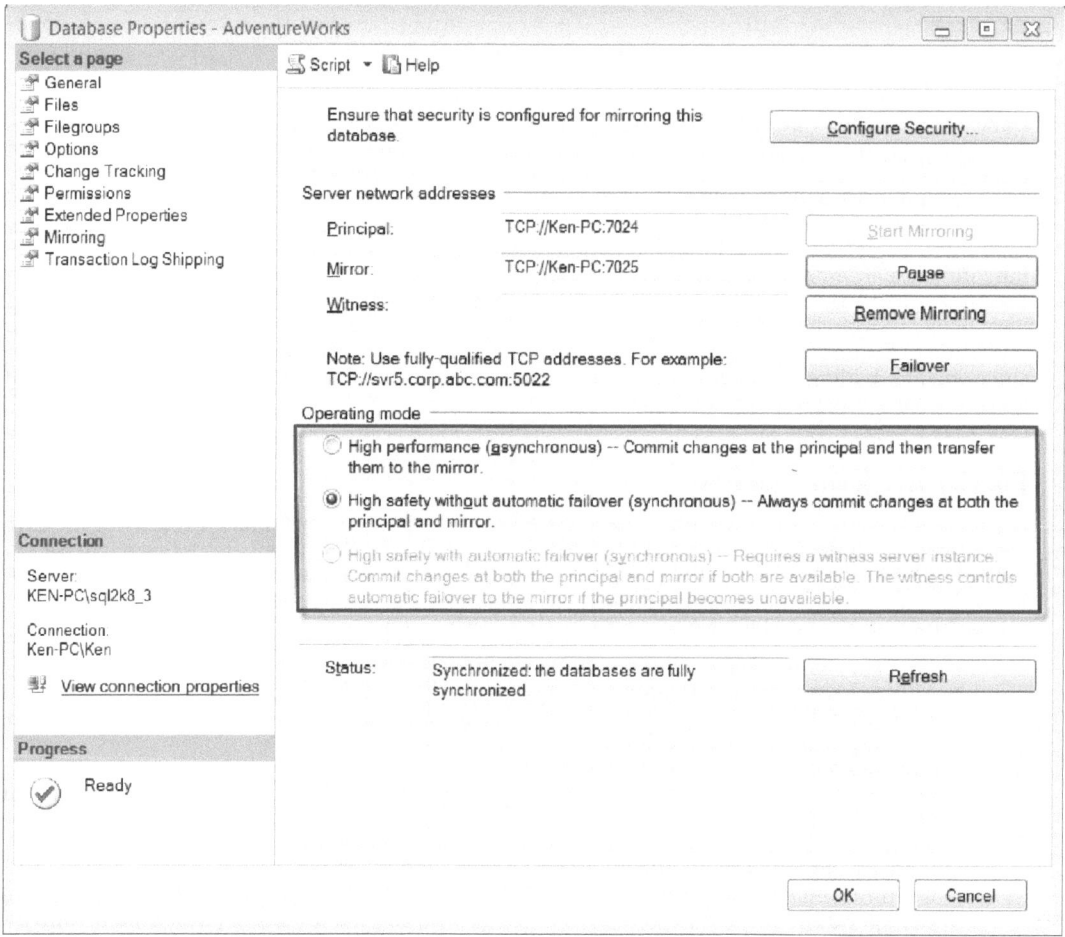

Figure 2-1. Database mirroring operating modes

All three operating modes have the same concept, but depending on the safety level, the order in which a transaction is committed is slightly different. With high-performance mode, the transaction is committed on the principal server before the mirror. This enables the application to move forward without having to wait for the transaction to commit on the mirror. With the high-safety modes, the transaction is committed on the mirror before being committed on the principal. This causes the application to wait until the transaction has been committed on both servers before moving forward.

The biggest difference between the two high-safety modes is that one mode uses a witness to form a quorum that allows for automatic failover, while the other does not use a witness and the failover must occur manually. The reason we don't say that this is the only difference is that there are some behavioral differences when it comes to failover when losing the witness. We will discuss this a little more in the "Understanding Mirroring States" section later in this chapter. Because using a witness provides minimal downtime during a failure, high-safety mode with automatic failover is also commonly referred to as high-availability mode.

The operating modes can be broken further into synchronous processing and asynchronous processing. The transaction safety on the principal database determines whether database mirroring runs synchronously or asynchronously. While running database mirroring synchronously, the database SAFETY is set to FULL, and when running asynchronously the database SAFETY is set to OFF. High-availability mode and high-safety mode are performed using synchronous processing, while the high-performance mode is performed using asynchronous processing. Keep in mind the following differences between synchronous and asynchronous processing when choosing a database-mirroring operating mode:

- Synchronous processing ensures zero data loss. Asynchronous processing trades the chance of some data loss for increased performance.
- Asynchronous processing requires the Enterprise Edition of SQL Server. Synchronous processing can be performed in the Standard or Enterprise editions of SQL Server.
- Synchronous processing can cause application performance issues on slower networks. Asynchronous processing avoids performance issues by not waiting for the mirror to commit first (hence, the risk of data loss).
- Recovery is faster when using synchronous processing because no uncommitted transactions need to be applied or undone.
- For the same reason, failover can be automatic with synchronous processing but not with asynchronous processing.

We know that all the different options and terminology can be confusing when discussing operating modes. If you follow the flow in Figure 2-2, you can see the factors that determine the three possible operating modes.

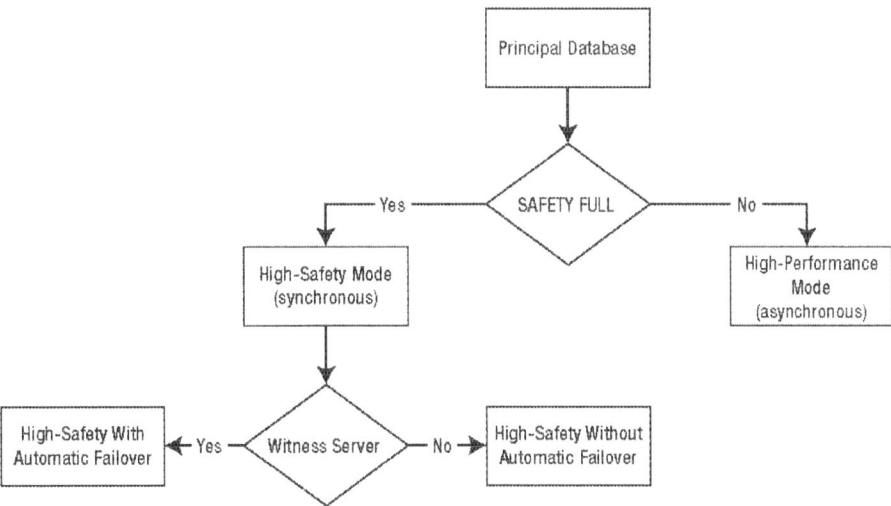

Figure 2-2. Flow to determine the operating mode for a database

No matter which mode you choose, you must have the principal database configured to use the full recovery model. Let's take a closer look at the operating modes in a little more detail.

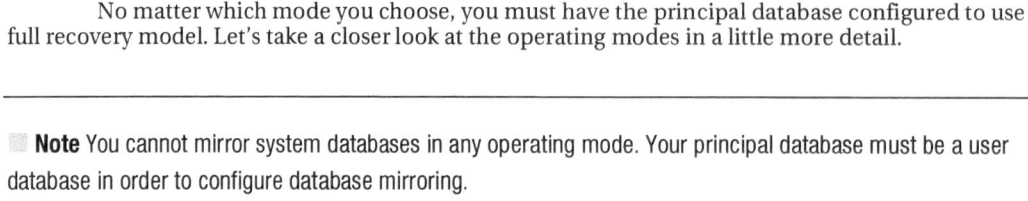

Note You cannot mirror system databases in any operating mode. Your principal database must be a user database in order to configure database mirroring.

High-Safety Mode

You can use high-safety mode in database mirroring to provide a duplicate copy of the principal database on a mirror server in a synchronous fashion so there is no chance of data loss between the principal and the mirror. In order for a transaction to commit on the principal database, it must first commit on the mirror. This also means that your application will actually have to wait for a transaction to commit on two databases instead of just one, which may cause performance issues, especially on slower networks. High-safety mode is supported in the Enterprise and Standard editions of SQL Server, with one caveat being that the principal and the mirror must be running the same edition.

Tip SQL Server 2008 introduces the capability to compress the individual transactions being transmitted to the mirror database to help improve performance on slow networks with bandwidth limitations. This may increase performance enough to allow you to implement high-safety mode when using database mirroring in SQL Server 2008 on networks that may have forced you to use high-performance mode in SQL Server 2005.

In order to provide the highest level of availability, you can use a witness server to verify connectivity between the principal and the mirror. The witness server is not a requirement for high-safety mode, but it is a requirement for automatic failover capabilities. The witness server runs an instance of SQL Server that consumes very little resources and can even run using SQL Server Workgroup and Express editions. Using a witness provides a communication check between the principal and the mirror, similar to the heartbeat in failover clustering. This communication check provides the ability for the mirror to assume the role of the principal if the principal becomes unavailable.

The witness is not a single point of failure and does not actually perform the failover; it just provides verification to the mirror server that the principal server is down. If the witness server crashes, database mirroring is still operational and completely functioning between the principal and the mirror, and you will just lose the ability to automatically fail over. The reason for this behavior is to prevent unnecessary failovers due to network connectivity. In order for a server to become a principal server, it has to be able to communicate with at least one other server; therefore, the only purpose of the witness is to answer the question, "Is the principal down?" In order to automatically recover from a failure, the witness and the mirror servers must agree that the principal is actually down.

The life cycle, or data flow, of a transaction is the key to ensuring zero data loss. Let's look at Figure 2-3 to review the order of operations in which a transaction occurs using high-safety mode that guarantees zero data loss.

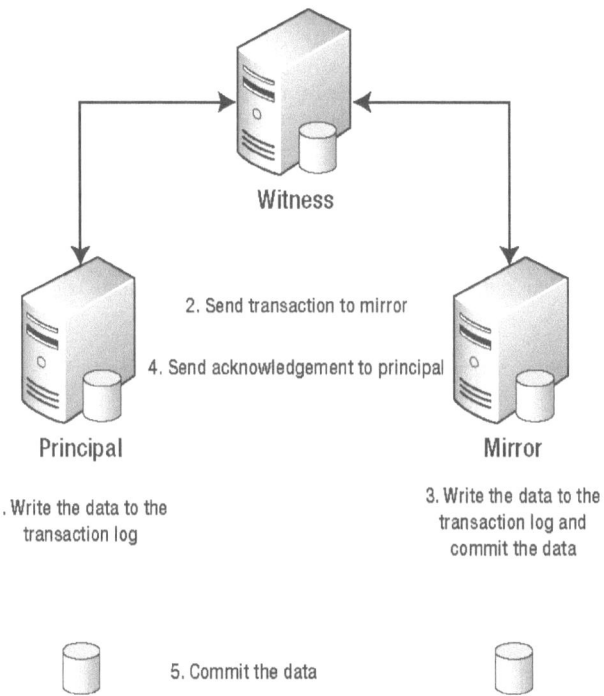

Figure 2-3. Database mirroring high-safety mode with witness server

You can see by examining the steps in Figure 2-3 how high-safety mode could cause performance issues within your application and why it is important to have a good network connection between the principal and mirror servers along with comparable I/O capacity as well.

1. An incoming transaction is written to the transaction log on the principal server.
2. The transaction is then sent to the transaction log on the mirror server.
3. The transaction is then committed to the transaction log on the mirror server. Notice that the transaction is still uncommitted on the principal server.
4. The mirror server sends an acknowledgement to the principal server that the transaction has successfully committed.
5. Finally, the transaction is committed on the principal server and control is returned to the calling application.

High-Performance Mode

You can use high-performance mode in database mirroring to perform asynchronous operations between the principal and mirror databases. High-performance mode supports only a manual failover with the possibility of data loss. There is no need to use a witness server in high-performance mode because there is no automatic failover capability. Since the principal database does not have to wait for acknowledgement from the mirror server in order to keep processing requests, high-performance mode could increase application performance if you have a slow network connection or latency issues between the principal and mirror servers. You may also want to use high-performance mode if your mirror server has less I/O capacity than your principal server does. Asynchronous processing also means that the mirror server can be several minutes behind when processing a high volume of transactions, which may or may not be acceptable, depending on the requirements agreed upon in the Service Level Agreement (SLA). High-performance mode is only supported if you are using the Enterprise Edition of SQL Server.

■ **Note** You can also configure high-performance mode to run with a witness, but this is not recommended since the witness adds no value for failover and your mirror would need to be able to communicate with the witness in the event of a failover.

Figure 2-4 shows the typical configuration of database mirroring using high-performance mode. Notice the order of operations using high-performance mode that allows the application to perform requests without having to wait for the transactions to commit on the mirror.

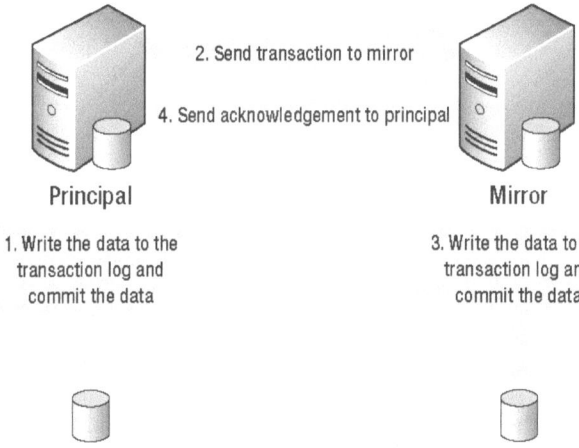

Figure 2-4. *Database mirroring high-performance mode*

By examining the steps in Figure 2-4 you can see how it would be faster from an application perspective. You can also see how you could possibly lose data if a failure occurs before all of the transactions have committed on the mirror server.

1. An incoming transaction is written to the transaction log on the principal server. The transaction is immediately committed, and control is returned to the calling application.
2. The transaction is sent to the transaction log on the mirror server.
3. The transaction is committed to the transaction log on the mirror server.
4. The mirror server sends an acknowledgement to the principal server that the transaction has successfully committed.

Understanding Sessions

Once you have configured database mirroring, you can start a database mirroring session. When all the servers are communicating, they maintain information about the state of each other. We will cover what exactly these states are in the next section, "Understanding Mirroring States." This state information is maintained until you stop the database mirroring session. Starting a database mirroring session essentially starts the process of synchronizing your principal database with your mirror database.

Pausing and Resuming Sessions

You can pause and resume a database mirroring session in order to suspend sending transactions to the mirror database while still maintaining the state of the session. Pausing a database session can be useful if you are having performance issues on your server. You can temporarily pause the database mirroring session in order to alleviate some of the strain on your server. You have to keep in mind that while a database mirroring session is paused, the transactions remain active in the principal database and SQL Server cannot truncate the transaction log. If you leave the database mirroring session in a paused state for too long, you run the risk of filling up the transaction log on the principal database server, which could cause major issues with any other database that resides on that server as well.

You can pause a database mirroring session from the Database Properties dialog box on the Mirroring page of the principal server by simply clicking the Pause button. After you are prompted and accept the changes, the button text will change to Resume. Alternatively, you can run `ALTER DATABASE <DatabaseName> SET PARTNER SUSPEND` against either the principal or the mirror database to pause a database mirroring session and `ALTER DATABASE <DatabaseName> SET PARTNER RESUME` to resume the database mirroring session.

When you start a database mirroring session, the principal server starts to send transactions to the mirror server. Any transactions that have not been sent to the mirror server are collected in what is called a *send queue*. If you are running database mirroring in high-safety mode, the only time transactions will build up in the send queue is when database mirroring is paused. If you are running database mirroring in high-performance mode, transactions can build up in the send queue not only due to pausing the database mirroring session, but also high server activity, slow network connectivity, a large redo queue on the mirror server, or any other reason that would cause database mirroring to fall behind.

On the mirror server, transactions are constantly being written from the transaction log to the database. The transactions that remain in the transaction log that haven't been written to the database make up what is called the *redo queue*. If for any reason the redo operation fails, the mirror server pauses the session until you manually fix the issue that caused the redo failure.

Running Multiple Sessions

You cannot mirror a single database to multiple servers. If you need more than one copy of your database, you can use log shipping in conjunction with database mirroring. Although you can only have one session per database, you can have multiple sessions per server. Let's take a look at a couple of examples of running multiple database mirroring sessions.

Let's say you have one big consolidation server you are running a couple of databases on and two smaller servers you can use for disaster recovery purposes. If you look at Figure 2-5, you can see that the server hosting the principal databases is sending transactions from database A to one server and database B to another. In this case, each database is running a separate database mirroring session. Also, if there is a failure to either database on the principal server, its respective mirror server would take over as the principal and the old principal would now become the mirror. This means that a single server could actually host both a principal and a mirror database.

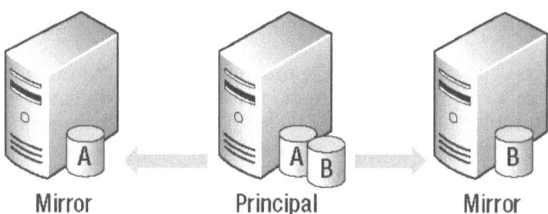

Figure 2-5. *Running multiple sessions on three servers*

Knowing that a single server can play the role of both partners, let's take a look at the database mirroring configuration in Figure 2-6. In this example, each server hosts a principal database and a mirror database. Both of these servers are running multiple sessions, and either server could hold any combination of the principal or mirror databases at any given time. Unlike failover clustering, the databases do not fail over as a group. In this scenario, you should make sure your server is powerful enough to handle the load of both databases until you can bring the other server back online.

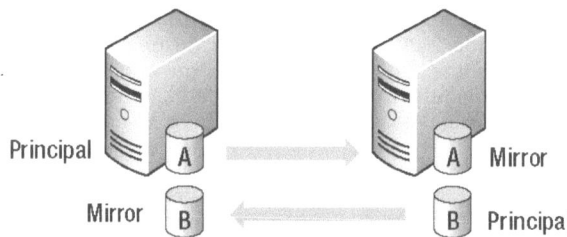

Figure 2-6. *Running multiple sessions on two servers*

Understanding Mirroring States

Database mirroring can be in one of a few different mirroring states during the context of a session in relation to its partner. You can use the mirroring state to identify the condition of a session or where exactly database mirroring is in the process of synchronizing the database between the servers. The possible mirroring states include:

- *SYNCHRONIZING*: You will generally see this state when you first enable the database mirroring session. This means that the mirror server is substantially behind the principal server and the mirror server is trying its best to catch up.
- *SYNCHRONIZED*: You should generally be in this state most of the time during the database mirroring session. Once the initial burst of transactions are sent to the mirror server, the state changes from SYNCHRONIZING to SYNCHRONIZED. This does not necessarily mean that you will not lose data in high-performance mode; it just means that the mirror server is keeping up with the principal. When you are running in high-performance mode, there is always a chance for data loss.
- *SUSPENDED*: Database mirroring is in a SUSPENDED state when the principal server is not sending transactions to the mirror server. You will see this state after a failover has occurred. The database mirroring state can become SUSPENDED for a couple of other reasons as well, such as manually pausing a database mirroring session or in the event of redo log errors.

- *PENDING_FAILOVER*: You will only see this state on the principal server when it is in the process of killing user connections and becoming the role of the mirror.
- *DISCONNECTED*: You will see this state when the partners have lost connectivity with each other.

Other than the PENDING_FAILOVER state, the principal server and the mirror server will always have the same state. The witness server, however, can have one of three states in correlation to either partner involved in a database mirroring session: CONNECTED, DISCONNECTED, and UNKNOWN. As long as the state of the witness is CONNECTED to one partner, there is a quorum between the witness and the partner, which allows for failover. If the witness is not connected to a partner, the state is either UNKNOWN or DISCONNECTED, and in the event of a failure, the database becomes unavailable. If you are running database mirroring with a witness, it takes at least two servers to form a quorum. If the witness is DISCONNECTED and the mirror server crashes, your database will be inaccessible even if it is the principal database. For this reason, if your witness becomes DISCONNECTED, you can turn off the witness, which disables the need for a quorum, by running the following statement ALTER DATABASE <DatabaseName> SET WITNESS OFF until you have resolved any connectivity issues between the witness and the partners.

You can find information about the mirroring states, along with several other useful data points, by querying the sys.database_mirroring catalog view. Figure 2-7 shows some sample output from the sys.database_mirroring catalog view. You can tell that we ran the query on the principal database that is running FULL SAFETY. The database is synchronized with the mirror, and we are not connected to the witness.

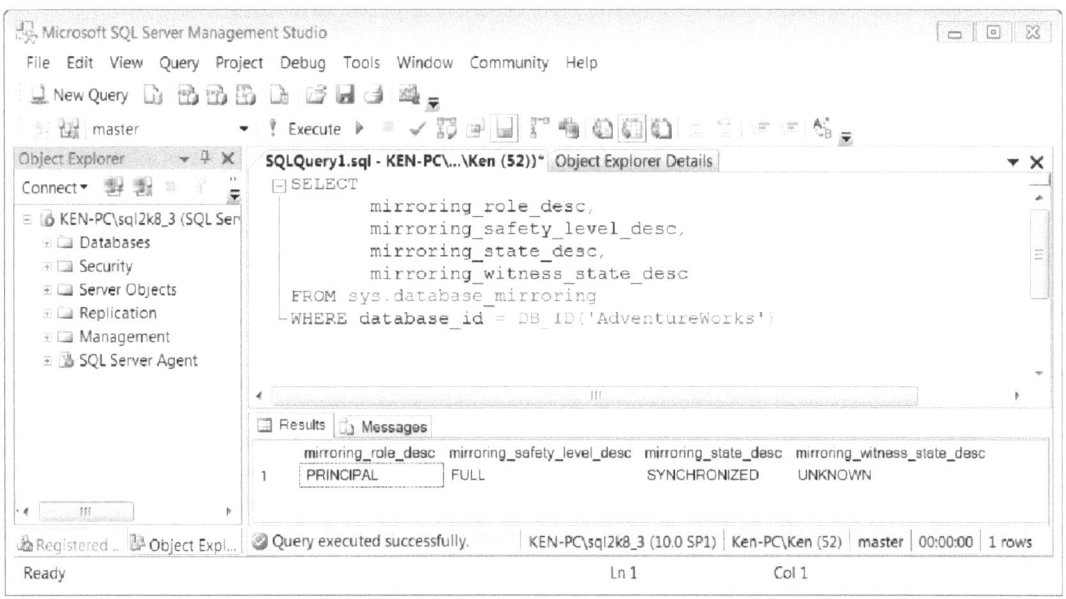

Figure 2-7. Mirroring states in sys.database_mirroring catalog view

Switching Roles

One of the nice features in database mirroring is the ability to easily switch roles. If you have ever used other high-availability techniques such as log shipping, you know that making the secondary database the primary database is not so hard, but making the primary database the new secondary usually takes a little more work. There are three ways to switch roles in database mirroring:

- Manual failover
- Automatic failover
- Forced service with possible data loss

With manual failover, you can switch roles by simply clicking the Failover button on the Mirroring page of the Database Properties dialog box or running the following statement on the principal server. ALTER DATABASE <DatabaseName> SET PARTNER FAILOVER. However, you should be aware that manual failover is not supported in high-performance mode.

Automatic failover occurs when you are running database mirroring in high-safety mode with a witness and a failure occurs on the principal server. The mirror server becomes the new principal. When the original principal server becomes available again, it will take on the role of mirror.

The last role change, forced service with possible data loss, is supported in both high-performance mode and high-safety mode without a witness. In the event that the principal server has a failure, you can run the following command on the mirror server to bring the database online while potentially incurring data loss:

```
ALTER DATABASE <DatabaseName> SET PARTNER FORCE_SERVICE_ALLOW_DATA_LOSS
```

Transparent Client Redirection

Transparent client redirection is a feature provided by SQL Native Client (SNAC) that works with database mirroring to allow client applications to automatically redirect in the case of a failover. You can specify both partners in the database connection string by adding the Failover_Partner keyword and supplying the mirror server name. If the application is unable to connect to the principal database, a connection to the mirror database is attempted. Even though you specify the mirror as the Failover_Partner, it doesn't have to be the mirror in order for the connection string to work correctly because at any given time you can only connect to either the principal database or the mirror database. The application will successfully connect to whichever partner contains the current principal database. In other words, you don't have to make any application changes due to failovers. However, if you are already connected when a failover occurs, the application should be coded to attempt to reconnect to the database.

Enhanced Features

Microsoft has added a handful of new features to database mirroring in SQL Server 2008. As an added bonus, you will automatically benefit from these new features without having to make any special configuration changes. Ultimately, the new features lead to enhanced performance, reduced downtime, and the ability to automatically recover from certain page errors.

Log Stream Compression

One of the most prominent enhancements in database mirroring is stream compression between the principal and the mirror server to minimize network bandwidth. This feature will add more value to networks having latency issues by reducing the amount of traffic that is being sent between servers.

However, if you have a high-speed network with plenty of bandwidth, the effects of stream compression may hardly be noticeable at all. Your server may experience higher CPU utilization as a result of stream compression because it takes more cycles to compress and decompress the data. Also, the server will be processing more transactions per second, requiring more CPU cycles.

Automatic Page Recovery

Another nice new feature is the ability to automatically recover from a corrupted page. Automatic recovery from a corrupted page consists of one mirroring partner requesting the unreadable page from the other as shown in Figure 2-8. If a query is executed that contains data that resides on a corrupted page, an error will be raised and a new page will be copied from the mirror to replace the corrupted page. In most cases, by the time the query is executed again, the page will have been restored from the mirror, and the query will execute successfully.

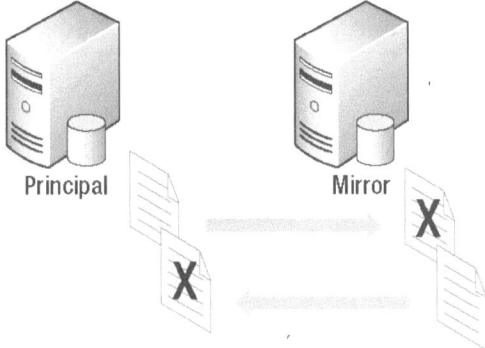

Figure 2-8. *Automatic page recovery*

There are certain pages that database mirroring cannot recover such as the file header (page 0), and the database boot page (page 9). Database mirroring also can't recover allocation pages including the Global Allocation Map (GAM), Shared Global Allocation Map (SGAM), and Page Free Space (PFS). Database mirroring can, however, recover from the following errors:

- *Error 823*: Operating system Cyclic Redundancy Check (CRC) failure
- *Error 824*: Logical errors including a bad page checksum or torn write
- *Error 829*: Page has been marked as restore pending

Having the knowledge of these errors when you are designing and writing your application gives you an advantage in the high-availability arena. You can look for these errors in your application, gracefully capture the error, and then have your application retry the query. Although the chances of encountering a corrupt page are slim, this is yet another way database mirroring allows you to abstract what could be perceived as a negative experience from the user.

Availability Enhancements

There are also some enhancements that will help increase availability in the event of a failure. Log send buffers are used more efficiently by appending log records of the next log-flush operation to the most recently used log cache if it contains sufficient free space. Write-ahead events have been enhanced by asynchronously processing incoming log records and log records that have already been written to disk. In a failover, read-ahead during the undo phase is enhanced by the mirror server sending read-ahead hints to the principal to indicate the pages that will be requested so the principal server can put it in the copy buffer.

Features by Edition

We have covered several features in this chapter. You can use Table 2-1 as a quick reference guide to determine what features are available in each edition of SQL Server 2008. There are a few nice benefits you get when using Enterprise Edition instead of Standard Edition. In fact, one of the biggest determining factors may be that high-performance mode is only supported by Enterprise Edition. The Developer Edition of SQL Server 2008 supports exactly the same features as the Enterprise Edition because it uses the same engine, so we have omitted the Developer Edition from Table 2-1.

Table 2-1. Mirroring Features by Edition

Feature	Enterprise	Standard	Workgroup	Web	Express
Act as partner	Yes	Yes	No	No	No
Act as witness	Yes	Yes	Yes	Yes	Yes
High-safety mode with automatic failover	Yes	Yes	No	No	No
High-safety mode without automatic failover	Yes	Yes	No	No	No
High-performance mode	Yes	No	No	No	No
Automatic page repair	Yes	Yes	No	No	No
Log stream compression	Yes	Yes	No	No	No
Reporting capabilities	Yes	No	No	No	No
Available after undo	Yes	No	No	No	No
Parallel redo	Yes	No	No	No	No

Summary

This chapter has provided you with the fundamental knowledge you need to understand before implementing database mirroring. Taking the time to understand how all of the components in database mirroring interact with each other will help you throughout the book as we dive deeper into each topic. We have also introduced the new features available in SQL Server 2008 along with laying out what edition of SQL Server you need in order to use these features. In the next chapter, we will cover some of the things you should consider before implementing database mirroring along with some best-practice recommendations you should be aware of before moving on to the actual setup process.

CHAPTER 3

Planning and Best Practices

You can avoid the pitfalls that others have encountered and have a smooth deployment of database mirroring with a little careful planning. You just need to know the right questions to ask before configuring database mirroring and to understand what to expect during the process.

This chapter leads you through a three-step process for thinking through a deployment of mirroring. After those steps is an example plan. To round everything out at the end, we provide a list of best practices. Following them, or at least being careful about when you don't, will help ensure a successful and ongoing deployment.

Step One: Know Your Environment

First, you need to learn about your current environment. There are several questions you should be able to answer about your environment that will help you plan a mirroring deployment.

You can probably find many of the answers to the questions in this section on your own. If you do not personally have access to your servers, you will need to be able to provide a list of questions for someone else to answer. You may need to work closely with your system administrators.

The questions covered in this section are:

- Are your servers ready?
- Is your database ready?
- Do you know your service accounts?
- Do you know your database size?
- Is your mirror comparable to your principal?
- Are you combining with other techniques?

Are Your Servers Ready?

You need to check that all servers are running the same build of SQL Server and are on at least SQL Server 2005 SP1 (service pack 1) or SQL Server 2008. SQL Server 2005 SP1 was the first version of SQL Server that fully supported database mirroring. If you are on a build prior to SP1 for SQL Server 2005, you will need to include upgrading the SQL build prior to implementing database mirroring. You can include a trace flag that will allow you to configure database mirroring prior to SQL Server 2005 SP1, but you really should take the time to make sure you are running the most recent service packs during the process. The only exception you may have to make is for vendor-supported applications. Many times vendors will not certify a specific version of SQL Server until they have fully tested their applications, so in certain cases you may have to go with the latest version that the vendor will support.

▪ **Note** If you need to include upgrading SQL Server 2005 in your plan, you should consider upgrading to at least CU6 (cumulative update 6) for SP2. CU6 for SP2 included an important bug fix for database mirroring. See knowledge base article KB947462 at http://support.microsoft.com/kb/947462 for more information.

The principal and mirror servers can be running different operating systems or have different architectures. However, it is crucial that the principal and mirror be running the same edition of SQL Server, either Enterprise Edition or Standard Edition. You should make sure you are running the same version of SQL Server on both servers as well. It is also important to have identical drive letters and file paths for the data and log files. Any changes to the principal database are replicated on the mirror database, and if the drive structure is different, some structural changes to the principal database could cause mirroring to fail. The witness server however, can run the Workgroup or Express Edition of SQL Server 2005 or SQL Server 2008.

Is Your Database Ready?

You need to make sure your database does not have a filegroup that uses the filestream option. Database mirroring does not support databases using filestream. Filestream is a new feature in SQL Server 2008 that actually stores data on the file system that is retrieved using T-SQL. If you fail over to the mirror server, database mirroring has no way to retrieve the data from the file system on the principal server.

Database mirroring also requires the Full Recovery model. If your database is using the Simple or Bulk-logged Recovery model, you will need to change the recovery model to Full before taking the initial full backup for mirroring setup. You can run the following query to determine the current recovery model of your database:

```
SELECT recovery_model_desc
FROM sys.databases
WHERE name = 'DatabaseName'
```

If you are not using the Full Recovery model, you can change the recovery model of your database to Full by running the following script.

```
USE master
GO

ALTER DATABASE [DatabaseName] SET RECOVERY FULL
```

Do You Know Your Service Accounts?

The simplest way to deploy database mirroring is to use the same domain account for the SQL Server service on all servers involved in database mirroring. If all servers are using the same service account, you do not have to grant permissions on the endpoint. This may not be possible or allowable in all environments.

You can use the Network Service built-in system account as an alternate to a domain account. You can use the Network Service account like a domain account. When the Network Service account tries to access another machine, it presents itself as Domain\MachineName$. For example, if you are using Network Service for SQL Servers named SQLServer1 and SQLServer2 in the domain ProdDomain, the domain accounts will be ProdDomain\SQLServer1$ and ProdDomain\SQLServer2$.

A less-favorable alternative is using the Local System built-in account. Local System is a special built-in system account that is highly privileged on the local system. Local System does not have permissions to access resources on any server other than its own, and you are not able to grant permissions to another server's Local System account. If you use the Local System for the SQL Server service account on a server involved in database mirroring, you must use certificate authentication instead of Windows authentication.

■ **Caution** The certificates used for certificate authentication expire annually. Be aware that there are long-term maintenance requirements when using certificate authentication.

Do You Know Your Database Size?

How big is your database? If you are planning to mirror a large database, you will need to factor the time required to create the full backup, copy it to the mirror server, and restore it. For very large databases, this can add many hours to your plan. You can perform the backup, copy, and restore in advance of the mirroring deployment. One tactic that has worked well for us in the past when preparing to mirror a very large database is to set up log shipping first and let log shipping keep the databases in sync until you are ready to deploy mirroring. You need to make sure you use the NORECOVERY option when restoring the database instead of the STANDBY option if you are planning to use log shipping as an interim process when configuring database mirroring. Once you are ready to start database mirroring, you can disable the backup job, make sure all the logs are copied to the mirror server before disabling the copy job, and then run the restore job one last time before disabling it to apply the remaining logs. You should then be able to start database mirroring with minimal time to synchronize the principal and the mirror.

Is Your Mirror Comparable to Your Principal?

It's best if your mirror server is comparable in terms of CPU and disk capacity to your principal server. That's not an absolute requirement, but we highly recommend that your mirror server be capable of handling the same load as the principal server in case of a failover. If your mirror server is not comparable to your principal server, you may want to consider using mirroring without automatic failover. If running in a diminished capacity for a minimal amount of time is permissible, you can set up a process to fail back to the original server as soon as it is online and synchronized again. We explain how to set up this process in Chapter 6. Also, if your mirror server cannot keep up with your principal server, the mirror server will slow down your application if you are using synchronous mirroring.

Are You Combining with Other Techniques?

You will need to take additional care when combining database mirroring with replication, log shipping, or failover clustering. You should be aware of the steps required to deploy the combined solutions.

Step Two: Know Your Applications

In addition to knowing about your hardware environment, you should also learn about the applications that are running in that environment. However, application-specific knowledge might not be readily available to you. That's particularly true in the case of third-party applications that your organization has purchased and installed. Those applications may be like "black boxes." You may have to seek out developers and testers or administrators and users of your applications. If you have access to application source code or configuration files, you may be able to determine what you need to know on your own. Following are some questions you should answer about each application that you plan to support in your mirrored environment:

- How are your applications connecting to the servers?
- Do any components not support automatic failover?
- Do your applications have dependencies on other databases?
- Do your applications rely on external resources?

How Are Your Applications Connecting to the Servers?

To support database mirroring, your applications should create their connections using the SQL Native Client, the ADO.Net 2.0 Data Provider, or the JDBC 1.1 Driver for SQL Server. The connection strings should utilize the failover partner attribute. You will need to ensure that someone makes the proper modifications to the client connection strings. You can deploy the updated client connection strings with or in advance of database mirroring.

Do Any Components Not Support Automatic Failover?

If your applications have components such as legacy DTS packages, SSIS packages, or external executables using connection protocols that do not support mirroring, you will need to evaluate whether you can upgrade the components to support database mirroring. You will have to decide how to handle the components that you are not able to upgrade.

One way to manage these components is to set up copies of the components on the mirror server configured to connect to the mirror database. You will need to set up a process that detects a mirroring failover and takes steps to enable any jobs or scheduled tasks required to run these components. We will explain two different ways to monitor for failover events and automatically perform specific tasks after detecting a failover.

Another frequently used option when a failover is not going to be for an extended period is to allow certain components not to run. In these scenarios, you will want to set up a process to fail mirroring back to the original principal as soon as it is online and synchronized.

Do Your Applications Have Dependencies on Other Databases?

If your applications have dependencies on databases other than the one that you plan to mirror, check to see whether any of those other databases run on the same server as your primary database. Out of the box, database mirroring does not support cross-database dependencies. In the event of a single database failure, only the failed database will automatically fail over to the mirror. If there are other databases that need to be active on the same server as the failed database, you have several options for handling this:

- You can mirror all databases with cross-dependencies and monitor for a failover event. When you detect a failover, query for the state of the other databases and automatically trigger a failover of the remaining databases. This failover process can include additional tasks such as disabling or enabling SQL jobs or setting configuration options of the mirrored database.
- Asynchronous mirroring without automatic failover is an option worth exploring. When mirroring asynchronously (often called high-performance mode), failover is performed manually. With this option, when you respond to a failure, you can make a decision as to whether to fail over all databases to the mirroring partners or simply try to resolve the failing database.

- Another option is to maintain a live copy of the interdependent databases on the other server using technologies such as merge replication. This strategy ensures that there is always a live version of the other databases on both the mirror and principal to use as needed.

Don't worry too much about the details of these options now. We will cover these options in greater detail throughout the rest of the book. However, cross-database dependencies is something you should be aware of during the planning stages of your database mirroring configuration.

Do Your Applications Rely on External Resources?

If your database has processes that access external resources on the local server, this will cause failures since your application will not be able to access those resources in the event of a failure. You may be able to work around the issue by coding the process to use UNC paths to access the resource through a share. Ideally, you would place the share on a remote server that will likely be accessible even if one of the SQL Servers is offline. Alternatively, you can set up a process that keeps the contents of the resource locations in sync.

Step Three: Know Your Plan

The key to any successful plan is to know it and practice it. Run through your mirroring-deployment plan several times in a non-production environment to see whether you encounter any challenges. Here is a list of additional items you will need to account for in your plan.

- Set up all logins on the mirror server to match the logins on the principal server.
- When you restore the database on the mirror server, you will be the owner of the database. You will not be able change the owner of the database while the database is offline. We suggest that you set up a process to check the owner of the database when it is brought online and reassign the owner if it is not owned by the sa login. The other option is to perform a test failover of the database after setting up mirroring and manually change the database owner.
- If your database has a dependency on the TRUSTWORTHY option being set for CLR processes, you will need to set this option after the initial failover. You can handle this option the same as the database owner. If a process is set up to check the owner of the database when the mirror comes online, you can check this option in the same process and set it if needed.
- Make sure all database backup jobs are disabled for the duration of the mirroring setup. Full backups and log backups affect the log chain and may cause your log restores to fail on the mirror server. However, it may not be practical to stop the transaction log backups in a high-volume environment. You will need to copy and apply any transaction log backups that have taken place on the database before you can create a database mirroring session.
- If you are changing the recovery model from bulk-logged or simple to the Full Recovery model (a requirement for database mirroring), you may not have a maintenance task in place already to perform log backups. It is important to perform proper maintenance on the log files when using the Full Recovery model. You should have this process created and ready to enable.

Sample Plan

Table 2-1 shows a sample plan for a single database mirroring deployment. This deployment plan is an example of the most common and simplest database mirroring project you are likely to encounter. The plan doesn't go into a lot of detail. It just lays out the steps to perform and their probable execution times.

Don't underestimate the value of a simple list like that in Table 2-1. It is all too easy in the heat of deployment to overlook a crucial step. Having a checklist to follow will help ensure, for example, that you don't omit restoring the transaction log backup on the mirror server, an omission which might result in much lost time and frustration as you go back and do the entire process all over again. And thinking about the time required for each step helps ensure that you allocate enough time for the overall process. You don't want to come up short when 8:00 a.m. rolls around and your company's entire workforce sits down to try to log in.

Table 2-1. Sample Mirroring Deployment Plan

Time	Step Detail	Step Duration
8:00 p.m.	Disable all SQL jobs and scheduled tasks	3 min.
8:03 p.m.	Verify that the database is using Full Recovery	2 min.
8:05 p.m.	Create full backup of database	10 min.
8:15 p.m.	Copy and restore full backup on mirror server	10 min.
8:20 p.m.	Create transaction log backup of database	2 min.
8:22 p.m.	Copy and restore transaction log backup on mirror server	3 min.
8:25 p.m.	Configure database mirroring	10 min.
8:35 p.m.	Deploy new configuration files to web site and web service	5 min.
8:40 p.m.	Enable all SQL jobs and scheduled tasks	5 min.
8:45 p.m.	Install database mirroring maintenance procedures	5 min.
8:50 p.m.	Give testers green light to begin testing	5 min.

Best Practices

Following is a collection of best practices to help you simplify and standardize how you deal with database mirroring on a daily basis. These practices will help you maximize performance and minimize challenges while establishing a consistent method of handling database mirroring.

- Use a mirror server that is comparable to the principal and able to handle the load in the event of a failover.
- Use a dedicated network interface card (NIC) for mirroring traffic to optimize performance of data throughput.
- Do not use a witness server when running in high-performance mode. Using a witness in high-performance mode introduces a risk of service loss. If the witness server disconnects while either the principal or the mirror is down, the other partner remains offline due to loss of quorum.
- Use the same database file layout for the mirror partner, including the drive letters and the paths of the data and log files. If file layout is different, you may be required to suspend mirroring in order to add files to the database later.

- Test your system in a non-production environment with a production level load running in both asynchronous and synchronous modes to determine which operating mode is best suited for your system.
- Start out with asynchronous mirroring in your production environment. Once you are satisfied that database mirroring is performing fine, switch to synchronous mirroring. If synchronous mirroring is working fine, then add the witness server to the mix.
- Upgrade your systems to at least CU6 for SP2 if running SQL Server 2005, or use SQL Server 2008.
- Use the same service pack level and edition of SQL Server for the principal and mirror servers.
- Use the same collation for the principal and mirror SQL Server instances.
- Use larger batch sizes when performing bulk operations to increase performance.
- Make sure you perform regular maintenance on the log file. The more frequently you back up the log file, the better. Thirty minutes should be your minimum frequency for log backups. For a very busy transactional server, you should backup the log more frequently such as every five or fifteen minutes.
- You should use encryption to secure the data sent between the principal and the mirror servers. Encryption has very little overhead compared to the security benefits it provides.
- Consider switching to high-performance mode when running large batch operations such as a large data import or during long-running transactions such as index rebuilds.
- Use larger batch sizes when performing bulk insert operations to increase performance.
- Use T-SQL scripts or stored procedures rather than database maintenance plans for performing routine maintenance. Maintenance plans do not support database mirroring and will fail if they attempt to perform maintenance on the mirror partner. Have your scripts or procedures check the `state` or `state_desc` columns of the `sys.databases` system view for values of zero (0) or online, respectively.
- Store the expected database mirroring configuration locally on the servers as a reference point for maintenance and troubleshooting processes. After setting up database mirroring, query the mirroring system tables for the key data and insert it into a table in a separate database used for operational procedures.
- Modify the Partner Timeout property on the principal partner to allow the cluster ample time to perform a failover when adding mirroring to a failover cluster. If the timeout property is too short, a clustering failover may appear to be a failure and initiate a mirroring failover.
- Do not set the Partner Timeout property to less than 10 seconds in order to avoid unnecessary failovers.
- Consider using log shipping instead of database mirroring when setting up mirroring across a wide area network (WAN) or on a system with high network latency. Mirroring in high-safety mode may not be able to keep the mirror in sync and could cause considerable delays in query processing. When high network latency exists, log shipping is likely to be preferable over asynchronous (high-performance) mirroring. Log shipping has a lower management overhead, and high network latency negates the advantages of mirroring.
- Set up maintenance tasks to synchronize logins between the mirroring partner servers. If SQL authentication is used, use the SID (security identifier) of the SQL logins when recreating the logins on the mirror partner. The SID of the SQL login is cached on the client, and in the event of a failover, the attempts to connect to the mirror server will fail if the client is using a SQL login and the SID on the mirror server does not match the SID in the client's cache. However, if you are using Windows Authentication you can avoid this issue altogether.
- Perform maintenance on the mirror server first when patching or upgrading SQL Server. Once the maintenance on the mirror is complete, fail over to the mirror database, patch the original principal, and then fail back to the original principal. If a witness server is involved, you can patch or upgrade the witness at any point in the process. You can patch or upgrade the witness first, second, or last. The key practice is to make sure you are not patching, upgrading, or rebooting multiple servers at the same time.

- You should only use certificate authentication as a last resort. Certificates expire annually and add a layer of maintenance overhead that can be easily overlooked, which introduces additional potential for failure.
- Set up a job to check the size of the log file and shrink it if it gets above 5 GB if you are using a SQL Server 2005 build prior to CU6 for SP2. There was a bug fixed in CU6 that caused the initialization of mirroring to fail if the log file was too large. However, if at all possible, you should apply the latest service packs to avoid this issue altogether.
- You should monitor the suspect_pages system table in the msdb database for repaired torn pages if you are using SQL Server 2008. If SQL Server detects a torn page in the principal database, SQL Server will try to recover the torn page from the mirror database. If there was physical corruption, this recovery process could mask a larger problem.
- You should make sure that your database mirroring partner servers are not on the same switch or router if they are in the same data center or lab. If your servers are on the same switch or router and the switch or router fails, you lose both sides of the mirror, and your whole system is down. Having the servers on the same switch or router would introduce a single point of failure into the environment.

Summary

This chapter has covered several things you should consider before you even start configuring database mirroring. You should know that your environment is ready to implement database mirroring and your applications can take advantage of database mirroring once it has been configured. Finally, you should come up with an implementation plan and practice that plan in a test environment. We also included a list of best practices you should consider while coming up with your plan. Ultimately, taking a little more time to plan in the beginning leads to a more successful implementation of database mirroring.

Database Mirroring Setup

When you set up database mirroring, the experience can range from the incredibly simple to the overly complex. SQL Server offers a database mirroring wizard to guide you through the simple setups. The wizard is quick and easy and really is the way to go when you just need to get the basics up and running.

If you have multiple databases to mirror, the wizard can be cumbersome and slow you down. Likewise, if you want to use the more advanced features of database mirroring, you will have to set up mirroring with T-SQL. Once you get accustomed to setting up mirroring with T-SQL, this method will be much faster for you. We will cover both methods of database mirroring setup in this chapter.

Note For the screenshots and sample code included in this chapter, we are using a database named `MirrorTest`. You should replace `MirrorTest` with your own database's name when you use the provided code.

Before You Begin

You need to perform certain steps before setting up mirroring. You need to perform these preparatory steps regardless of the strategy you are planning to use for setting up mirroring. The database mirroring wizard does not prepare the database for mirroring.

You can split the preparation into two separate parts. Perform the first part in advance of the database mirroring setup. For the most part, it really doesn't matter how far in advance you perform the steps in part one; these are just prerequisites for database mirroring and your application. You will need to perform the second part immediately prior to setting up mirroring because it interrupts the routine maintenance of your database such as backups.

Part One: Advanced Preparation

You should configure as much as you can prior to actually setting up database mirroring. This is especially helpful if you are setting up database mirroring during an outage window. The more you can do in advance, the more time you have to focus on the tasks you need to perform immediately prior to setting up database mirroring. Follow these steps to prepare your environment for database mirroring:

1. Set the recovery model of the database to the Full Recovery model if not already set. You can make this change in SQL Server Management Studio (SSMS) on the Options tab of the Database Properties dialog. You can also manually make the change with the following T-SQL code:

```
Alter Database [MirrorTest] Set Recovery Full;
```

2. Set the compatibility level of your database to level 90 or higher. Level 90 is SQL Server 2005 compatibility, and level 100 is SQL Server 2008 compatibility. You can set the compatibility level of your database in SSMS on the Options tab of the Database Properties dialog, or you can manually make the change with T-SQL. You can use the following commands to change your database's compatibility level.

   For SQL Server 2005:

   ```
   Exec sp_dbcmptlevel @dbname = 'MirrorTest', @new_cmptlevel = 90
   ```

   For SQL Server 2008:

   ```
   Alter Database [MirrorTest] Set Compatibility_Level = 100;
   ```

3. Copy all server logins from the principal server instance to the mirror server instance. There are several ways to do this.

   - SQL Server Integration Services (SSIS) has a transfer logins task you can use to copy logins to the other server.
   - You can use the Generate Scripts wizard by right-clicking on your database, highlighting Tasks, and clicking on Generate Scripts. Select the option to script logins and select all Users as the objects to script. Output the script to a new query window and run the login create statements on the mirror server instance.
   - Query the system security views to create your own T-SQL code to create the logins. We will show you how to script this approach in Chapter 6 so you can set up a maintenance process to keep the logins in sync.

4. Set up any external resources that you need on the mirror server such as SSIS packages, routine maintenance jobs, file shares, and so on.

Depending on how far in advance you perform the preliminary setup, you may need to validate that what you already set up is current. Even if there was a code freeze on the servers, you may need to add or delete server logins or change the permissions for a login. If logins or external resources have been added or changed on the principal server, you need to make sure the changes are applied to the mirror server as well.

Part Two: Pre-setup Configuration

The purpose of part two is to move a current copy of the principal database to the mirror server. Your data needs to be as current as possible so database mirroring does not have to try to apply too many transactions to the mirror database while they are trying to synchronize. Perform the following steps immediately before you begin configuring database mirroring:

1. Disable any jobs on the server that perform full backups or log backups. If a full or log backup is created in between the time that you create your full backup (in the next step) and the time that you create your log backup (in Step 4), you will not be able to restore the log backup that you created over the full backup that you created.
2. Create a full backup of your database and copy it to the mirror server instance.
3. Restore the full backup on the mirror instance using the NORECOVERY option. If you are using the Restore Database User Interface, you can specify NORECOVERY on the Options tab under Recovery State. Select the second recovery state (Restore With NoRecovery).
4. Create a log backup of your database and copy it to the mirror server instance.
5. Restore the log backup on the mirror instance using the NORECOVERY flag. If you are using the Restore Database User Interface, you can specify NORECOVERY on the Options tab under Recovery State. Select the second recovery state (Restore With NoRecovery).

■ **Caution** If at any point during this process you do not restore the database using the NORECOVERY option, you will have to start over by applying another full backup and any transaction log backups.

Now that you have prepared your database, you can move on to setting up database mirroring. If your database is under a heavy load during mirroring setup, you will want to move through the setup steps as quickly as you can without the risk of making mistakes. If your mirror partner gets too far out of sync with the principal partner, you may want to create another log file and restore it to the mirror database again with the NORECOVERY option. If it is not feasible to turn off your transaction log backups during this process, you can continue to back up the logs. You will just need to apply all of them to the mirror database prior to configuring database mirroring.

Following the Wizard

The wizard is straightforward, but it can sometimes be a little counterintuitive. You may not even realize that there is a database mirroring wizard just from looking around. You will not find the wizard listed under the database mirroring topics in SQL Server Books Online.

You can access the database mirroring wizard from Object Explorer within SQL Server Management Studio. This is how you start the wizard:

1. Expand the Databases node.
2. Right-click on the database that you want to mirror.
3. Click on Properties.
4. Click on Mirroring in the left pane to switch to the Database Properties Mirroring page. Figure 4-1 shows the Database Properties Mirroring page.

CHAPTER 4 ■ DATABASE MIRRORING SETUP

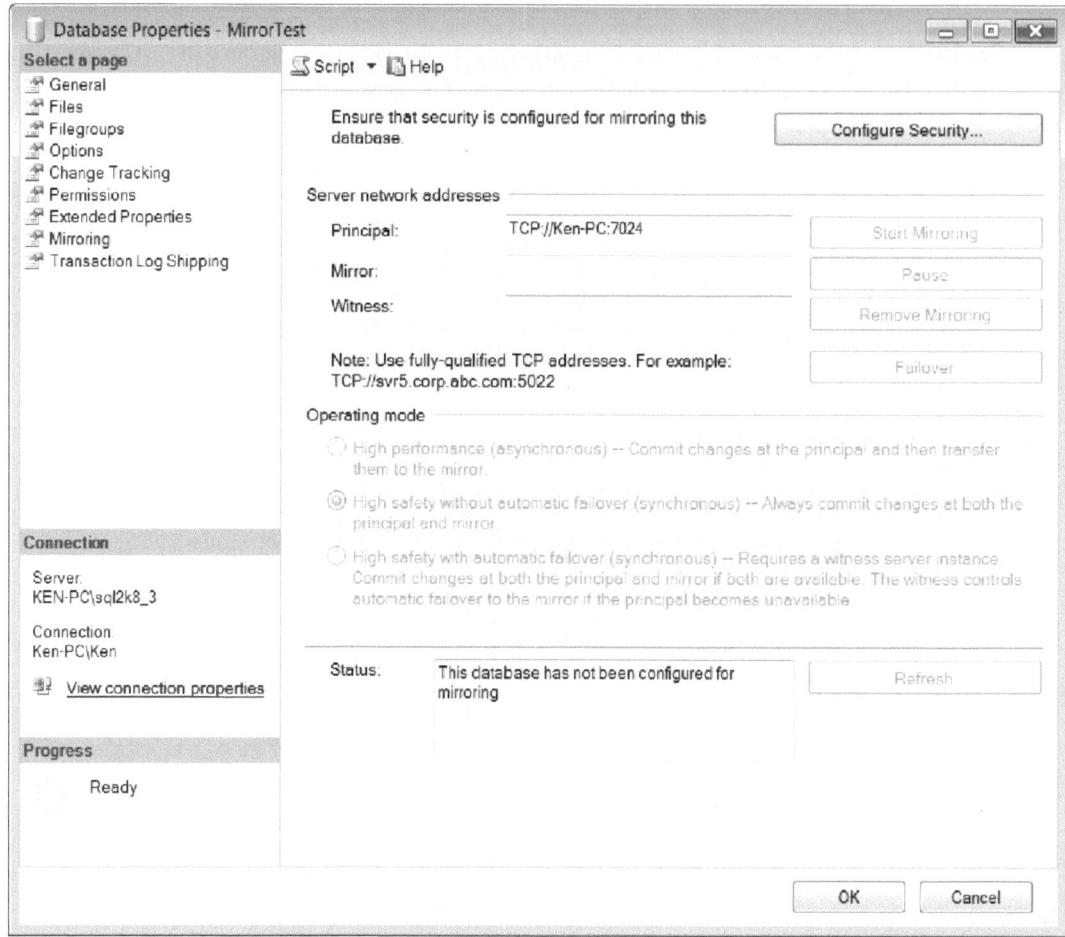

Figure 4-1. *Database Properties Mirroring page*

5. Click the Configure Security button to start the Configure Database Mirroring Security Wizard shown in Figure 4-2.

Figure 4-2. Database Mirroring Security Wizard

At this point, you can see that the actual name of the wizard is the *Configure Database Mirroring Security Wizard*. That is a lot to say, plus the wizard does a lot more than just configure security for database mirroring, so we prefer to call it the database mirroring wizard. Whenever we use the term *database mirroring wizard*, we are referring to the *Configure Database Mirroring Security Wizard*.

The first screen of the database mirroring wizard is merely a title screen. You can check the box at the bottom if you want to skip this screen when you run this wizard in the future. To set up mirroring from this point, follow these general steps:

1. Click the Next button on the title screen to display the Include Witness Server screen shown in Figure 4-3.

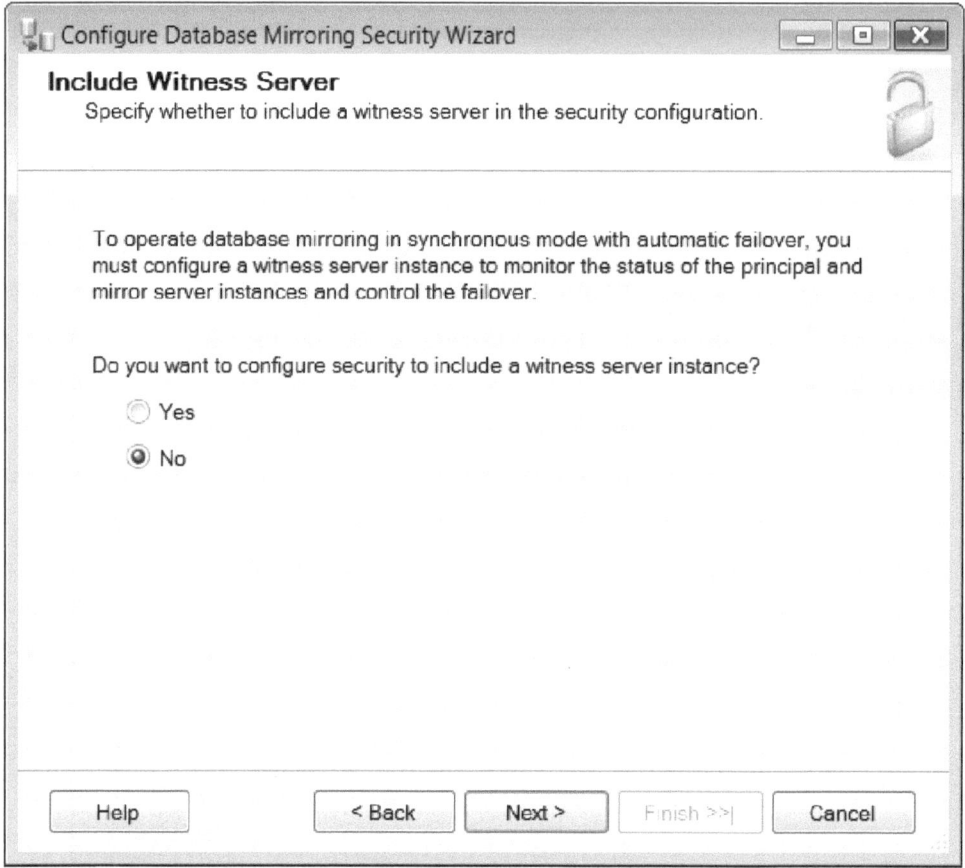

Figure 4-3. Include Witness Server screen

2. Select Yes or No to designate whether you want to set up a witness and click Next.
3. If you selected to include a witness, the next screen shown in Figure 4-4 asks which servers you want to configure. For a new mirroring setup, the principal and mirror are required.

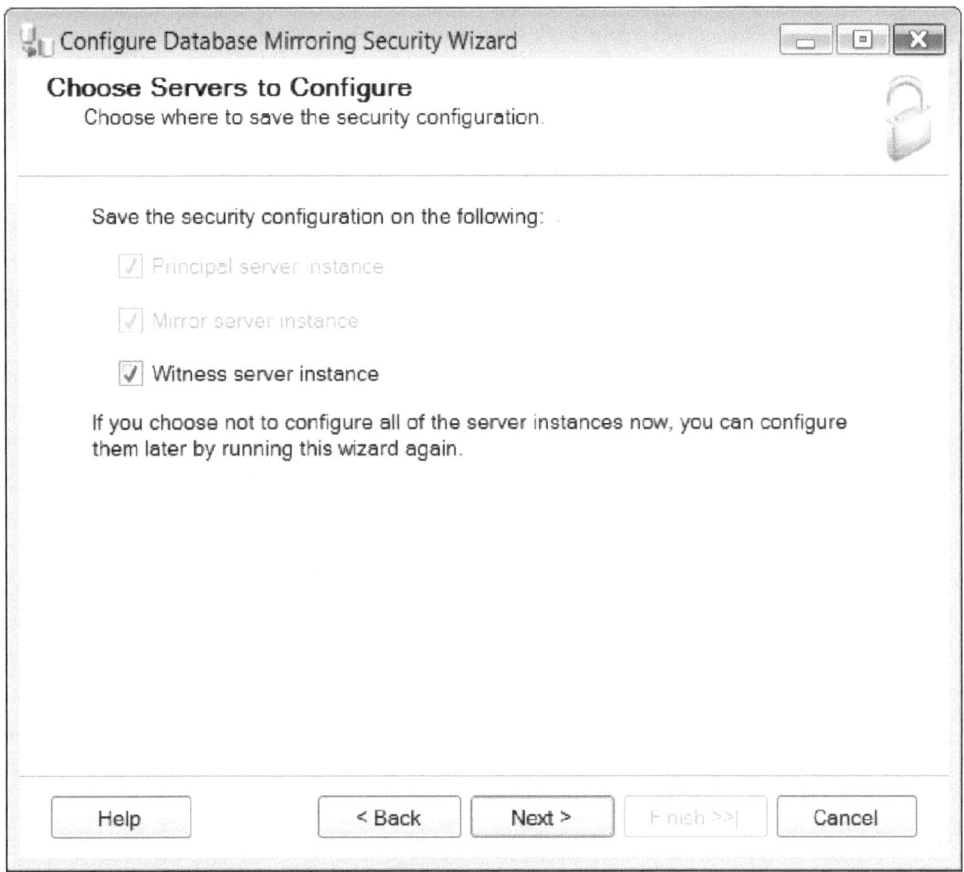

Figure 4-4. Choose Servers to Configure screen

Check the box for the witness server instance and click Next to move to the Principal Server Instance screen shown in Figure 4-5.

Figure 4-5. Principal Server Instance screen

4. Configure the "Principal server instance" setting. If a mirroring endpoint already exists, you will not be able to change the endpoint configuration. If no endpoint exists, you can configure it here. Customize the settings for the endpoint or just click Next to accept the default settings. You will now see the Mirror Server Instance screen shown in Figure 4-6.

Figure 4-6. Mirror Server Instance screen

5. Configure the "Mirror server instance" setting. This screen is similar to the previous screen. The big difference is the Connect button. Click Connect to select the mirror server instance and to set up the security configuration. A standard connection dialog box opens. The only authentication methods you can configure with the wizard are Windows Authentication or SQL Authentication. If you need to use certificate authentication or special encryption algorithms, you must set up mirroring manually with T-SQL. Once you have configured the mirror server, click Next.

6. If you selected to configure a witness at this time, configure the witness server instance. The page for the witness instance is identical to the page for the mirror instance. Once you have configured the witness server, click Next to display the Service Accounts screen shown in Figure 4-7.

Figure 4-7. *Service Accounts screen*

7. Specify your service accounts for the instances. If you are using the same domain account for all instances of the SQL Server service, do not enter anything in this page; just click Next. If the servers use different domain accounts, you will need to enter the accounts on this page for each server instance. Click Next to display the Complete the Wizard screen shown in Figure 4-8.

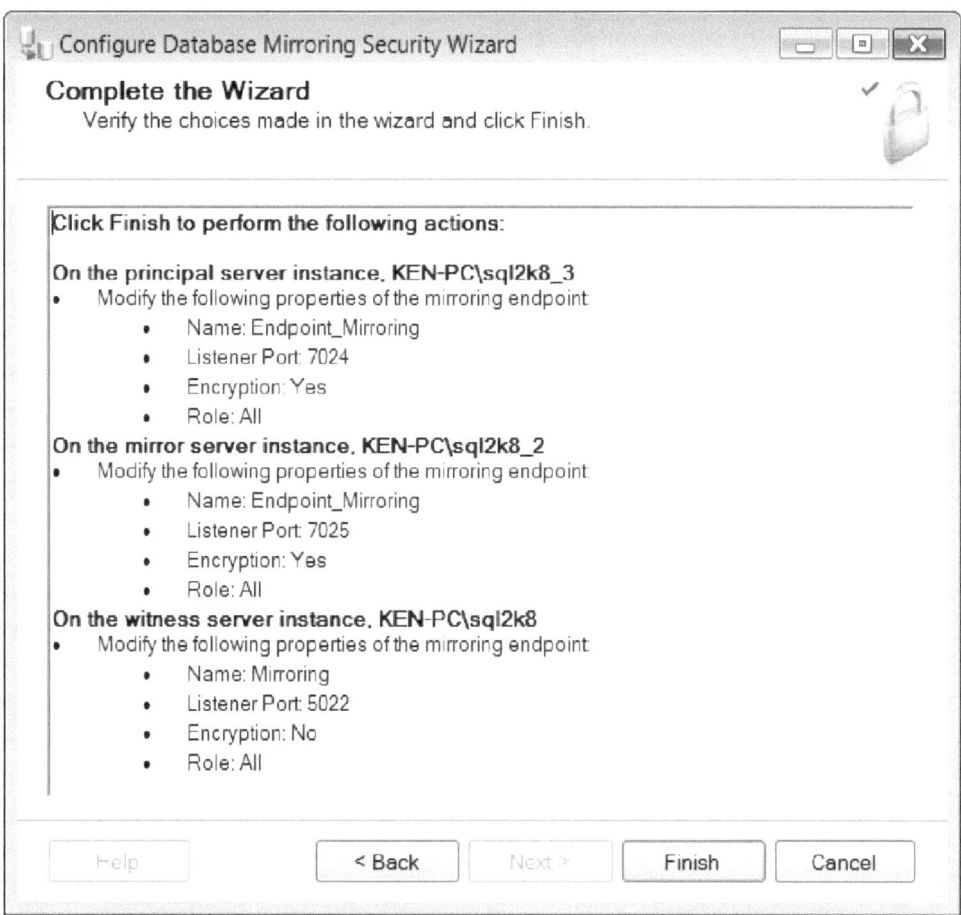

Figure 4-8. *Complete the Wizard screen*

8. The Complete the Wizard screen shows a summary of your settings. Verify your settings and click Finish to display the Configuring Endpoints screen shown in Figure 4-9.

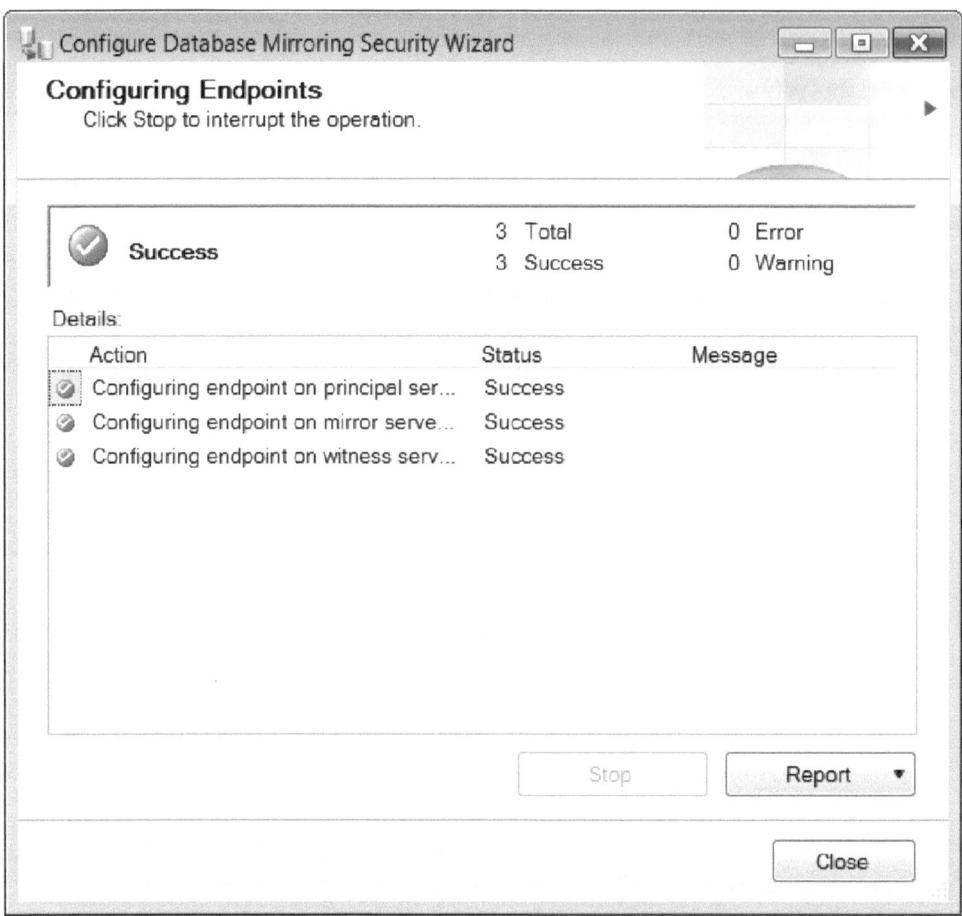

Figure 4-9. Configuring Endpoints screen

9. The wizard creates and configures the endpoints. If you see errors reported, review the messages or use the Report button on the Configuring Endpoints screen to view or save the report. If you do not see any errors, click Close to display the Database Properties dialog box shown in Figure 4-10.

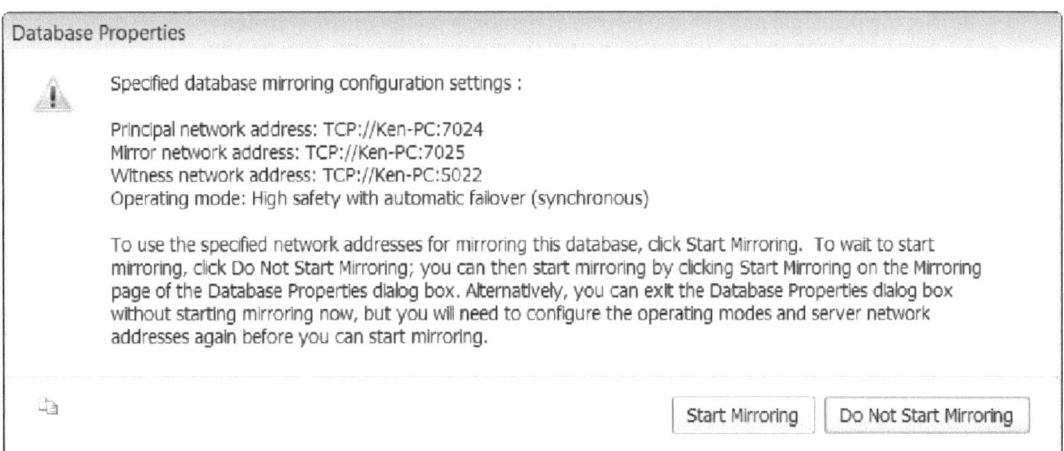

Figure 4-10. Database Properties dialog box

10. Review the configuration settings and click Start Mirroring if you are happy with the settings. If you do not want to start database mirroring in synchronous mode, you need to select Do Not Start Mirroring. You will need to change the mode to asynchronous and select Start Mirroring from the Database Properties dialog box.

11. You are now on the Database Properties Mirroring page again. Here you will see a little glitch in the mirroring wizard. If you configured database mirroring without a witness, the "Operating mode" field is set to "High safety without automatic failover (synchronous)." At this point, you can change the setting to "High performance (asynchronous)," but you cannot save the change if you selected Start Mirroring from the Database Properties dialog box in Figure 4-10. To change to asynchronous mirroring, you must first save the configuration by clicking the OK button. Then you can open the Database Properties Mirroring page again and change the operating mode.

Now that you have database mirroring set up, you can verify that mirroring is running as expected by looking at the principal or mirror partners in Object Explorer in SSMS. You should see the mirroring role and the mirroring state next to the database name. The principal database should say (Principal, Synchronized) if the databases are in sync or (Principal, Synchronizing) if they are still in the process of synchronizing. The mirror database should report its mirroring role and mirroring state in a similar fashion in SQL Server 2005. The mirror database will also display its database state of Restoring. SQL Server 2008 only displays the database state.

Setting Up Mirroring Manually

It may seem like there are a lot steps to setting up database mirroring, and it may seem complex in the beginning. However, some steps are only required one time on a server. For example, you only set up a mirroring endpoint once on an instance no matter how many databases you plan to mirror.

Use the following manual steps to set up database mirroring. We will explain each of these steps in detail following this list.

1. Create endpoints on all of the instances.
2. Create a login for the service accounts of the other instances if they do not exist.
3. Grant connect permissions to the service accounts of the other instances on the endpoint.

4. Set the principal partner for the mirror database on the mirror partner.
5. Set the mirror partner for the principal database on the principal partner.
6. If using a witness server, set the witness partner on the principal partner to enable automatic failover.
7. If not using a witness server, you may want to change the operating mode from "High safety (synchronous)" to "High performance (asynchronous)."

Step 1: Create Endpoints

A database mirroring endpoint is the mechanism through which all database mirroring traffic flows. It is the point of entry for the other servers participating in the mirroring session. Each server instance must have an endpoint to be able to join a database mirroring session.

You create an endpoint using the Create Endpoint statement. Since you can have only one database mirroring endpoint on a server instance, you need to check to see whether an endpoint already exists. There are several system views that contain information about the database mirroring endpoint, but for simplicity's sake, you should use sys.database_mirroring_endpoints and sys.tcp_endpoints. These two views contain everything you need to know about the endpoint.

Listing 3-1 gives an example of how to query to see whether an endpoint exists. The sys.database_mirroring_endpoints catalog view limits the endpoints only used for database mirroring. The sys.tcp_endpoints catalog view shows all endpoints; for example, the endpoint used by the dedicated administrator connection (DAC). However, by adding the sys.tcp_endpoints catalog view you can see additional information such as the port number and IP address used by the endpoint.

Listing 3-1. Querying for the Endpoint Data

```
SELECT DME.name,
        DME.protocol_desc,
        DME.type_desc,
        DME.state_desc,
        role_desc,
        TE.port,
        TE.ip_address
FROM sys.database_mirroring_endpoints AS DME
INNER JOIN sys.tcp_endpoints AS TE ON TE.endpoint_id = DME.endpoint_id
```

If an endpoint does not exist, you will then need to create one. Listing 3-2 shows how to do that. It creates an endpoint named DatabaseMirroring.

Listing 3-2. Creating an Endpoint If One Does Not Exist

```
IF NOT EXISTS (SELECT 1 FROM sys.database_mirroring_endpoints)
  BEGIN
    CREATE ENDPOINT [DatabaseMirroring]
        State = Started
        AS TCP (Listener_Port = 5022, Listener_IP = ALL)
        FOR Database_Mirroring (Role = ALL);
  END
```

There are many aspects of the `CREATE ENDPOINT` statement that we want to call out. Listing 3-2 shows the most common way to create an endpoint for database mirroring and will work well in nearly all scenarios. However, you may want to customize some of the properties of the endpoint to suit your needs. Following are some properties that you may want to change:

Listener_Port: A port can only have one process listening on it at a time. It is crucial to setting up a database mirroring session that you choose a port not already in use. The database mirroring wizard will default to port 5022. If you have multiple instances on a server that participate in mirroring, you must specify a different port for each instance.

Listener_IP: The default listener IP is all available IP addresses. The endpoint will send and receive database mirroring traffic across any IP address in this configuration. One suggestion for performance improvements is to dedicate a network card to database mirroring. You can specify the IP address of the dedicated network card as the Listener_IP, and SQL Server will direct all traffic related to database mirroring across the dedicated network card. You can improve performance of mirroring as well as the server as a whole by separating the traffic streams.

Role: There are three options available for role: partner, witness, or all. If you designate an endpoint as serving the role of a witness or a partner, you cannot use the endpoint for the other role. If you need to change the role of the endpoint, you can do so later by using an Alter Endpoint statement. We suggest always setting the role to all to avoid complications later. The database mirroring wizard creates endpoints with the role specified as partner or witness, not all.

Authentication: If you do not specify an authentication method, the default method is Windows authentication with the Negotiate authorization. You can specify NTLM or Kerberos authorization or use the Negotiate option. The Negotiate option will cause the endpoint to choose the best available authorization scheme. If you are using certificate authentication, this endpoint property defines that.

Step 2: Create Logins

If your instances are all using the same domain accounts for the SQL Server service, you can skip this step. You will need to create a login for the other server instances' service accounts if they do not already exist. You can create the logins in SSMS by right-clicking on the Logins node under Security in Object Explorer and clicking New Login. Another way you can create the logins is by using the Create Login statement:

```
CREATE LOGIN [Domain\Username] FROM Windows;
```

Step 3: Grant Connect on Endpoint to Logins

You can skip this step as well if your server instances are using the same domain account. In that case, the accounts will already have permission to connect to the endpoint. The only privilege you need to grant is Connect. You can use the following code to grant connect permissions:

```
GRANT CONNECT ON ENDPOINT::[DatabaseMirroring] TO [Domain\Username];
```

Step 4: Set the Principal Partner on Mirror

You define the mirroring partnership on the mirror partner first to get the database ready to initialize mirroring. Define the partnership with the Alter Database statement. The key component of the command is the server network address of the partner.

The format of this command is as follows:

```
ALTER DATABASE <Database Name>
SET PARTNER = 'TCP:\<Server Address>:Port';
```

The server address is the string address that uniquely identifies the principal server, and the port is the port that the endpoint on the principal server uses. It is highly recommended that you use either the IP address or the fully qualified domain name of the server.

If we performed this on our mirror database MirrorTest, the code would be:

```
ALTER DATABASE [MirrorTest]
SET PARTNER = 'TCP:\v-rodav4.mydomain.com:5022';
```

Step 5: Set the Mirror Partner on Principal

When you define the mirroring partnership on the principal database, the process is identical to how you defined it on the mirror partner. Use the Alter Database statement to define the partnership. Once again, the server address must uniquely identify the mirror partner, and the port designation must match the port that the endpoint on the mirror server is using.

You will notice in the following example that our server address is the same as our principal, but the port is different. When a partner is on a named instance, you do not use the instance name in the server address. This is another reason why using different ports for each instance on a server is required.

We would perform this on our principal database MirrorTest with the following:

```
ALTER DATABASE [MirrorTest]
SET PARTNER = 'TCP:\v-rodav4.mydomain.com:5023';
```

If there are no errors, database mirroring is officially running at this point. The mirror and principal partners are synchronizing or synchronized. You can validate this quickly by looking at the databases in Object Explorer in SSMS. However, you will need to refresh the databases in order to see the new status. You should see the mirroring role and the mirroring state next to the database name. The principal database should say "(Principal, Synchronized)" if the databases are in sync or "(Principal, Synchronizing)" if they are still in the process of synchronizing. The mirror database should report its mirroring role and mirroring state in a similar fashion in SQL Server 2005. The mirror database will also display its database state of Restoring. SQL Server 2008 only displays the database state.

Step 6: Set the Witness Partner on Principal

If you want to include a witness partner in the database mirroring session, you can define it at any point after mirroring is up and running. You can define a witness partner in the same manner that you defined the mirror and principal partners. You define the witness on the principal server. Use a slightly different Alter Database statement to set up the witness.

The format of this command is:

```
ALTER DATABASE <Database Name>
SET WITNESS = 'TCP:\<Server Address>:Port';
```

The server address is the string address that uniquely identifies the witness server, and the port is the port that the endpoint on the witness server uses. Again, it is highly recommended that you use either the IP address or the fully qualified domain name of the server for the server address.

If we added a witness for our mirrored database `MirrorTest`, the code would be:

```
ALTER DATABASE [MirrorTest]
SET WITNESS = 'TCP:\v-rodav4.mydomain.com:7022';
```

Once again, notice that our witness is on a named instance and is using a different port number than the principal or mirror servers.

Step 7: Change the Operating Mode

When you initialized the database mirroring session, mirroring started in synchronous mode. If you want automatic failover, and you are using a witness server, then do not change the operating mode at this time. If you are not using a witness server, you may want to change the operating mode to asynchronous.

You can change the operating mode by issuing an Alter Database statement:

```
ALTER DATABASE [MirrorTest]
SET SAFETY OFF;
```

If you change the operating mode to asynchronous, you should realize that you cannot manually fail over the mirroring session while in asynchronous mode. You have to change the operating mode back to synchronous mode, wait for the databases to synchronize, and then fail over the database.

Special Case: Mirroring with Certificates

If your servers are using Local System for the SQL Server service accounts, you will need to use certificate authentication. Certificate authentication will also be required if your servers are not able to authenticate the accounts of the other servers or if you do not want to grant permissions to a Windows login.

Repeat the following steps on each server instance to configure mirroring with certificate authentication. The subsections that follow describe each step in detail.

1. Create a database master key in master if one does not already exist.
2. Create a certificate in master database encrypted by the master key.
3. Create an endpoint using the certificate for authentication.
4. Back up the certificate to a file.
5. Create login on server for the other instances.
6. Create users in master database mapped to the logins you created.
7. Assign the certificates to the users.
8. Grant connect permissions on the endpoint.
9. Set the principal partner for the mirror database on the mirror partner.
10. Set the mirror partner for the principal database on the principal partner.
11. If using a witness server, set the witness partner on the principal partner to enable automatic failover.
12. If not using a witness server, you may want to change the operating mode from "High safety (synchronous)" to "High performance (asynchronous)."

Step 1: Create Database Master Key

The database master key is required to create encrypted certificates. You will need to provide a strong password for the database master key. Take note of this password and store it somewhere safe. Create the database master key with the following code:

```
USE master
GO

CREATE MASTER KEY ENCRYPTION BY PASSWORD = 'My$tr0nGPa$$w0rd!!';
```

Step 2: Create a Certificate

Use the Create Certificate command to create an encrypted certificate from the database master key. Be aware that certificates expire one year from creation date unless you provide an expiration date when you create it. The following code creates the certificate with an expiration date in the year 2015 to give us a little more leeway for dealing with this issue:

```
USE master
GO

CREATE CERTIFICATE Host_1_Cert
WITH Subject = 'Host_1 Certificate',
Expiry_Date = '1/1/2015';
```

Step 3: Create an Endpoint

For the sake of brevity, we will not repeat the detailed information about endpoints cited above. For more details on endpoints, please see the previous section on endpoints.

To create an endpoint that uses certificate authentication create the endpoint in this manner:

```
IF NOT EXISTS (SELECT 1 FROM sys.database_mirroring_endpoints)
  BEGIN
    CREATE ENDPOINT [DatabaseMirroring]
        State = Started
        AS TCP (Listener_Port = 5022, Listener_IP = ALL)
        FOR Database_Mirroring (
            Authentication = Certificate Host_1_Cert,
            Encryption = Required Algorithm AES,
            Role = ALL);
  END
```

Step 4: Back Up the Certificate

You will need to back up the certificate to a file and copy it to the other servers so that it can be imported. You can recreate the certificate easily, so there is no need to store the certificate in a safe location.

You can back up the certificate with the following command:

```
BACKUP CERTIFICATE Host_1_Cert
TO FILE = 'E:\mssql\bak\certificates\Host_1_Cert.cer';
```

Step 5: Create Logins

Create a server login for each of the other servers.

```
CREATE LOGIN Host_2_Login WITH PASSWORD = 'My$trOnGPa$$wOrd!!';
```

Step 6: Create Users

Create a user in the master database for each of the other servers mapped to the associate login.

```
CREATE USER Host_2_User For Login Host_2_Login;
```

Step 7: Assign the Certificate

Create a new certificate by importing the certificates copied from the other servers. Map the new certificate to the appropriate user that you created.

```
CREATE CERTIFICATE Host_2_Cert
Authorization Host_2_User
FROM FILE = 'E:\mssql\bak\certificates\Host_2_Cert.cer';
```

Step 8: Grant Connect on Endpoint to Logins

The only privilege you need to grant is Connect. You can use the following code to grant connect permissions:

```
GRANT CONNECT ON ENDPOINT::[DatabaseMirroring] TO [Host_2_Login];
```

Step 9: Configure Database Mirroring

The remaining steps are the same as explained in the previous section. There are no special considerations with regards to certificates for the remainder of the process.

Test, Monitor, and Wrap Up

Now that you have database mirroring configured and running, you should perform some basic tests. The most basic test is to fail the database over to the mirror partner and then fail it back. If you are running in asynchronous mode, you will need to change the operating mode first.

The following code changes the operating mode, waits 30 seconds, and then fails over the database:

```
ALTER DATABASE [MirrorTest]
SET SAFETY ON
GO

WaitFor Delay '00:00:30';
GO
```

```
ALTER DATABASE [MirrorTest]
SET PARTNER FAILOVER;
```

After testing the failover, open Database Mirroring Monitor. Database Mirroring Monitor will create a job on the servers to update the database mirroring monitor history. This allows you to check the historical state of database mirroring. There are two ways to open Database Mirroring Monitor. The easiest way is to right-click on the mirrored database in Object Explorer in SSMS, highlight Tasks, and click on Launch Database Mirroring Monitor. This will open the monitor to the correct pane with the mirrored database already registered.

The other way you can run Database Mirroring Monitor is to click Start, click Run, enter SQLMonitor and press Enter or click OK. When SQL Monitor opens, it will open to the Replication Monitor pane. Switch to the Database Mirroring Monitor pane by clicking Go on the menu bar and clicking Database Mirroring Monitor. If your database is not already registered, you will have to register the database manually.

Note When you first look at a database mirroring session in the monitor, it connects to the principal partner first and then the mirror partner. For a short period, the monitor will display as disconnected from the mirror partner. This only means that the monitor has not yet established a connection to the mirror partner. This does not mean that the mirror partner is in a disconnected state.

If mirroring is running correctly and configured to your specifications, you just need to wrap up a few things. If you disabled any jobs such as maintenance routines, you should re-enable them at this point. Deploy any website or application configuration files that have new connection strings. If you have testers available to test the application, alert them that they can begin their testing.

Troubleshooting Common Setup Issues

As you can see, there are several steps involved in setting up database mirroring. If your environment is not configured 100 percent correct, you will encounter errors during setup. There are generally three issues you may encounter when setting up database mirroring: restore issues, transaction log issues, and communication issues. We will discuss each of these issues, including the error messages you will receive and how to resolve them.

Restore Issues

If you did not restore your database on the mirror server using the NORECOVERY option, you will receive the following error.

Error 1416 - Database <DatabaseName> is not configured for mirroring.

In order to resolve this issue you will have to take a full backup of the principal database and restore it on the mirror server using the NORECOVERY option. You will then need to take one more transaction log backup and restore it on the mirror server using the NORECOVERY option as well. If at any time during the setup process you restore a backup using any other option than NORECOVERY, you will have to start over with a new full backup.

Transaction Log Issues

If you did not restore a transaction log on the mirror server before trying to start database mirroring or you have taken transaction log backups of the principal database since you restored the database on the mirror server, you will receive the following errors.

Error 1412 - The remote copy of database <DatabaseName> has not been rolled forward to a point in time that is encompassed in the local copy of the database log.

Error 1478 - The mirror database, <DatabaseName>, has insufficient transaction log data to preserve the log backup chain of the principal database. This may happen if a log backup from the principal database has not been taken or has not been restored on the mirror database.

To solve either one of these errors, you need to apply one or more transaction log backups to the database on the mirror server. If you have not taken a backup of the transaction log of the database on the principal server and restored it to the database on the mirror, you will need to do so in order to resolve error 1478, which will allow you to start database mirroring. If you did not turn off your transaction log backup job on your principal server, you will need to apply all of the transaction logs that have occurred since the last log you applied on the mirror server in order to resolve error 1412, which will allow you to start database mirroring.

Communication Issues

Communication issues are the hardest of all issues to resolve, since there are many components that may be the culprit. Also, the error message does not indicate which server is the cause of the communication issue; you have to troubleshoot both servers that are trying to communicate. You will see the following errors if you are having communication issues when trying to start database mirroring.

Error 1418 - The server network address <NetworkAddress> can not be reached or does not exist. Check the network address name and that the ports for the local and remote endpoints are operational.

Error 1486 - Database Mirroring Transport is disabled in the endpoint configuration.

Error 1456 - The ALTER DATABASE command could not be sent to the remote server instance <NetworkAddress>. The database mirroring configuration was not changed. Verify that the server is connected, and try again.

Error 1456 specifically deals with communication between the witness server and one of the partner servers. Error 1418 and 1456 are communication errors between each of the partner servers. However, you can use the following list to help you resolve communication issues for all three errors. Error 1418 even has its own page in SQL Server Books Online located at http://msdn.microsoft.com/en-us/library/aa337361.aspx.

- Make sure SQL Server is not using the Local System account. You will need to use Network Service or a domain account unless you set up database mirroring using certificates.
- Try to telnet to each port locally and remotely. If you can telnet locally and not remotely, you probably have a firewall issue.
- Query the sys.database_mirroring_endpoints catalog view on each server to make sure all of the settings such as encryption and authentication methods are the same for each endpoint.
- Query the sys.tcp_enpoints catalog view to make sure the database mirroring endpoints are started. If not, you can start an endpoint using the following command:

```
ALTER ENDPOINT EndpointName STATE = STARTED
```

Summary

After you have performed a few database mirroring setups, you will realize that mirroring really is much simpler than it sounds at first. Our suggestion is to try to practice the setup a couple of times using both the wizard and T-SQL. Once you are comfortable using both methods for setting up database mirroring, you will be ready to tackle any database mirroring needs that arise.

We especially think understanding and practicing the T-SQL method is important because it offers greater control over the process and helps you to understand how database mirroring works. With greater insight into how mirroring works, you will be able to respond quickly if problems arise and create processes to manage and maintain mirroring.

CHAPTER 5

Automating Setup

If you need to set up one or two mirrored databases, the information you learned in the previous chapter will serve you well. What do you do if you need to mirror more than a hundred databases spread across ten servers? The answer is that you automate. Automation is one of the DBA's most important tools.

When faced with a complex, multistep task, we have found that the simplest and least problematic way to automate the task is to break it down into individual steps, automate each individual step, and then create a master process to control the flow and logic of the overall process. We follow this methodology for the solutions in this chapter, which are based upon both T-SQL and PowerShell.

Each of the sections that follow shows you a stored procedure to execute just one step in the overall process of configuring a mirroring environment. In order to use those procedures, you should create each of them on all servers that you plan to involve in your mirroring configuration. You can put the procedures in the master database or in a database of your own choosing. We prefer to create an operations database on each server for our operations and maintenance scripts. The important thing to remember is to make sure you put the stored procedures in the same database on every server.

After walking through and explaining each of the procedures, we show how to invoke the master procedure that ties them all together. We do that in the section named "The Master Procedure" in this chapter. Be sure that you also create the master procedure on all involved servers.

Remember that as a DBA, you are responsible for your environment. We've tested the code in this chapter to the best of our ability. It is code that we use on an almost daily basis. However, you should be sure to read and understand the code before unleashing it in your own environment. Automation is powerful, but it's still important to understand what the automation is doing.

Note You can find the code for the procedures in this chapter in the example download for this book. That download is available from the Source Code section on the Apress web site.

Prepare the Database for Mirroring

The procedure dba_ConfigureDBForMirroring introduced in this section automatically prepares a database for mirroring. All you have to do is pass to the procedure the name of the database that you would like to mirror, and the procedure does the rest. The first thing it does after setting a few variables and confirming that there is actually a database with the name you passed is to verify that the database is not participating in mirroring. If the database is already participating in mirroring, the procedure returns an error. The next thing the procedure does is check to make sure the compatibility level is 90, which is the minimum level required for database mirroring, or greater. If the value is less than 90, the procedure sets the compatibility level to the highest setting supported by the version of SQL Server. The last thing the procedure does is check to make sure the database is using the Full Recovery model. If not, the procedure changes the recovery model for you. Following is the code for this procedure.

```
CREATE PROCEDURE dbo.dba_ConfigureDBForMirroring
        @DBName sysname
AS

DECLARE @RecoveryModel INT,
        @Compatibility INT,
        @DBID INT,
        @MaxCompat INT,
        @SQL NVARCHAR(500),
        @MirrState INT,
        @Server sysname

SET NOCOUNT ON

SET @DBID = DB_ID(@DBName)
SET @MaxCompat = PARSENAME(CAST(SERVERPROPERTY('ProductVersion') AS sysname), 4)*10
SET @Server = @@SERVERNAME

IF @DBID IS NULL
  BEGIN
        RAISERROR('Database [%s] not found on server [%s].',
                               16, 1, @DBName,  @Server);
        RETURN;
  END

SELECT @Compatibility = D.compatibility_level,
               @RecoveryModel = D.recovery_model,
               @MirrState = DM.mirroring_state
FROM   sys.databases D
INNER JOIN sys.database_mirroring DM ON DM.database_id = D.database_id
WHERE D.database_id = @DBID

IF @MirrState IS NOT NULL
  BEGIN
    RAISERROR('Database [%s] is already configured for mirroring on server [%s].',
                   16, 1, @DBName, @Server);
    RETURN;
  END

IF @Compatibility < 90
  BEGIN
        PRINT 'Changing compatibility level to ' + CAST(@MaxCompat AS NVARCHAR);
        IF @MaxCompat = 90 -- SQL Server 2005
          BEGIN
```

```
                    EXEC sp_dbcmptlevel @dbname = @DBName,
                                   @new_cmptlevel = @MaxCompat;
            END
        ELSE IF @MaxCompat >= 100 -- SQL Server 2008+
            BEGIN
                    SET @SQL = 'Alter Database ' + QUOTENAME(@DBName) +
                            ' Set Compatibility_Level = ' +
                            CAST(@MaxCompat AS NVARCHAR) + ';';
                    EXEC sp_executesql @SQL;
            END
    END

IF @RecoveryModel <> 1 -- Full Recovery Model
    BEGIN
        PRINT 'Changing Recovery Model to Full';
        SET @SQL = 'Alter Database ' + QUOTENAME(@DBName) +
                ' Set Recovery Full;';
        EXEC sp_executesql @SQL;
    END
```

Back Up the Principal Database

Here we have the opportunity to accomplish two tasks with a single procedure. The process of creating a full backup is almost identical to the process of creating a log backup. If you make the procedure generic enough, you can use the same procedure for both tasks. The procedure *dba_BackupDB* handles both full and log backups. First, the procedure checks to make sure the database you supplied is a valid database and is online. Then, if you did not supply a backup location, the procedure attempts to select the default location from the registry, and as a last resort, the last backup location that is stored in the msdb database. Finally, the procedure adds the appropriate file extension based on the backup type, creates the file directory if needed, and performs the backup. Following is the code.

```
CREATE PROCEDURE dbo.dba_BackupDB
        @DBName sysname,
        @BackupType bit = 0, -- 0 = Full, 1 = Log
        -- Location where you want the backups saved
        @BackupLocation NVARCHAR(255) = NULL,
        @Debug bit = 0, -- 0 = Execute, 1 = Return SQL for execution
        @BackupFile NVARCHAR(500) = NULL OUTPUT
AS

DECLARE @BakDir NVARCHAR(255),
        @Exists INT,
        @DBID INT,
        @SQL NVARCHAR(1000),
        @Backup NVARCHAR(500),
        @DateSerial NVARCHAR(35),
        @ErrNumber INT,
```

```
        @ErrSeverity INT,
        @ErrState INT,
        @ErrProcedure sysname,
        @ErrLine INT,
        @ErrMsg NVARCHAR(2048),
        @BAKExtension NVARCHAR(10),
        @BackupName sysname,
        @BAKDesc sysname,
        @BackupTypeStr NVARCHAR(20),
        @BAKName sysname

DECLARE @FileExists TABLE (FileExists INT NOT NULL,
                      FileIsDirectory INT NOT NULL,
                      ParentDirectoryExists INT NOT NULL)

SET NOCOUNT ON

SET @DateSerial = CONVERT(NVARCHAR, GETDATE(), 112) +
                REPLACE(CONVERT(NVARCHAR, GETDATE(), 108), ':', '');
SET @DBID = DB_ID(@DBName)

IF @DBID IS NULL
  BEGIN
        RAISERROR ('The specified database [%s] does not exist.', 16, 1, @DBName);
        RETURN;
  END

IF EXISTS (SELECT 1 FROM sys.databases
        WHERE name = @DBName
        AND state > 0)
  BEGIN
        RAISERROR ('The specified database [%s] is not online.', 16, 1, @DBName);
        RETURN;
  END

IF EXISTS (SELECT 1 FROM sys.databases
        WHERE name = @DBName
        AND source_database_id IS NOT NULL)
  BEGIN
        RAISERROR ('The specified database [%s] is a database snapshot.',
                            16, 1, @DBName);
        RETURN;
  END

IF @BackupLocation IS NULL
```

```
   BEGIN
        EXEC xp_instance_regread N'HKEY_LOCAL_MACHINE',
                                 N'Software\Microsoft\MSSQLServer\MSSQLServer',
                                 N'BackupDirectory',
                                 @BakDir output,
                                 'no_output';
        IF @BakDir IS NOT NULL
          BEGIN
                INSERT INTO @FileExists
                EXEC sys.xp_fileexist @BakDir;

                SELECT @Exists = ParentDirectoryExists
                FROM @FileExists

                IF @Exists = 1
                  BEGIN
                        SET @BackupLocation = @BakDir;
                  END
          END
   END

IF @BackupLocation IS NULL
  BEGIN
    SELECT TOP 1 @BakDir = LEFT(MF.physical_device_name,
             LEN(MF.physical_device_name) -
             CHARINDEX('\', REVERSE(MF.physical_device_name)))
    FROM msdb.dbo.backupset BS INNER JOIN
        msdb.dbo.backupmediafamily MF
         ON MF.media_set_id = BS.media_set_id
    ORDER BY BS.type ASC, -- full backups first, then differentials, then log backups
        BS.backup_finish_date DESC; -- oldest first

        IF @BakDir IS NOT NULL
          BEGIN
                DELETE FROM @FileExists

                INSERT INTO @FileExists
                EXEC sys.xp_fileexist @BakDir;

                SELECT @Exists = ParentDirectoryExists
                FROM @FileExists

                IF @Exists = 1
                  BEGIN
                        SET @BackupLocation = @BakDir;
                  END
```

```
            END
    END

IF @BackupLocation IS NOT NULL
  BEGIN
        IF RIGHT(@BackupLocation, 1) <> '\'
                SET @BackupLocation = @BackupLocation + '\';
    END
ELSE
  BEGIN
        RAISERROR ('Backup location not specified or not found.', 16, 1);
        RETURN;
    END

/* Set backup extension and with option */
IF @BackupType = 0
  BEGIN
        SET @BAKExtension = '.bak'
        SET @BackupTypeStr = 'Database'
    END
ELSE
  BEGIN
        SET @BAKExtension = '.trn'
        SET @BackupTypeStr = 'Log'
    END

IF RIGHT(@BackupLocation, 1) <> '\'
  BEGIN
          SET @BackupLocation = @BackupLocation + '\'
    END

SET @BAKName = @DBName + '_backup_' + @DateSerial + @BAKExtension;
SET @Backup = @BackupLocation + @DBName;
SET @BackupName = @DBName + ' Backup';
SET @BAKDesc = 'Backup of ' + @DBName;
SET @SQL = 'Backup ' + @BackupTypeStr + SPACE(1) +
        QUOTENAME(@DBName) + CHAR(10) + CHAR(9) +
        'To Disk = ''' + @Backup + '\' + @BAKName + '''' + CHAR(10) + CHAR(9) +
        'With Init,' + CHAR(10) + CHAR(9) + CHAR(9) +
        'Description = ''' + @BAKDesc + ''',' + CHAR(10) + CHAR(9) + CHAR(9) +
        'Name = ''' + @BackupName + ''';';

-- Make sure backup location exists
-- Will not overwrite existing files, if any
IF @Debug = 0
  BEGIN
```

```
        EXEC xp_create_subdir @Backup;
    END
ELSE
  BEGIN
        PRINT 'Exec xp_create_subdir ' + @Backup + ';';
    END

BEGIN TRY
        IF @Debug = 0
          BEGIN
                PRINT 'Backing up ' + @DBName;
                EXEC sp_executesql @SQL;
            END
        ELSE
          BEGIN
                PRINT 'Print ''Backing up ' + @DBName + '''';';
                PRINT @SQL;
            END
END TRY
BEGIN CATCH
        SET @ErrNumber = ERROR_NUMBER();
        SET @ErrSeverity = ERROR_SEVERITY();
        SET @ErrState = ERROR_STATE();
        SET @ErrProcedure = ERROR_PROCEDURE();
        SET @ErrLine = ERROR_LINE();
        SET @ErrMsg = ERROR_MESSAGE();

        PRINT '';
        PRINT 'Database Name = ' + @DBName;
        PRINT 'Error Number = ' + CAST(@ErrNumber AS VARCHAR);
        PRINT 'Error Severity = ' + CAST(@ErrSeverity AS VARCHAR);
        PRINT 'Error State = ' + CAST(@ErrState AS VARCHAR);
        PRINT 'Error Procedure = ' + ISNULL(@ErrProcedure, '');
        PRINT 'Error Line = ' + CAST(@ErrLine AS VARCHAR);
        PRINT 'Error Message = ' + @ErrMsg;
        PRINT '';

        RAISERROR('Failed to back up database [%s].', 16, 1, @DBName);
        RETURN;
END CATCH

SET @BackupFile = @Backup + '\' + @BAKName
```

Restore Full Backup on the Mirror Database with No Recovery

The procedure dba_RestoreDB manages the restore of the backup file to the mirror database. This procedure drops the mirror database if it already exists before restoring the backup with the No Recovery option. There is no need to move the backup file you created in the previous section because the procedure uses the principal server name to create a Universal Naming Convention (UNC) path if you pass in the exact path of the file on the principal server. Following is the code.

```
CREATE PROCEDURE dbo.dba_RestoreDB
        @DBName sysname,
        @BackupFile NVARCHAR(500),
        @PrinServer sysname,
        @Debug bit = 0 -- 0 = Execute, 1 = Return SQL for execution
AS

DECLARE @DBID INT,
        @UNCBackupFile NVARCHAR(500),
        @Exists INT,
        @SQL NVARCHAR(MAX),
        @SQLVersion INT,
        @MaxID INT,
        @CurrID INT,
        @PhysicalName NVARCHAR(260),
        @Movelist NVARCHAR(MAX)
DECLARE @Files TABLE (FileID INT NOT NULL PRIMARY KEY,
                LogicalName NVARCHAR(128) NULL,
                PhysicalName NVARCHAR(260) NULL,
                [Type] CHAR(1) NULL,
                FileGroupName NVARCHAR(128) NULL,
                [Size] numeric(20,0) NULL,
                [MaxSize] numeric(20,0) NULL,
                CreateLSN numeric(25,0),
                DropLSN numeric(25,0) NULL,
                UniqueID uniqueidentifier,
                ReadOnlyLSN numeric(25,0) NULL,
                ReadWriteLSN numeric(25,0) NULL,
                BackupSizeInBytes bigint,
                SourceBlockSize INT,
                FileGroupID INT,
                LogGroupGUID uniqueidentifier NULL,
                DifferentialBaseLSN numeric(25,0) NULL,
                DifferentialBaseGUID uniqueidentifier,
                IsReadOnly bit,
                IsPresent bit,
```

```
                TDEThumbprint varbinary(32) NULL,
                NewPhysicalName NVARCHAR(260) NULL)

SET NOCOUNT ON

SET @DBID = DB_ID(@DBName);
SET @SQLVersion = PARSENAME(CAST(SERVERPROPERTY('ProductVersion') AS sysname), 4)

IF @DBID IS NOT NULL
  BEGIN
        IF EXISTS (SELECT 1 FROM sys.databases
                WHERE database_id = @DBID
                AND state = 0) -- online
            BEGIN
                SET @SQL = 'Alter Database ' + QUOTENAME(@DBName) +
                        ' Set Offline With Rollback Immediate;';

                IF @Debug = 1
                  BEGIN
                        PRINT @SQL;
                  END
                ELSE
                  BEGIN
                        EXEC sp_executesql @SQL;
                  END
          END

        PRINT 'Dropping existing database';
        SET @SQL = 'Drop Database ' + QUOTENAME(@DBName) + ';';
        IF @Debug = 1
          BEGIN
                PRINT @SQL;
          END
        ELSE
          BEGIN
                EXEC sp_executesql @SQL;
          END
  END

-- Convert bakup path to UNC
IF SUBSTRING(@BackupFile, 2, 2) = ':\'
  BEGIN
        SET @UNCBackupFile = '\\' + @PrinServer + '\' +
                        REPLACE(LEFT(@BackupFile, 2), ':', '$') +
                        RIGHT(@BackupFile, LEN(@BackupFile) - 2);
```

```
      END
ELSE
  BEGIN
        SET @UNCBackupFile = @BackupFile
  END

-- Verify backup file is accessible
EXEC xp_FileExist @UNCBackupFile, @Exists OUTPUT

IF @Exists = 0 -- Does not exist or is not accessible
  BEGIN
        RAISERROR('Unable to open backup file: %s', 16, 1, @UNCBackupFile);
        RETURN;
  END

SET @SQL  = 'Restore FileListonly From Disk = ''' + @UNCBackupFile + ''';';

-- Check file paths specified in backup
IF @SQLVersion = 9
  BEGIN
      INSERT INTO @Files (LogicalName, PhysicalName, [Type], FileGroupName, [Size],
                  [MaxSize], FileID, CreateLSN, DropLSN, UniqueId, ReadOnlyLSN,
                  ReadWriteLSN, BackupSizeInBytes, SourceBlockSize, FileGroupId,
                  LogGroupGUID, DifferentialBaseLSN, DifferentialBaseGUID,
                  IsReadOnly, IsPresent)
      EXEC sp_executesql @SQL
  END
ELSE
  BEGIN
      INSERT INTO @Files (LogicalName, PhysicalName, [Type], FileGroupName, [Size],
                  [MaxSize], FileID, CreateLSN, DropLSN, UniqueId, ReadOnlyLSN,
                  ReadWriteLSN, BackupSizeInBytes, SourceBlockSize, FileGroupId,
                  LogGroupGUID, DifferentialBaseLSN, DifferentialBaseGUID,
                  IsReadOnly, IsPresent, TDEThumbprint)
      EXEC sp_executesql @SQL;
  END

SELECT @MaxID = MAX(FileId), @CurrID = 1
FROM @Files

WHILE @CurrID <= @MaxID
  BEGIN
        SELECT @PhysicalName = PhysicalName
        FROM @Files
        WHERE FileID = @CurrID
```

```
        -- Check if file already exists
        EXEC xp_FileExist @PhysicalName, @Exists OUTPUT

        -- Change physical name if the file already exists
        IF @Exists = 1
          BEGIN
                SET @PhysicalName = LEFT(@PhysicalName, LEN(@PhysicalName) - 4) +
                                '_mirr' + RIGHT(@PhysicalName, 4)
          END

        UPDATE @Files
        SET NewPhysicalName = @PhysicalName
        WHERE FileID = @CurrID

        SET @CurrID = @CurrID + 1
    END

-- Build the "With Move" portion of the Restore command
SELECT @Movelist = ISNULL(@MoveList + ',' + CHAR(10) + CHAR(9), '') +
                'Move ''' + LogicalName + ''' To ''' +
                NewPhysicalName + ''''
FROM @Files
ORDER BY [Type]

SET @SQL = 'Restore Database ' + QUOTENAME(@DBName) + CHAR(10) + CHAR(9) +
        'From Disk = ''' + @UNCBackupFile + '''' + CHAR(10) + CHAR(9) +
        'With NoRecovery, Stats = 10, NoUnload,' + CHAR(10) + CHAR(9) +
        @Movelist

-- If not run in debug mode, execute, else print execute statement
IF @Debug = 0
  BEGIN
        EXEC sp_executesql @SQL;
  END
ELSE
  BEGIN
        PRINT '';
        PRINT @SQL;
  END
```

Back Up the Log of the Principal Database

You can reuse the procedure for the full backup—dba_BackupDB—for this task. We wrote the procedure dba_BackupDB with enough flexibility to handle full and log backups. You will see that there are slight differences in how the procedure handles the different backup types.

Restore the Log on the Mirror Database with No Recovery

Unlike the backup process, there are considerable differences between the restore processes. A single procedure for restoring the full and log backups would have to be overly complex to handle the differences. In light of that, execute the following dba_RestoreDBLog procedure to restore the log on the mirror with no recovery.

```
CREATE PROCEDURE dbo.dba_RestoreDBLog
        @DBName sysname,
        @BackupFile NVARCHAR(500),
        @PrinServer sysname,
        @Debug bit = 0 -- 0 = Execute, 1 = Return SQL for execution
AS

DECLARE @UNCBackupFile NVARCHAR(500),
        @Exists INT,
        @SQL NVARCHAR(MAX)

SET NOCOUNT ON

DECLARE @DBID INT ;

SET @DBID = DB_ID(@DBName);

-- Convert backup path to UNC
IF SUBSTRING(@BackupFile, 2, 2) = ':\'
  BEGIN
        SET @UNCBackupFile = '\\' + @PrinServer + '\' +
                REPLACE(LEFT(@BackupFile, 2), ':', '$') +
                RIGHT(@BackupFile, LEN(@BackupFile) - 2);
  END
ELSE
  BEGIN
        SET @UNCBackupFile = @BackupFile
  END

-- Verify backup file is accessible
EXEC xp_FileExist @UNCBackupFile, @Exists OUTPUT

IF @Exists = 0 -- Does not exist or is not accessible
```

```
  BEGIN
        RAISERROR('Unable to open backup file: %s', 16, 1, @UNCBackupFile);
        RETURN;
  END

SET @SQL = 'Restore Log ' + QUOTENAME(@DBName) + CHAR(10) + CHAR(9) +
        'From Disk = ''' + @UNCBackupFile + '''' + CHAR(10) + CHAR(9) +
        'With NoRecovery, Stats = 10'

-- If not run in debug mode, execute, else print execute statement
IF @Debug = 0
  BEGIN
        EXEC sp_executesql @SQL;
  END
ELSE
  BEGIN
        PRINT '';
        PRINT @SQL;
  END
```

Create Endpoints on Instances

You will need to create an endpoint on the principal, mirror, and witness if one does not already exist. The procedure dba_CreateEndPoint checks the existing endpoints to ensure that they are in the correct role and creates the endpoint when it does not exist. Following is the code.

```
CREATE PROCEDURE dbo.dba_CreateEndPoint
        @EndPointName sysname,
        @Port INT,
        @Debug bit = 0
AS

DECLARE @SQL NVARCHAR(4000),
        @ExPort INT,
        @ExEndPoint sysname,
        @ExRole INT,
        @ExState INT,
        @CurrEdition INT,
        @State NVARCHAR(200),
        @Role NVARCHAR(60)

SET @CurrEdition = CAST(SERVERPROPERTY('EngineEdition') AS INT)

SELECT @ExEndPoint = DME.name,
        @ExPort = TE.port,
```

```
        @ExRole = DME.role,
        @ExState = DME.state
FROM sys.database_mirroring_endpoints DME
INNER JOIN sys.tcp_endpoints TE ON TE.endpoint_id = DME.endpoint_id

IF @ExEndPoint IS NOT NULL
  BEGIN
        IF @ExRole <> 'All'
                AND @CurrEdition <> 4 -- Express
          BEGIN
                SET @Role = 'All'
          END
        ELSE
          BEGIN
                SET @Role = @ExRole
          END

        IF @ExState <> 3 -- Started
          BEGIN
                SET @State = 'State = Started ' + CHAR(10) + CHAR(9)
          END
        ELSE
          BEGIN
                SET @State = ''
          END

        SET @SQL = 'Alter Endpoint ' + QUOTENAME(@ExEndPoint) + CHAR(10) + CHAR(9) +
                @State + 'For Database_Mirroring (Role = ' + @Role + ');';

        IF @Debug = 1
          BEGIN
                PRINT @SQL
          END
        ELSE
          BEGIN
                EXEC sp_executesql @SQL;
          END
  END
ELSE
  BEGIN
        SET @SQL = 'Create Endpoint ' + QUOTENAME(@EndPointName) +
                CHAR(10) + CHAR(9) +
                'State = Started' + CHAR(10) + CHAR(9) +
                'As TCP (Listener_Port = ' + CAST(@Port AS NVARCHAR) + ',' +
                CHAR(10) + CHAR(9) +
```

```
                    'Listener_IP = ALL)' + CHAR(10) + CHAR(9) +
                    'For Database_Mirroring (Role = ALL)'


        IF @Debug = 1
          BEGIN
                PRINT @SQL
          END
        ELSE
          BEGIN
                EXEC sp_executesql @SQL;
          END
    END
```

Create Login for the Service Accounts and Grant Connect

The dba_CheckLogins stored procedure creates the logins for the service accounts if they do not already exist and then grants the permissions to those accounts. You can choose to configure a single partner, or pass in both server names to configure both partners. All you are really required to enter is the server or servers you would like to configure and the name of the endpoint. Use the following code to make sure you have the proper logins configured for database mirroring.

```
CREATE PROCEDURE dbo.dba_CheckLogins
        @Server1 sysname,
        @Server2 sysname = NULL,
        @EPName sysname,
        @Debug bit = 0
AS

DECLARE @SQLServAcct sysname,
        @Domain sysname,
        @SQL NVARCHAR(500)
DECLARE @LoginConfig TABLE (Name sysname,
                        ConfigValue sysname)

SET NOCOUNT ON

INSERT INTO @LoginConfig
EXEC xp_loginconfig 'default domain'

SELECT @Domain = ConfigValue
FROM @LoginConfig

EXEC xp_instance_regread N'HKEY_LOCAL_MACHINE',
                N'System\CurrentControlSet\Services\MSSQLSERVER',
                N'ObjectName',
```

```
                @SQLServAcct OUTPUT,
                N'no_output'

IF @SQLServAcct = 'NT AUTHORITY\NetworkService'
        SET @SQLServAcct = @Domain + '\' +
        CAST(SERVERPROPERTY('MachineName') AS sysname) + '$'


-- Server 1
SET @SQL = 'If Not Exists (Select 1' + CHAR(10) +
        'From ' + QUOTENAME(@Server1) + '.master.sys.server_principals' +
        CHAR(10) + 'Where name = ''' + @SQLServAcct + ''')' + CHAR(10) + CHAR(9) +
        'Create Login ' + QUOTENAME(@SQLServAcct) + ' From Windows;'

IF @Debug = 1
  BEGIN
        PRINT @SQL;
  END
ELSE
  BEGIN
        EXEC sp_executesql @SQL;
  END

SET @SQL = 'If Not Exists (Select 1' + CHAR(10) + 'From ' +
        QUOTENAME(@Server1) + '.master.sys.server_principals P' + CHAR(10) +
        'Inner Join ' + QUOTENAME(@Server1) + '.master.sys.server_permissions SP ' +
        CHAR(9) + 'On SP.grantee_principal_id = P.principal_id' + CHAR(10) +
        'Inner Join ' + QUOTENAME(@Server1) +
        '.master.sys.database_mirroring_endpoints E' +
        CHAR(10) + CHAR(9) + 'On E.name = Object_Name(SP.major_id)' + CHAR(10) +
        'Where SP.permission_type = ''CO''' + CHAR(10) +
        'And SP.state = ''G'')' + CHAR(10) + CHAR(9) +
        'Grant Connect On EndPoint::' + QUOTENAME(@EPName) +
        ' To ' + QUOTENAME(@SQLServAcct) + ';';

IF @Debug = 1
  BEGIN
        PRINT @SQL;
  END
ELSE
  BEGIN
        EXEC sp_executesql @SQL;
  END

-- Server 2
IF @Server2 IS NOT NULL
```

```
BEGIN
    SET @SQL = 'If Not Exists (Select 1' + CHAR(10) +
            'From ' + QUOTENAME(@Server2) +
            '.master.sys.server_principals' +
            CHAR(10) + 'Where name = ''' + @SQLServAcct + ''')' +
            CHAR(10) + CHAR(9) +
            'Create Login ' + QUOTENAME(@SQLServAcct) + ' From Windows;'

    IF @Debug = 1
      BEGIN
            PRINT @SQL;
      END
    ELSE
      BEGIN
            EXEC sp_executesql @SQL;
      END

    SET @SQL = 'If Not Exists (Select 1' + CHAR(10) +
            'From ' + QUOTENAME(@Server2) + '.master.sys.server_principals P' +
            CHAR(10) + 'Inner Join ' + QUOTENAME(@Server2) +
            '.master.sys.server_permissions SP ' + CHAR(10) + CHAR(9) +
            'On SP.grantee_principal_id = P.principal_id' + CHAR (10) +
            'Inner Join ' + QUOTENAME(@Server2) +
            '.master.sys.database_mirroring_endpoints E' + CHAR(10) +
            CHAR(9) + 'On E.name = Object_Name(SP.major_id)' + CHAR(10) +
            'Where SP.permission_type = ''CO''' + CHAR(10) +
            'And SP.state = ''G'')' + CHAR(10) + CHAR(9) +
            'Grant Connect On EndPoint::' + QUOTENAME(@EPName) +
            ' To ' + QUOTENAME(@SQLServAcct) + ';';

    IF @Debug = 1
      BEGIN
            PRINT @SQL;
      END
    ELSE
      BEGIN
            EXEC sp_executesql @SQL;
      END
END
```

Set the Mirroring and Witness Partners

The process for setting the mirroring partners is the same on the mirror and principal servers. There is only a slight difference in the wording of the command to set a witness partner. You can use a single procedure for all three steps of the process. The procedure dba_SetPartner follows. It builds the connection string for the specified partner and sets the partnership on the server. The master procedure will call the procedure on the mirror server first and the principal server second. The procedure will only be called for the witness partner if you provide a witness server to the master procedure.

```
CREATE PROCEDURE dbo.dba_SetPartner
        @Partner sysname,
        @DBName sysname,
        @Port INT,
        @IsWitness bit = 0
        @Debug bit = 0
AS

DECLARE @PartnerFQDN NVARCHAR(300),
        @PartnerRole NVARCHAR(7 )
        @SQL NVARCHAR(100),
        @OrigShowAdvanced INT,
        @OrigXPCmdShell INT,
        @CmdShell NVARCHAR(200)
DECLARE @Ping TABLE (PingID INT IDENTITY(1, 1) NOT NULL PRIMARY KEY,
                    PingText VARCHAR(1000) NULL)

SET NOCOUNT ON

-- If SQL Instance, parse out machine name
IF CHARINDEX('\', @Partner) > 0
        SET @Partner = LEFT(@Partner, CHARINDEX('\', @Partner) - 1)

IF @IsWitness = 0
  BEGIN
        SET @PartnerRole = 'Partner'
  END
ELSE
  BEGIN
        SET @PartnerRole = 'Witness'
  END


-- Check if xp_cmdshell and show advanced options is enabled
SELECT @OrigShowAdvanced = CAST(value_in_use AS INT)
FROM sys.configurations
WHERE name = 'show advanced options'

SELECT @OrigXPCmdShell = CAST(value_in_use AS INT)
FROM sys.configurations
```

```
WHERE name = 'xp_cmdshell'

-- If disabled, enable xp_cmdshell
IF @OrigXPCmdShell = 0
  BEGIN
        IF @OrigShowAdvanced = 0
          BEGIN
                EXEC sp_configure 'show advanced options', 1;
                RECONFIGURE;
          END
        EXEC sp_configure 'xp_cmdshell', 1;
        RECONFIGURE;
  END

SET @CmdShell = 'ping ' + @Partner

INSERT INTO @Ping (PingText)
EXEC xp_cmdshell @CmdShell

-- If originally disabled, disable xp_cmdshell again
IF @OrigXPCmdShell = 0
  BEGIN
        EXEC sp_configure 'xp_cmdshell', 0;
        RECONFIGURE;

        IF @OrigShowAdvanced = 0
          BEGIN
                EXEC sp_configure 'show advanced options', 0;
                RECONFIGURE;
          END
  END

DELETE FROM @Ping
WHERE PingText NOT LIKE 'Pinging%'
OR PingText IS NULL

SELECT @PartnerFQDN = SUBSTRING(PingText, 9, CHARINDEX(SPACE(1), PingText, 9) - 9)
FROM @Ping

SET @PartnerFQDN = 'TCP://' + @PartnerFQDN + ':' + CAST(@Port AS NVARCHAR)

SET @SQL = 'Alter Database ' + QUOTENAME(@DBName) +
        ' Set ' + @PartnerRole + ' = ''' + @PartnerFQDN + ''';'

IF @Debug = 1
```

```
   BEGIN
         PRINT @SQL;
   END
ELSE
   BEGIN
         EXEC sp_executesql @SQL;
   END
```

Change the Operating Mode If Not Using a Witness

If you are not using a witness server, you cannot utilize automatic failover. Without automatic failover, we suggest running your mirroring session in high-performance mode. High-performance mode commits transactions asynchronously to the mirror database. There can be a performance hit with synchronous mirroring in periods of high transactions. Without the benefit of automatic failover, we do not think the performance hit is justifiable unless zero data loss is a requirement.

If you do not provide a witness server when you run the master procedure, it will use the following procedure to change the operating mode to high-performance (asynchronous). This gives you time to make sure that your system is handling the transaction load before switching to high-safety (synchronous) mode. Create the following stored procedure called dba_SetOperatingMode so the master stored procedure can use it to set the appropriate operating mode for database mirroring.

```
CREATE PROCEDURE dbo.dba_SetOperatingMode
        @DBName sysname,
        @Debug bit = 0
AS

DECLARE @SQL NVARCHAR(100)

SET NOCOUNT ON

SET @SQL = 'Alter Database ' + QUOTENAME(@DBName) +
        ' Set Safety Off;';

IF @Debug = 1
   BEGIN
         PRINT @SQL;
   END
ELSE
   BEGIN
         EXEC sp_executesql @SQL;
   END
```

Helper Procedure to Manage Linked Servers

Several tasks are going to require the use of linked servers. The master procedure uses this helper procedure to create a linked server for the mirror and witness servers if they do not already exist. The name of this procedure is dba_ManageLinkedServer, and the code is as follows.

```
CREATE PROCEDURE dbo.dba_ManageLinkedServer
        @ServerName sysname,
        @Action VARCHAR(10) = 'create'
AS
IF @ServerName = @@ServerName
        RETURN

IF @Action = 'create'
 BEGIN
        IF NOT EXISTS (SELECT 1 FROM sys.servers
                        WHERE name = @ServerName
                        AND is_linked = 1)
          BEGIN
                EXEC master.dbo.sp_addlinkedserver @server = @ServerName,
                                        @srvproduct = N'SQL Server';
                EXEC master.dbo.sp_serveroption @server = @ServerName,
                                        @optname = N'collation compatible',
                                        @optvalue = N'false';
                EXEC master.dbo.sp_serveroption @server = @ServerName,
                                        @optname = N'data access',
                                        @optvalue = N'true';
                EXEC master.dbo.sp_serveroption @server = @ServerName,
                                        @optname = N'dist',
                                        @optvalue = N'false';
                EXEC master.dbo.sp_serveroption @server = @ServerName,
                                        @optname = N'pub',
                                        @optvalue = N'false';
                EXEC master.dbo.sp_serveroption @server = @ServerName,
                                        @optname = N'rpc',
                                        @optvalue = N'true';
                EXEC master.dbo.sp_serveroption @server = @ServerName,
                                        @optname = N'rpc out',
                                        @optvalue = N'true';
                EXEC master.dbo.sp_serveroption @server = @ServerName,
                                        @optname = N'sub',
                                        @optvalue = N'false';
                EXEC master.dbo.sp_serveroption @server = @ServerName,
                                        @optname = N'connect timeout',
                                        @optvalue = N'0';
```

```
                    EXEC master.dbo.sp_serveroption @server = @ServerName,
                                           @optname = N'collation name',
                                           @optvalue = NULL;
                    EXEC master.dbo.sp_serveroption @server = @ServerName,
                                           @optname = N'lazy schema validation',
                                           @optvalue = N'false';
                    EXEC master.dbo.sp_serveroption @server = @ServerName,
                                           @optname = N'query timeout',
                                           @optvalue = N'0';
                    EXEC master.dbo.sp_serveroption @server = @ServerName,
                                           @optname = N'use remote collation',
                                           @optvalue = N'true';
                    EXEC master.dbo.sp_addlinkedsrvlogin @rmtsrvname = @ServerName,
                                           @locallogin = NULL ,
                                           @useself = N'True';
              END
    END
ELSE IF @Action = 'drop'
 BEGIN
         IF EXISTS (SELECT 1 FROM sys.servers
                 WHERE name = @ServerName
                 AND is_linked = 1)
            BEGIN
                 EXEC master.dbo.sp_dropserver @server = @ServerName,
                                           @droplogins = NULL
            END
    END
```

The Master Procedure

The master procedure is the procedure that you will call to set up mirroring. It will handle the logic and the flow of the process. We've named the master procedure dba_SetupMirroring, and it is the only procedure you need to thoroughly understand. Let's begin by looking at the parameters and then an example execution. Then we'll look at the code. Once you understand how to invoke the procedure, you'll be better able to follow the logic in the code.

Parameters

Following are the parameters to the master procedure, dba_SetupMirroring.

@DBName: Name of database, sysname (nvarchar(128)) data type, required

@MirrorServer: Name of mirror instance, sysname data type, required

@PrincipalPort: Port number for endpoint on principal, int data type, optional, defaults to 5022

@MirrorPort: Port number for endpoint on mirror, int data type, optional, defaults to 5023

@WitnessServer: Name of witness instance, sysname data type, optional

@WitnessPort: Port number for endpoint on witness, int data type, optional, defaults to 5024

@Debug: Flag indicating whether SQL code should be executed or returned to caller, bit data type, optional, defaults to 0, 0 = execute code, 1 = return SQL without executing

Sample Execution

We will give you a couple of sample calls to the procedure. The first example demonstrates execution without a witness server. The second example shows how to configure mirroring with a witness server using the master procedure.

Following is how you execute the procedure to configure mirroring without a witness server.

```
EXEC dbo.dba_SetupMirroring
            @DBName = 'MirrorTest',
            @MirrorServer 'MirrorServer',
            @PrincipalPort = 7022,
            @MirrorPort int = 7023
```

Notice that we've only passed in the first four parameters. We are not configuring a witness server. There is thus no need to pass the witness server name and port number. We are also not debugging, so we've omitted the debug flag as well.

Now let's look at an invocation involving the configuration of a witness server. This time, we pass in the witness server's name and port number. And for completeness, we pass in the debug flag as well, even though we're still not debugging. Following is our procedure call.

```
EXEC dbo.dba_SetupMirroring
            @DBName = 'MirrorTest',
            @MirrorServer 'MirrorServer',
            @PrincipalPort = 7022,
            @MirrorPort int = 7023,
            @WitnessServer sysname = 'WitnessServer',
            @WitnessPort int = 7024,
            @Debug bit = 0
```

As before, mirroring will be configured for you. The witness server—named WitnessServer in this case—will also be automatically configured.

The Code

Now it's time to look at the code for the dba_SetupMirroring procedure. The code follows, and it's quite long. Read it carefully though, and be sure that you understand how it works before unleashing it in your production environment. And remember, you can download the code from the example files available on the Source Code section on the Apress web site.

```
CREATE PROCEDURE dbo.dba_SetupMirroring
      @DBName sysname,
```

```
        @MirrorServer sysname,
        @PrincipalPort INT = 5022,
        @MirrorPort INT = 5023,
        @WitnessServer sysname = NULL,
        @WitnessPort INT = 5024,
        @Debug bit = 0
AS

DECLARE @PrincipalServer sysname,
        @CurrDBName sysname,
        @BackupFile NVARCHAR(500),
        @Results INT,
        @Exists INT,
        @SQL NVARCHAR(MAX),
        @EPName sysname

SET NOCOUNT ON

SET @PrincipalServer = @@ServerName
SET @CurrDBName = DB_NAME()
SET @EPName = 'MirroringEndPoint'

-- Make sure linked server to mirror exists
EXEC @Results = dbo.dba_ManageLinkedServer
                @ServerName = @ MirrorServer,
                @Action = 'create'

IF @Results <> 0
  BEGIN
        RETURN @Results;
  END

-- Make sure linked server to witness exists, if provided
IF @WitnessServer IS NOT NULL
  BEGIN
        EXEC @Results = dbo.dba_ManageLinkedServer
                        @ServerName = @WitnessServer,
                        @Action = 'create'

        IF @Results <> 0
          BEGIN
                RETURN @Results;
          END
  END
```

```
-- Configure database for mirroring
EXEC @Results = dbo.dba_ConfigureDBForMirroring @DBName = @DBName

IF @Results <> 0
  BEGIN
        RETURN @Results;
  END

-- Back up the principal database
EXEC @Results = dbo.dba_BackupDB @DBName = @DBName,
        @BackupType = 0, -- 0 = Full, 1 = Log
        -- Location where you want the backups saved
        -- Allow procedure to choose the best location
        -- @BackupLocation nvarchar(255) = null,
        @Debug = @Debug, -- 0 = Execute, 1 = Return SQL for execution
        @BackupFile = @BackupFile OUTPUT

IF @Results <> 0
  BEGIN
        RETURN @Results;
  END

IF @BackupFile IS NULL
  BEGIN
        RAISERROR('Full backup failed for unknown reason.', 16, 1);
        RETURN;
  END

-- Verify new backup exists
EXEC @Results = xp_FileExist @BackupFile, @Exists OUTPUT

IF @Results <> 0
  BEGIN
        RETURN @Results;
  END

IF @Exists = 0
  BEGIN
        RAISERROR('Full backup file not found after backup.', 16, 1);
        RETURN;
  END

-- Restore full backup
SET @SQL = 'Exec ' + QUOTENAME(@MirrorServer) + '.' +
        QUOTENAME(@CurrDBName) + '.dbo.dba_RestoreDB' + CHAR(10) + CHAR(9) +
```

```
            '@DBName = ''' + @DBName + ''',' + CHAR(10) + CHAR(9) +
            '@BackupFile = ''' + @BackupFile + ''',' + CHAR(10) + CHAR(9) +
            '@PrinServer = ''' + @PrincipalServer + ''',' + CHAR(10) + CHAR(9) +
            '@Debug = ' + CAST(@Debug AS NVARCHAR) + ';'
EXEC @Results = sp_executesql @SQL

IF @Results <> 0
  BEGIN
        RETURN @Results;
  END


-- Backup log of principal database
SET @BackupFile = NULL

EXEC @Results = dbo.dba_BackupDB @DBName = @DBName,
        @BackupType = 1, -- 0 = Full, 1 = Log
        -- Location where you want the backups saved
        -- Allow procedure to choose the best location
        -- @BackupLocation nvarchar(255) = null,
        @Debug = @Debug, -- 0 = Execute, 1 = Return SQL for execution
        @BackupFile = @BackupFile OUTPUT

IF @Results <> 0
  BEGIN
        RETURN @Results;
  END

IF @BackupFile IS NULL
  BEGIN
        RAISERROR('Log backup failed for unknown reason.', 16, 1);
        RETURN;
  END

-- Verify new log backup exists
EXEC @Results = xp_FileExist @BackupFile, @Exists OUTPUT

IF @Results <> 0
  BEGIN
        RETURN @Results;
  END

IF @Exists = 0
  BEGIN
        RAISERROR('Log backup file not found after backup.', 16, 1);
        RETURN;
```

```
        END

-- Restore log backup
SET @SQL = 'Exec ' + QUOTENAME(@MirrorServer) + '.' +
        QUOTENAME(@CurrDBName) + '.dbo.dba_RestoreDBLog' + CHAR(10) + CHAR(9) +
        '@DBName = ''' + @DBName + ''',' + CHAR(10) + CHAR(9) +
        '@BackupFile = ''' + @BackupFile + ''',' + CHAR(10) + CHAR(9) +
        '@PrinServer = ''' + @PrincipalServer  + ''',' + CHAR(10) + CHAR(9) +
        '@Debug = ' + CAST(@Debug AS NVARCHAR) + ';'
EXEC @Results = sp_executesql @SQL

IF @Results <> 0
  BEGIN
        RETURN @Results;
  END

-- Create EndPoint on Principal
EXEC @Results = dbo.dba_CreateEndPoint
                @EndPointName = @EPName,
                @Port = @PrincipalPort,
                @Debug = @Debug

IF @Results <> 0
  BEGIN
        RETURN @Results;
  END

-- Create EndPoint on Mirror
SET @SQL = 'Exec ' + QUOTENAME(@MirrorServer) + '.' +
        QUOTENAME(@CurrDBName) + '.dbo.dba_CreateEndPoint' + CHAR(10) + CHAR(9) +
        '@EndPointName = ''' + @EPName + ''',' + CHAR(10) + CHAR(9) +
        '@Port = ' + CAST(@MirrorPort AS NVARCHAR) + ',' + CHAR(10) + CHAR(9) +
        '@Debug = ' + CAST(@Debug AS NVARCHAR) + ';'
EXEC @Results = sp_executesql @SQL

IF @Results <> 0
  BEGIN
        RETURN @Results;
  END

-- Create EndPoint on Witness, if provided
IF @WitnessServer IS NOT NULL
  BEGIN
        SET @SQL = 'Exec ' + QUOTENAME(@WitnessServer) + '.' +
                QUOTENAME(@CurrDBName) +
```

```
                    '.dbo.dba_CreateEndPoint' + CHAR(10) + CHAR(9) +
                    '@EndPointName = ''' + @EPName + ''',' + CHAR(10) + CHAR(9) +
                    '@Port = ' + CAST(@WitnessPort AS NVARCHAR) + ',' +
                    CHAR(10) + CHAR(9) +
                    '@Debug = ' + CAST(@Debug AS NVARCHAR) + ';'
            EXEC @Results = sp_executesql @SQL

            IF @Results <> 0
              BEGIN
                    RETURN @Results;
              END
    END

-- Create service account logins and grant Connect
-- On Principal
EXEC @Results = dbo.dba_CheckLogins
                    @Server1 = @MirrorServer,
                    @Server2 = @WitnessServer,
                    @EPName = @EPName,
                    @Debug = @Debug -- 0 = Execute, 1 = Return SQL for execution

IF @Results <> 0
  BEGIN
        RETURN @Results;
  END

-- Create service account logins and grant Connect
-- On Mirror
SET @SQL = 'Exec ' + QUOTENAME(@MirrorServer) + '.' +
        QUOTENAME(@CurrDBName) + '.dbo.dba_CheckLogins' + CHAR(10) + CHAR(9) +
        '@Server1 = ''' + @PrincipalServer + ''',' + CHAR(10) + CHAR(9) +
        CASE WHEN @WitnessServer IS NOT NULL THEN
        '@Server2 = ''' + @WitnessServer + ''',' + CHAR(10) + CHAR(9)
        ELSE '' END +
        '@EPName = ''' + @EPName + ''',' + CHAR(10) + CHAR(9) +
        '@Debug = ' + CAST(@Debug AS NVARCHAR) + ';'
EXEC @Results = sp_executesql @SQL;

IF @Results <> 0
  BEGIN
        RETURN @Results;
  END

-- Create service account logins and grant Connect
-- On Mirror
```

```
IF @WitnessServer IS NOT NULL
  BEGIN
        SET @SQL = 'Exec ' + QUOTENAME(@MirrorServer) + '.' +
                QUOTENAME(@CurrDBName) + '.dbo.dba_CheckLogins' +
                CHAR(10) + CHAR(9) +
                '@Server1 = ''' + @PrincipalServer + ''',' + CHAR(10) + CHAR(9) +
                '@Server2 = ''' + @MirrorServer + ''',' + CHAR(10) + CHAR(9) +
                '@EPName = ''' + @EPName + ''',' + CHAR(10) + CHAR(9) +
                '@Debug = ' + CAST(@Debug AS NVARCHAR) + ';'
        EXEC @Results = sp_executesql @SQL;

        IF @Results <> 0
          BEGIN
                RETURN @Results;
            END
  END

-- Configure Partner on Mirror
SET @SQL = 'Exec ' + QUOTENAME(@MirrorServer) + '.' +
        QUOTENAME(@CurrDBName) + '.dbo.dba_SetPartner' + CHAR(10) + CHAR(9) +
        '@Partner = ''' + @PrincipalServer + ''',' + CHAR(10) + CHAR(9) +
        '@DBName = ''' + @DBName + ''',' + CHAR(10) + CHAR(9) +
        '@Port = ' + CAST(@PrincipalPort AS NVARCHAR) + ',' + CHAR(10) + CHAR(9) +
        '@IsWitness = 0,' + CHAR(10) + CHAR(9) +
        '@Debug = ' + CAST(@Debug AS NVARCHAR) + ';'
EXEC @Results = sp_executesql @SQL;

IF @Results <> 0
  BEGIN
        RETURN @Results;
  END

-- Configure Partner on Principal
EXEC @Results = dbo.dba_SetPartner
                @Partner = @MirrorServer,
                @DBName = @DBName,
                @Port = @MirrorPort,
                @IsWitness = 0,
                @Debug = @Debug;

IF @Results <> 0
  BEGIN
        RETURN @Results;
  END
```

81

```
-- Configure Witness on Principal, if provided
IF @WitnessServer IS NOT NULL
  BEGIN
        EXEC @Results = dbo.dba_SetPartner
                        @Partner = @WitnessServer,
                        @DBName = @DBName,
                        @Port = @WitnessPort,
                        @IsWitness = 1,
                        @Debug = @Debug;

        IF @Results <> 0
          BEGIN
                RETURN @Results;
            END
  END

-- Change operating mode if no witness
IF @WitnessServer IS NULL
  BEGIN
        EXEC @Results = dbo.dba_SetOperatingMode
                        @DBName = @DBName,
                        @Debug = @Debug;

        IF @Results <> 0
          BEGIN
                RETURN @Results;
            END
  END

-- Display Mirroring status
SELECT DBName = DB_NAME(database_id),
        MirroringRole = mirroring_role_desc,
        MirroringState = mirroring_state_desc,
        SafetyLevel = mirroring_safety_level_desc,
        MirrorName = mirroring_partner_instance,
        MirrorFQDN = mirroring_partner_name,
        WitnessName = mirroring_witness_name
FROM sys.database_mirroring
WHERE database_id = DB_ID(@DBName)
```

Alternative Setup Using PowerShell

This section presents a PowerShell solution to automating setup that does not rely on procedures already existing on the SQL Server. In fact, the PowerShell script does not use any T-SQL at all.

One of the downsides of automation in T-SQL using linked servers is the infamous double-hop scenario mentioned previously. Instead of just being able to run a simple T-SQL script on a server, you have to create linked servers to allow SQL Server to run commands against both partners. The alternative is to write a script or executable that creates a connection to each server involved rather than using linked servers. If you already have the T-SQL solution in place, you can just write an executable, or a new master script of some sort, that invokes the individual stored procedures in the proper order. You would also have that new master script open individual connections to each of your servers. A better solution is one that does not involve replicating stored procedures at all.

One of the new features of SQL Server 2008 is the integration of PowerShell. This makes PowerShell a natural choice for a client-side solution to automating the setup of a mirroring environment.

PowerShell has the ability to load and use .Net objects. For the solution in this chapter, we load the SMO objects into PowerShell and use them directly in the script. The SQL Team separated some of the SMO functions into separate DLLs in SQL Server 2008. The script checks the internal version of SMO and loads the SMOExtended object if you are using the SQL Server 2008 version of SMO.

■ **Note** PowerShell is part of the SQL Server 2008 installation. If you need to install PowerShell, you can find download details at `http://www.microsoft.com/windowsserver2003/technologies/management/`↩ `powershell/download.mspx`.

The PowerShell Setup Script

Following is the PowerShell script that will automate the configuration of mirroring. You can find this script in the example download for this book. It is named AutomatingSetup.ps1. Explaining PowerShell commands is beyond the scope of this book, but if you would like to learn more about PowerShell you can read *Pro Windows PowerShell* by Hristo Deshev (Apress, 2008). For more information on invoking PowerShell scripts see "Running Windows PowerShell Scripts" at `http://www.microsoft.com/technet/scriptcenter/topics/winpsh/manual/run.mspx`.

```
param (
        [string] $SSPrincipal,
        [string] $SSMirror,
        [string] $Database,
        [string] $PrincipalPath,
        [string] $MirrorPath,
        [string] $SSWitness
)

## Path and name used to invoke script
$CUR_SCRIPT = $myinvocation.InvocationName

## Load SMO assemblies
[Reflection.Assembly]::LoadWithPartialName("Microsoft.SqlServer.ConnectionInfo")↩
|out-null
[Reflection.Assembly]::LoadWithPartialName("Microsoft.SqlServer.SmoEnum")|out-null
```

```
[Reflection.Assembly]::LoadWithPartialName("Microsoft.SqlServer.Smo")|out-null
$SMO = [Reflection.Assembly]::LoadWithPartialName("Microsoft.SqlServer.Smo")
## Parse out the internal version number
$SMOVer = $SMO.FullName.Split(",")[1].Split("=")[1].Split(".")[0]
## Load SMOExtended if not SQL Server 2005 (9)
if ($SMOVer -ne 9) {
        [Reflection.Assembly]::LoadWithPartialName("Microsoft.SqlServer.↵
SMOExtended")|out-null
}

## Declare empty array to hold ports already selected
$PortsUsed = @()

## Function to find an unused port
Function FindAPort ([string]$ServerToCheck) {
        $PortArray = ((5022..5025), (7022..7025), (5026..6000), (7026..8000))
        $socket = new-object System.Net.Sockets.TcpClient
        $PortAvailable = 0
        foreach ($Ports in $PortArray) {
                foreach ($Port in $Ports) {
                        if ($PortsUsed -notcontains $Port) {
                                $erroractionpreference = "SilentlyContinue"
                                $socket.Connect($ServerToCheck, $Port)
                                if (!$socket.Connected) {
                                        $PortAvailable = $Port
                                        $erroractionpreference = "Continue"
                                        $error.clear()
                                        $socket.Close()
                                        break
                                } else {
                                        $socket.Disconnect()
                                }
                        }
                }
                if ($PortAvailable -ne 0) { break }
        }
        write-host "`t Port $PortAvailable appears to be available" -f green
        return $PortAvailable
}

## Function to create endpoints
Function CreateEndPoint ([string]$EPName, [string]$EPServer, [int]$EPPort) {
        $MyEPServer = New-Object "Microsoft.SqlServer.Management.Smo.Server" ↵
$EPServer
```

```
        if ($MyEPServer.Edition -eq "Express Edition") {
                $EPRole = "Witness"
        } else {
                $EPRole = "All"
        }
        $EndPoint = New-Object "Microsoft.SqlServer.Management.Smo.EndPoint" ↵
$MyEPServer, $EPName
        $EndPoint.ProtocolType = "TCP"
        $EndPoint.EndPointType = "DatabaseMirroring"
        $EndPoint.Protocol.Tcp.ListenerPort = $EPPort
        $EndPoint.Payload.DatabaseMirroring.ServerMirroringRole = $EPRole
        $EndPoint.Create()
        $EndPoint.Start()
        if (!$error){
                write-host "`t Created Endpoint $EPName on $EPServer" -f green
        } else {
                RaisError "`t EndPoint Creation returned an error"
                Exit
        }
}

## Function to raise error
Function RaisError ([string]$ErrMsg){
        write-host $ErrMsg -f red
        $error.clear()
}

## Check user input, prompt for each value not provided as parameters
if(!$SSPrincipal) {
        $SSPrincipal = read-host "Enter Principal Server Name"
}
if(!$SSMirror) {
        $SSMirror = read-host "Enter Mirror Server Name"
}
if(!$Database) {
        $Database = read-host "Enter Database Name"
}
if(!$PrincipalPath) {
        $PrincipalPath = read-host "Enter Backup Directory for Principal"
}
if(!$MirrorPath) {
        $MirrorPath = read-host "Enter UNC Path to Backup Directory for Mirror"
}
if(!$SSWitness) {
```

```
        $SSWitness = read-host "Enter Witness Server Name (optional)"
}

## Make sure unique instance names were provided
if($SSPrincipal -eq $SSMirror -or $SSPrincipal -eq $SSWitness -or $SSMirror -eq ⏎
$SSWitness) {
        RaisError "`t All mirroring partners must be on unique SQL instances."
        exit
}

## Return Help and exit if any required input is missing
if(!$SSPrincipal -or !$SSMirror -or !$Database -or !$PrincipalPath -or ⏎
!$MirrorPath) {
        write-host "Usage: $CUR_SCRIPT options:
        string Principal SQL Server Instance
        string Mirror SQL Server Instance
        string Database Name
        string Backup Path for Principal Server
        string Backup Path for Mirror Server
        string Witness SQL Server Instance (optional)"
        exit
}

## Ensure backup directory exists
[System.IO.Directory]::CreateDirectory($PrincipalPath) | out-null

## Create server objects
$PrinSrv = New-Object "Microsoft.SqlServer.Management.Smo.Server" $SSPrincipal
$MirrSrv = New-Object "Microsoft.SqlServer.Management.Smo.Server" $SSMirror

## Check to see if SQL Edition meets requirements
$PrinEdition = $PrinSrv.Edition
$MirrEdition = $MirrSrv.Edition
$ValidEditions = "Developer Edition", "Standard Edition", "Enterprise Edition"

## Alert and exit if principal or mirror partner is not a valid edition
if (($ValidEditions -notcontains $PrinEdition) -or ($ValidEditions ⏎
-notcontains $MirrEdition)) {
        Write-host "`t Database Mirroring is only available in Developer, Standard," -f red
        Write-host "`t and Enterprise Editions." -f red
        Write-host "`t Principal Server: `t $PrinEdition" -f red
        Write-host "`t Mirror Server: `t`t $MirrEdition" -f red
        Exit
}
```

```
## Alert if principal and mirror are different editions and continue
if ($PrinEdition -ne $MirrEdition) {
        Write-host "`t Database Mirroring is not officially supported" -f yellow
        Write-host "`t with different Editions. You should use the same " -f yellow
        Write-host "`t Edition for both Principal and Mirror." -f yellow
        Write-host "`t Principal Server: `t $PrinEdition" -f yellow
        Write-host "`t Mirror Server: `t`t $MirrEdition" -f yellow
        Write-host ""
        Write-host "`t Proceeding with mirroring setup." -f yellow
}

## Get machine name of server -> get FQDN of server
$PrinMachine = $PrinSrv.NetName
$MirrMachine = $MirrSrv.NetName
$PrinFQDN = [system.net.dns]::GetHostEntry($PrinMachine).HostName
$MirrFQDN = [system.net.dns]::GetHostEntry($MirrMachine).HostName

## Create principal database object
$PrinDB = $PrinSrv.Databases[$Database]

## Return error and exit if database is already mirrored
if ($PrinDB.IsMirroringEnabled) {
        Write-host "Database $Database is already configured as a mirroring ↵
partner on $SSPrincipal." -f red
        exit
}

## Create Endpoint on Principal if not exists
$EPExist = $PrinSrv.Endpoints | where {$_.EndpointType -eq "DatabaseMirroring"}
if ($EPExist) {
        ## If existing Endpoint is for the witness role only, change role to all
        if ($EPExist.Payload.DatabaseMirroring.ServerMirroringRole -eq "Witness") {
                $EPExist.Payload.DatabaseMirroring.ServerMirroringRole = "All"
                $EPExist.Alter()
        }
        ## If existing Endpoint is not started, start it
        if ($EPExist.EndpointState -ne "started") {
                $EPExist.Start()
        }
        ## Get endpoint port
        $PrinPort = $EPExist.Protocol.Tcp.ListenerPort
} else {
        ## Find an unused port
```

```
        $PrinPort = FindAPort($SSPrincipal)
        ## Add port returned to array of ports used
        $PortsUsed = $PortsUsed + $PrinPort
        ## Create endpoint
        CreateEndPoint "MirroringEndPoint" $SSPrincipal $PrinPort
}


## Create Endpoint on Mirror if not exists
$EPExist = $MirrSrv.Endpoints | where {$_.EndpointType -eq "DatabaseMirroring"}
if ($EPExist) {
        ## If existing Endpoint is for the witness role only, change role to all
        if ($EPExist.Payload.DatabaseMirroring.ServerMirroringRole -eq "Witness") {
                $EPExist.Payload.DatabaseMirroring.ServerMirroringRole = "All"
                $EPExist.Alter()
        }
        ## If existing Endpoint is not started, start it
        if ($EPExist.EndpointState -ne "started") {
                $EPExist.Start()
        }
        ## Get endpoint port
        $MirrPort = $EPExist.Protocol.Tcp.ListenerPort
} else {
        ## Find an unused port
        $MirrPort = FindAPort($SSMirror)
        ## Add port returned to array of ports used
        $PortsUsed = $PortsUsed + $MirrPort
        ## Create endpoint
        CreateEndPoint "MirroringEndPoint" $SSMirror $MirrPort
}


## Check that principal database is ready for mirroring
## Checking compatibility level and recovery model
$dbCompatLevel = $PrinDB.Properties | where {$_.Name -eq "CompatibilityLevel"} ↩
| %{$_.value}
if ($dbCompatLevel -eq "Version80") {
        write-host "Compatibility level is set to SQL 2000 (80)." -f red
        write-host " Please change compatibility level to SQL 2005 (90) " -f red
        write-host "or SQL 2008 (10)." -f red
        exit
}
$dbRecoveryModel = $PrinDB.Properties | where {$_.Name -eq "RecoveryModel"} | ↩
%{$_.value}
if ($dbRecoveryModel -ne 1) {
        $PrinDB.RecoveryModel = 1
        $PrinDB.Alter()
```

```
        if (!$error){
                write-host "`t Changed recovery model to Full " -f green
                write-host "`t from $dbRecoveryModel" -f green
        } else {
                RaisError "`t Recovery model change returned an error."
                Exit
        }
}


## Create backup name
$BkDate = Get-Date -Format yyyyMMddHHmmss
$BkName = $Database + "_backup_$BkDate.bak"


## Backup the Principal database
$Backup = new-object "Microsoft.SqlServer.Management.Smo.Backup"
$BkFile = new-object "Microsoft.SqlServer.Management.Smo.BackupDeviceItem"
$BkFile.DeviceType = 'File'
$BkFile.Name = [System.IO.Path]::Combine($PrincipalPath, $BkName)
$Backup.Devices.Add($BkFile)
$Backup.Database = $Database
$Backup.Action = 'Database'
$Backup.Initialize = 1
$Backup.BackupSetDescription = "Backup of database $Database"
$Backup.BackupSetName = "$Database Backup"
$Backup.PercentCompleteNotification = 5
$Backup.SqlBackup($PrinSrv)
if (!$error){
        write-host "`t Database $Database backed up to $PrincipalPath" -f green
} else {
        RaisError "`t Database $Database backup returned an error."
        Exit
}


## If database exists on Mirror, delete it
$DBExists = $MirrSrv.Databases[$Database]
if ($DBExists) {
        if ($dbExists.IsMirroringEnabled) {
                RaisError "`t Database $DBExists is already configured as a ↩
Mirroring partner on $SSMirror."
                Exit
        }
        if ($DBExists.status -eq "online") {
                $MirrSrv.KillDatabase($Database)
        } else {
```

```
                $DBExists.drop()
        }
        if (!$error){
                write-host "`t Dropping existing database on Mirror server" -f green
        } else {
                RaisError "`t Drop of existing database on Mirror server ↵
returned an error."
                Exit
        }
}


## Restore the Mirror database
$Restore = new-object "Microsoft.SqlServer.Management.Smo.Restore"
$Restore.Database = $Database
$Restore.Action = 'Database'
$BkFile.Name = [System.IO.Path]::Combine($MirrorPath, $BkName)
$Restore.Devices.Add($BkFile)
$Restore.ReplaceDatabase = $false
## Check file list and generate new file names if files already exists
$DataFiles = $Restore.ReadFileList($SSMirror)
ForEach ($DataRow in $DataFiles) {
        $LogicalName = $DataRow.LogicalName
        $PhysicalName = $DataRow.PhysicalName
        $FileExists = Test-Path $PhysicalName
        if ($FileExists) {
                $PhysicalName = $PhysicalName -replace(".mdf", "_mirr.mdf")
                $PhysicalName = $PhysicalName -replace(".ldf", "_mirr.ldf")
                $PhysicalName = $PhysicalName -replace(".ndf", "_mirr.ndf")
                $Restore.RelocateFiles.Add((new-object microsoft.sqlserver.↵
management.smo.relocatefile -ArgumentList $LogicalName, $PhysicalName))|out-null;
        }
}
$Restore.NoRecovery = $true
$Restore.PercentCompleteNotification = 5
$Restore.SqlRestore($SSMirror)
if (!$error){
        write-host "`t Database $Database restored from $MirrorPath" -f green
} else {
        RaisError "`t Restore of database $Database on Mirror server returned ↵
an error."
        Exit
}

## Create backup name
```

```
$BkDate = Get-Date -Format yyyyMMddHHmmss
$BkName = $Database + "_backup_$BkDate.trn"

## Backup the log on Principal database
$LogBackup = new-object "Microsoft.SqlServer.Management.Smo.Backup"
$BkFile.DeviceType = 'File'
$BkFile.Name = [System.IO.Path]::Combine($PrincipalPath, $BkName)
$LogBackup.Devices.Add($BkFile)
$LogBackup.Database = $Database
$LogBackup.Action = 'Log'
$LogBackup.Initialize = 1
$LogBackup.BackupSetDescription = "Log backup of database $Database"
$LogBackup.BackupSetName = "$Database Log Backup"
$LogBackup.PercentCompleteNotification = 5
$LogBackup.SqlBackup($PrinSrv)
if (!$error){
        write-host "`t Database $Database log backed up to $PrincipalPath" -f green
} else {
        RaisError "`t Database $Database log backup returned an error."
        Exit
}


## Restore the log on Mirror Database
$LogRestore = new-object "Microsoft.SqlServer.Management.Smo.Restore"
$LogRestore.Database = $Database
$LogRestore.Action = 'log'
$BkFile.Name = [System.IO.Path]::Combine($MirrorPath, $BkName)
$LogRestore.Devices.Add($BkFile)
$LogRestore.NoRecovery = $true
$LogRestore.PercentCompleteNotification = 5
$LogRestore.SqlRestore($SSMirror)
if (!$error){
        write-host "`t Database $Database log restored from $MirrorPath" -f green
} else {
        RaisError "`t Database $Database log restore returned an error."
        Exit
}


## Set the Principal Partner on Mirror Partner
$MirrDB = $MirrSrv.Databases[$Database]
$MirrDB.MirroringPartner = "TCP://" + $PrinFQDN.ToString() + ":$PrinPort"
$MirrDB.Alter()
if (!$error){
        write-host "`t Set Principal Partner on Mirror " -f green
} else {
```

```
            RaisError "`t Setting Principal Partner on Mirror returned an error."
            Exit
}

## Set the Mirror Partner on Principal Partner
$PrinDB.MirroringPartner = "TCP://" + $MirrFQDN.ToString() + ":$MirrPort"
$PrinDB.Alter()
if (!$error){
        write-host "`t Set Mirror Partner on Principal" -f green
} else {
        RaisError "`t Setting Mirror Partner on Principal returned an error."
        Exit
}

## Verify that mirroring is started
$PrinDB.Refresh()
if ($PrinDB.MirroringStatus) {
        write-host ""
        write-host "`t Database Mirroring started" -f green
}

## Process Mirror database if provided
if (!$SSWitness) {
        ## Set Safety off if no witness and if
        ## running Enterprise or Developer Edition on both partners
        if ($PrinEdition -ne "Standard Edition" -and $MirrEdition -ne "Standard ↵
Edition") {
                $PrinDB.MirroringSafetyLevel = "Off"
                $PrinDB.Alter()
                if (!$error){
                        Write-host "`t Turning transaction safety off." -f green
                } else {
                        RaisError "`t Turning transaction safety off returned ↵
an error."
                        Exit
                }
        }
} else {
        ## Connect to Witness server
        $WitSrv = New-Object "Microsoft.SqlServer.Management.Smo.Server" $SSWitness
        ## Get machine name of server -> get FQDN of server
        $WitMachine = $WitSrv.NetName
        $WitFQDN = [system.net.dns]::GetHostEntry($WitMachine).HostName
```

```
        ## Create Endpoint on Witness if not exists
        $EPExist = $WitSrv.Endpoints | where {$_.EndpointType -eq ↵
"DatabaseMirroring"}
        if ($EPExist) {
                ## If existing Endpoint is for the Partner role only, change ↵
role to all
                ## No need to check for Express Edition due to existing Partner role
                if ($EPExist.Payload.DatabaseMirroring.ServerMirroringRole -eq ↵
"Partner") {
                        $EPExist.Payload.DatabaseMirroring.ServerMirroringRole ↵
= "All"

                        $EPExist.Alter()
                }
                ## If existing Endpoint is not started, start it
                if ($EPExist.EndpointState -ne "started") {
                        $EPExist.Start()
                }
                ## Get endpoint port
                $WitPort = $EPExist.Protocol.Tcp.ListenerPort
        } else {
                ## Find an unused port
                $WitPort = FindAPort($SSWitness)
                ## Create endpoint
                CreateEndPoint "MirroringEndPoint" $SSWitness $WitPort
        }

        ## Set Witness server on Principal
        $PrinDB.MirroringWitness = "TCP://" + $WitFQDN.ToString() + ":$WitPort"
        $PrinDB.Alter()
        if (!$error){
                Write-host "`t Set Witness Partner on Principal" -f green
        } else {
                RaisError "`t Setting Witness Partner on Principal returned an ↵
error."
                Exit
        }
}

## Refresh connections to reload stale properties
$MirrDB.Refresh()
$PrinDB.Refresh()
## Get and display mirroring status
$PrinPart = $MirrDB.MirroringPartner
$PrinStatus = $PrinDB.MirroringStatus
```

```
$MirrPart = $PrinDB.MirroringPartner
$MirrStatus = $MirrDB.MirroringStatus
$Safety = $PrinDB.MirroringSafetyLevel
write-host "`t Principal: `t $PrinPart"  -f green
write-host "`t Status: `t $PrinStatus"  -f green
write-host "`t Mirror: `t $MirrPart"  -f green
write-host "`t Status: `t $MirrStatus"  -f green
if ($SSWitness) {
        $WitPart = $PrinDB.MirroringWitness
        $WitStatus = $PrinDB.MirroringWitnessStatus
        write-host "`t Witness: `t $WitPart"  -f green
        write-host "`t Status: `t $WitStatus"  -f green
}
write-host "`t Safety Level: `t $Safety" -f green
```

Summary

We have demonstrated a lot of code in this chapter, but if you take the time to examine and comprehend the code, you will have a far greater understanding of how database mirroring really works. Using these automation techniques and these scripts will make your administrative life a lot easier if you set up and manage mirrored databases. We specifically tailored the scripts to be generic enough to be usable for most situations. We have commented the scripts pretty well, and if you need to customize any of the scripts, you will find it to be easy and straightforward. If your end goal is to be able to cover the basic tasks of database mirroring, then you will make good use of these scripts. If you want to learn more about how the mirroring processes work, we suggest that you dig into these procedures and dissect them to get a good overview of the mirroring process.

CHAPTER 6

Maintenance Simplified

One of the biggest mistakes that you can make after setting up a high-availability solution is to think you are finished. All forms of high availability require monitoring and maintenance. Database mirroring is no different in that respect.

In this chapter, we will cover the routine maintenance that you will need to perform for mirrored databases and the servers that host them. You will learn how mirrored databases affect your existing maintenance routines. We will also show you automation techniques that will simplify the process of working with mirrored databases.

Routine Maintenance Considerations

All database maintenance should begin with a proper backup schedule, and this is especially true for mirrored databases. You will need to make special considerations when planning long-running, transaction-intensive processes such as checking database consistency, rebuilding indexes, and updating statistics for large tables. You may need to employ a strategy where you switch to asynchronous mirroring for the duration of the maintenance and then back to synchronous once the maintenance is complete and the databases are in a synchronized state.

Transaction Log Backups

Mirrored databases use the Full Recovery model. As a result, the database's transaction log can easily grow out of control if not kept in check. Even if you do not care about maintaining log backups for disaster recovery or point-in-time restores, it is crucial that you back up the log frequently. As a general rule of thumb, we recommend a log backup schedule no greater than every half hour. If the database handles a large number of transactions, you may need to increase the backup frequency to 15 minutes or less in order to avoid large transaction logs.

There was an important fix included in Cumulative Update 6 (CU6) for SQL Server 2005 Service Pack 2 (SP2). This bug could cause SQL Server to take both mirroring partners offline if the transaction log file was too large when the mirroring session needed to reinitialize. Even if you are using SQL Server 2008 or SQL Server 2005 SP2 CU6 or later, you should still try to keep your transaction logs a reasonable size. A large transaction file will increase the time for a database to start up. This will result in longer failover times and make failovers more noticeable to end users.

There was another important fix related to backups in Cumulative Update 5 (CU5) for SQL Server 2005 Service Pack 2 (SP2). Prior to CU5, if you use maintenance plans for your database and log backups, the maintenance plan will fail when it tries to back up the mirror partner. The mirror partner is in a recovering state; therefore, you cannot back it up. The maintenance plan will fail rather than skip the mirror database.

If you are not using at least SP2 CU5, then you should perform database and log backups using T-SQL rather than maintenance plans. Your T-SQL procedures for performing backups should check a database to ensure it is in a state that allows you to back it up before attempting to create the backup. If you are not using a maintenance plan, you will need to include a step to delete the old backups as well. You can use the two following procedures for automating log backups.

Backing Up the Log File

You need to be aware of several things before you generate a script to automatically back up transaction logs. You want your backups to proceed smoothly and not cause any unexpected problems. You also want to eliminate any common points of failure. When you are dealing with mirrored databases, it is essential that you be aware of their state and take action accordingly.

Write the Script

Here are some tips to follow when you write your own log backup script.

Check database state: When a database is in the mirror role, it is not online, and an attempt to back up the database or log file will result in an error. If the database transitions to the principal role, you will want to start backing up the log file. You can query sys.database_mirroring to check whether a database is a mirroring partner, and if so, what its role and state is. All you really need to do is check the database state in sys.databases. If state = 0 or state_desc = 'online', the database is in a state that allows you to perform backup operations.

Check recovery model: You can only back up the log file if the database in using the full or bulk-logged recovery models. If the database is using the simple recovery model, it will return an error when you try to back up the log. Check the recovery_model or recovery_model_desc columns in sys.databases. If the recovery model is 3 or the recovery model description is SIMPLE, do not try to back up the database.

Check for database snapshots: You cannot perform backup operations on a database snapshot. If you attempt to back up a database snapshot, it will return an error. You can differentiate database snapshots from regular databases by checking the source_database_id column in sys.databases. This column serves as a pointer to its source database. If source_database_id is not null, it is a snapshot, and you cannot back it up.

Check for log shipping: If you back up the transaction log of a log-shipped database outside of the log-shipping processes, you will break the log chain and log shipping will fail. A log backup of a log-shipped database will succeed, but you will create problems further down the line. Log-shipping secondary databases are not in an online state. If you are checking database state as described in the above section, you only need to check to see whether the database is a primary database for log shipping. You can determine this by checking for existence of the database name in the dbo.log_shipping_primary_databases table in the msdb database.

Check your core system databases: You cannot back up the log file of the tempdb and master databases. If you attempt to back up their log files, you will receive an error. Our personal preference is to exclude the model and msdb databases from log backups as well. The distribution database, if it exists on the server, makes heavy use of the transaction log, and you should back up its log file frequently.

The following query will give you a list of all databases on your server whose log files you can and should back up. This query follows the guidelines we described previously.

```
SELECT name
FROM sys.databases D
WHERE state = 0 AND
      recovery_model IN (1, 2) AND
      name NOT IN ('master', 'tempdb', 'msdb', 'model') AND
      source_database_id IS NULL AND
      NOT EXISTS (SELECT 1
                  FROM msdb.dbo.log_shipping_primary_databases
                  WHERE primary_database = D.name)
```

Make the Script Usable

When we write automation scripts, we always try to think of ways to make them generic so that you can use them for most scenarios. We also try to think of ways to simplify the execution of the script. If you make it easy to use, it will be more useful to others who use it. Ultimately, we prefer a script that can be deployed to many servers with very little or no customization of parameters. However, we also like to include parameters that make it easy to customize the script for special situations.

One way we do this is by including a parameter that allows you to specify a database by name. The parameter for database name has a default of NULL, and when the parameter is NULL, it processes the script for all databases as appropriate. You can add the following snippet to the above query to limit the output to a specific database if provided.

```
AND (name = @DBName
       OR @DBName IS NULL);
```

An example of when this may come in handy is when you have disabled the log backups during the setup of database mirroring. You will need to back up the log of your database as part of the setup process. You can easily call this script instead of going through the steps manually.

The script has a parameter that you can use to provide a base backup location for the backup. The parameter has a default of NULL, and when the parameter is NULL it makes a best effort attempt to determine the correct location for the backup. The procedure queries the system registry for the default backup location configured for the server. You set this value automatically during installation, and it should not return a NULL value. You can use xp_instance_regread to check the system registry.

```
EXEC xp_instance_regread N'HKEY_LOCAL_MACHINE',
                         N'Software\Microsoft\MSSQLServer\MSSQLServer',
                         N'BackupDirectory',
                         @BakDir output,
                         'no_output';
```

If the registry check returns a NULL value or if the specified backup directory does not exist, the procedure checks the system tables that log backup history. This particular query excludes backups for log-shipped databases because it is common for log-shipped databases to store their backups in a nonstandard location such as a file share on a different server.

```
SELECT TOP 1 @BakDir = LEFT(MF.physical_device_name,
      LEN(MF.physical_device_name) -
      CHARINDEX('\', REVERSE(MF.physical_device_name)))
```

```
FROM msdb.dbo.backupset BS INNER JOIN
     msdb.dbo.backupmediafamily MF
        ON MF.media_set_id = BS.media_set_id
WHERE NOT EXISTS (SELECT 1
                    FROM msdb.dbo.log_shipping_primary_databases
                    WHERE primary_database = BS.database_name)
-- log backups first, then differentials, then full backups
ORDER BY BS.type DESC,
       BS.backup_finish_date DESC; -- newest first
```

If you use a maintenance plan for log backups, one of the downsides is that if a backup fails, it stops processing backups. This means that any logs not backed up yet at the time of the failure are not processed. This is one reason that we prefer to use our own procedures rather than maintenance plans. The procedure we wrote performs the backup in a Try … Catch block and continues gracefully if a backup fails. When failures occur, the procedure will e-mail a list of failed backups to the recipients that you specify if you enable the alerts mechanism by passing in a value of 1 for the @SendAlerts parameter and if you have provided recipients for the @AlertRecipients parameter. The procedure also validates that Database Mail is enabled in sys.configurations and that a profile is configured before attempting to send the e-mail. The profile information is stored in msdb.dbo.sysmail_profile and msdb.dbo.sysmail_principalprofile.

```
IF @SendAlerts = 1 AND @AlertRecipients IS NOT NULL
  BEGIN
        IF EXISTS (SELECT 1
                    FROM sys.configurations
                    WHERE name = 'Database Mail XPs')
          BEGIN
                SELECT TOP (1) @ProfileName = name
                FROM msdb.dbo.sysmail_profile P LEFT JOIN
                    msdb.dbo.sysmail_principalprofile PP
                        ON PP.profile_id = P.profile_id
                ORDER BY PP.is_default DESC


                SET @Subject = 'Backup failures on ' +
                        CAST(@@SERVERNAME AS VARCHAR(255))


                SET @Body = 'Unable to back up the following databases: ' +
                        @FailedDBs


                EXEC msdb..sp_send_dbmail
                        @profile_name = @ProfileName,
                        @recipients = @AlertRecipients,
                        @Subject = @Subject,
                        @body = @Body
          END
  END
```

Automating Log Backups

You can use the following procedure to automate log backups of all databases using the guidelines described in the previous section. All parameters are optional, and you can use the script without providing any additional information. First, we will give you a brief explanation of the parameters.

@DBName: If you want to back up the log of a single database, you can pass in the database's name, and the procedure will back up the log of that database only. The procedure will consider all databases for log backups if you do not provide a database name.

@LogBackupLocation: The procedure will make a best effort determination to discover the best location for the log backups unless you provide a location with this parameter.

@FileExtension: The system procedure that this procedure calls requires that you tell it the file extension of the backup files. You can use any file extension you want to use, but it is a common practice to use the file extension trn for transaction log backups. This procedure defaults to this extension.

@SendAlerts: If the procedure is unable to back up any of the database log files, it will continue on to the next database. It keeps track of which databases failed. With this parameter, you can tell the procedure to send an e-mail if there are any backup failures. A value of 1 indicates to send alerts, and the default value of 0 means do not send any alerts.

@AlertRecipients: If you are going to send alerts, you use this parameter to pass in the list of recipients.

@Debug: We like to include a debug parameter for troubleshooting purposes. If you pass in a value of 1 for this parameter, the procedure will output the SQL to create the logins and grant the permissions without executing it. The default value of 0 will result in execution of the code.

```
CREATE PROCEDURE dbo.dba_BackupDBLogs
  -- Database name or null for all databases
  @DBName sysname = NULL,
   -- Location where you want the backups
  @LogBackupLocation NVARCHAR(255) = NULL,
  -- log backup extension
  @FileExtension NVARCHAR(3) = 'trn',
  -- 0 = do not send alerts, 1 = send alerts
  @SendAlerts bit = 0,
  @AlertRecipients VARCHAR(500) = NULL,
  -- 0 = execute log backup, 1 = output the code without executing
  @Debug bit = 0
AS

DECLARE @BakDir NVARCHAR(255),
        @Exists INT,
        @CurrID INT,
        @MaxID INT,
        @SQL NVARCHAR(1000),
        @LogBackup NVARCHAR(500),
```

```
        @DateSerial NVARCHAR(35),
        @ErrNumber INT,
        @ErrSeverity INT,
        @ErrState INT,
        @ErrProcedure sysname,
        @ErrLine INT,
        @ErrMsg NVARCHAR(2048),
        @FailedDBs NVARCHAR(4000),
        @Subject VARCHAR(255),
        @Body VARCHAR(8000),
        @ProfileName sysname

DECLARE @DBs TABLE (DBID INT IDENTITY(1, 1) NOT NULL PRIMARY KEY,
                    DBName sysname NOT NULL)

DECLARE @FileExists TABLE (FileExists INT NOT NULL,
                           FileIsDirectory INT NOT NULL,
                           ParentDirectoryExists INT NOT NULL)

DECLARE @Failures TABLE (FailId INT IDENTITY(1, 1) NOT NULL PRIMARY KEY,
                         DBName sysname NOT NULL,
                         ErrNumber INT NULL,
                         ErrSeverity INT NULL,
                         ErrState INT NULL,
                         ErrProcedure sysname NULL,
                         ErrLine INT NULL,
                         ErrMsg NVARCHAR(2048) NULL)

SET NOCOUNT ON

SET @DateSerial = CONVERT(NVARCHAR, GETDATE(), 112) +
        REPLACE(CONVERT(NVARCHAR, GETDATE(), 108), ':', '')

IF @DBName IS NOT NULL
  BEGIN
    IF NOT EXISTS (SELECT 1
                   FROM sys.databases
                   WHERE name = @DBName)
      BEGIN
        RAISERROR ('The specified database [%s] does not exist.
                   Please check the name entered or do not supply
                   a database name if you want to back up the log
                   for all online databases using the full or
                   bulk-logged recovery model.', 16, 1, @DBName);
        RETURN;
```

```
            END

IF EXISTS (SELECT 1
            FROM sys.databases
            WHERE name = @DBName AND
                  state > 0)
  BEGIN
    RAISERROR ('The specified database [%s] is not online.
                Please check the name entered or do not supply
                a database name if you want to back up the log
                for all online databases using the full or
                bulk-logged recovery model.', 16, 1, @DBName);
    RETURN;
  END

IF EXISTS (SELECT 1
            FROM sys.databases
            WHERE name = @DBName AND
                  recovery_model = 3)
  BEGIN
    RAISERROR ('The specified database [%s] is using the simple
                recovery model. Please check the name entered or
                do not supply a database name if you want to back up
                the log for all online databases using the full or
                bulk-logged recovery model.', 16, 1, @DBName);
    RETURN;
  END

IF EXISTS (SELECT 1
            FROM sys.databases
            WHERE name = @DBName AND
                  source_database_id IS NOT NULL)
  BEGIN
    RAISERROR ('The specified database [%s] is a database snapshot.
                Please check the name entered or do not supply
                a database name if you want to back up the log
                for all online databases using the full or
                bulk-logged recovery model.', 16, 1, @DBName);
    RETURN;
  END

IF EXISTS (SELECT 1
            FROM msdb.dbo.log_shipping_primary_databases
            WHERE primary_database = @DBName)
  BEGIN
```

```
            RAISERROR ('The specified database [%s] is a log shipping
                        primary and cannot have its log file backed up.
                        Please check the name entered or do not supply
                        a database name if you want to back up the log
                        for all online databases using the full or
                        bulk-logged recovery model.', 16, 1, @DBName);
            RETURN;
        END
    END

IF @LogBackupLocation IS NULL
  BEGIN
    EXEC xp_instance_regread
            N'HKEY_LOCAL_MACHINE',
            N'Software\Microsoft\MSSQLServer\MSSQLServer',
            N'BackupDirectory',
            @BakDir output,
            'no_output';
    IF @BakDir IS NOT NULL
      BEGIN
        INSERT INTO @FileExists
        EXEC sys.xp_fileexist @BakDir;

        SELECT @Exists = ParentDirectoryExists
        FROM @FileExists

        IF @Exists = 1
          BEGIN
            SET @LogBackupLocation = @BakDir;
          END
      END
    END

IF @LogBackupLocation IS NULL
  BEGIN
    SELECT TOP 1 @BakDir = LEFT(MF.physical_device_name,
          LEN(MF.physical_device_name) -
          CHARINDEX('\', REVERSE(MF.physical_device_name)))
    FROM msdb.dbo.backupset BS INNER JOIN
        msdb.dbo.backupmediafamily MF
          ON MF.media_set_id = BS.media_set_id
    WHERE NOT EXISTS (SELECT 1
                    FROM msdb.dbo.log_shipping_primary_databases
                    WHERE primary_database = BS.database_name)
    -- log backups first, then differentials, then full backups
```

```
    ORDER BY BS.type DESC,
            BS.backup_finish_date DESC; -- newest first

    IF @BakDir IS NOT NULL
      BEGIN
        DELETE FROM @FileExists

        INSERT INTO @FileExists
        EXEC sys.xp_fileexist @BakDir;

        SELECT @Exists = ParentDirectoryExists
        FROM @FileExists

        IF @Exists = 1
          BEGIN
            SET @LogBackupLocation = @BakDir;
          END
      END
  END

IF @LogBackupLocation IS NOT NULL
  BEGIN
    IF RIGHT(@LogBackupLocation, 1) <> '\'
      SET @LogBackupLocation = @LogBackupLocation + '\';
  END
ELSE
  BEGIN
    RAISERROR ('Backup location not specified or not found.', 16, 1);
    RETURN;
  END

INSERT INTO @DBs (DBName)
SELECT name
FROM sys.databases D
WHERE state = 0 AND --online
      -- 1 = Full, 2 = Bulk-logged, 3 = Simple
      -- (log backups not needed for simple recovery model)
      recovery_model IN (1, 2) AND
      -- No log backups for core system databases
      name NOT IN ('master', 'tempdb', 'msdb', 'model') AND
      -- If is not null, database is a database snapshot
      -- and can not be backed up
      source_database_id IS NULL AND
      -- Backing up the log of a log-shipped database will
      -- break the log shipping log chain
```

```
      NOT EXISTS (SELECT 1
                    FROM msdb.dbo.log_shipping_primary_databases
                    WHERE primary_database = D.name) AND
        (name = @DBName OR
         @DBName IS NULL);

SELECT @MaxID = MAX(DBID), @CurrID = 1
FROM @DBs;

WHILE @CurrID <= @MaxID
  BEGIN
    SELECT @DBName = DBName
    FROM @DBs
    WHERE DBID = @CurrID;

    SET @LogBackup = @LogBackupLocation + @DBName + '\';

    -- Make sure backup location exists
    -- Will not overwrite existing files, if any
    IF @Debug = 0
      BEGIN
        EXEC xp_create_subdir @LogBackup;
      END
    ELSE
      BEGIN
        PRINT 'Exec xp_create_subdir ' + @LogBackup + ';';
      END

    SET @LogBackup =
        @LogBackup + @DBName + @DateSerial + '.' + @FileExtension

    SET @SQL = 'Backup Log ' + QUOTENAME(@DBName) +
               ' To Disk = ''' + @LogBackup + ''';';

    BEGIN TRY
      IF @Debug = 0
        BEGIN
          PRINT 'Backing up the log for ' + @DBName;
          EXEC sp_executesql @SQL;
        END
      ELSE
        BEGIN
          PRINT 'Print ''Backing up the log for ' + @DBName + ''';';
          PRINT @SQL;
        END
```

```
    END TRY
    BEGIN CATCH
      SET @ErrNumber = ERROR_NUMBER();
      SET @ErrSeverity = ERROR_SEVERITY();
      SET @ErrState = ERROR_STATE();
      SET @ErrProcedure = ERROR_PROCEDURE();
      SET @ErrLine = ERROR_LINE();
      SET @ErrMsg = ERROR_MESSAGE();

      INSERT INTO @Failures
         (DBName, ErrNumber, ErrSeverity, ErrState,
          ErrProcedure, ErrLine, ErrMsg)
      SELECT @DBName, @ErrNumber, @ErrSeverity, @ErrState,
             @ErrProcedure, @ErrLine, @ErrMsg
    END CATCH

    SET @CurrID = @CurrID + 1;
  END

IF EXISTS (SELECT 1
           FROM @Failures)
  BEGIN
    SELECT @MaxID = MAX(FailId), @CurrID = 1
    FROM @Failures

    WHILE @CurrID <= @MaxID
      BEGIN
        SELECT @DBName = DBName,
               @ErrNumber = ErrNumber,
               @ErrSeverity = ErrSeverity,
               @ErrState = ErrState,
               @ErrProcedure = ErrProcedure,
               @ErrLine = ErrLine,
               @ErrMsg = ErrMsg
        FROM @Failures
        WHERE FailId = @CurrID

        PRINT '';
        PRINT 'Database Name = ' + @DBName;
        PRINT 'Error Number = ' + CAST(@ErrNumber AS VARCHAR);
        PRINT 'Error Severity = ' + CAST(@ErrSeverity AS VARCHAR);
        PRINT 'Error State = ' + CAST(@ErrState AS VARCHAR);
        PRINT 'Error Procedure = ' + ISNULL(@ErrProcedure, '');
        PRINT 'Error Line = ' + CAST(@ErrLine AS VARCHAR);
        PRINT 'Error Message= ' + @ErrMsg;
```

```
    PRINT '';

    SET @CurrID = @CurrID + 1
  END

  SELECT @FailedDBs =
          ISNULL(@FailedDBs + ', ', '') + QUOTENAME(DBName)
  FROM @Failures

  IF @SendAlerts = 1 AND
     @AlertRecipients IS NOT NULL
    BEGIN
      IF EXISTS (SELECT 1
                  FROM sys.configurations
                  WHERE name = 'Database Mail XPs')
        BEGIN
          SELECT TOP (1) @ProfileName = name
          FROM msdb.dbo.sysmail_profile P WITH(nolock) LEFT JOIN
              msdb.dbo.sysmail_principalprofile PP
                ON PP.profile_id = P.profile_id
          ORDER BY PP.is_default DESC

          SET @Subject = 'Backup failures on ' +
                          CAST(@@SERVERNAME AS VARCHAR(255))
          SET @Body = 'Unable to back up the following databases: ' +
                        @FailedDBs

          EXEC msdb..sp_send_dbmail
                      @profile_name = @ProfileName,
                      @recipients = @AlertRecipients,
                      @Subject = @Subject,
                      @body = @Body
        END
    END

  RAISERROR ('Unable to back up the following databases: %s',
            1, 1, @FailedDBs);
END
```

Managing Log Backup Retention

You want to be sure that your log backups do not fill up the disk drive. It is important that you delete the old log files. If you are performing log backups with a maintenance plan, be sure to include a step to delete the old log backups as well. If you are using a procedure to back up the log files, it is a very simple process to delete the old log files.

The procedure we wrote reuses a lot of code from the log backup procedure. By reusing the code, you can ensure that you are determining the log backup location in the same manner as the log backup procedure. It is important to know that if you are not explicitly providing a location for the backup, both procedures will find the same backup location. It uses the same logic detailed previously.

Other than finding the correct backup location, there was only one bit of logic to worry about. You can use a system procedure that already encapsulates the remaining logic. The procedure sys.xp_delete_file requires a backup location, file extension, and a date in order to perform the deletion. The system procedure also accepts parameters for specifying whether you want backup files or report files deleted and for specifying whether to delete from the first-level subdirectories as well. Our procedure does not customize these last two parameters. When you pass in the required parameters, the system procedure does the rest.

Deleting Log Backups

You can use the following procedure to automate the deletion of log backups of all databases following the same guidelines used for creating log backups. All parameters are optional, and you can use the script without any additional customization. Following is a brief explanation of the parameters.

@DBName: If you want to delete the log of a single database, you can pass in the database's name and the procedure will process the log backups for that database only. The procedure will consider all databases for log backup deletion if you do not provide a database name.

@LogBackupLocation: The procedure will make a best effort determination to discover the location of the log backups unless you provide a location with this parameter. This logic for this process is identical to the logic of the log backups. If you provide a value for this parameter in the log backup procedure, you should provide the same value for this one.

@FileExtension: The system procedure that this procedure calls requires that you tell it the file extension of the backup files. You can use any file extension you want to use, but it is a common practice to use the file extension trn for transaction log backups. This procedure defaults to this extension.

@Retention: This parameter is the number of days for which you want to retain the log backups on the server. The parameter defaults to four days' worth of log files, but you may want to retain more or fewer backups depending on your particular requirements. If you want to be able to support point-in-time restores, then you may want to save more. If you are not concerned about point-in-time recovery, you may want to retain fewer backups.

@Debug: We like to include a debug parameter for troubleshooting purposes. If you pass in a value of 1 for this parameter, the procedure will output the SQL to create the logins and grant the permissions without executing it. The default value of 0 will result in execution of the code.

```
CREATE PROCEDURE dbo.dba_DeleteLogBackups
    -- Name of database, all databases if null
    @DBName sysname = NULL,
    -- Location of log backups
    @LogBackupLocation NVARCHAR(255) = NULL,
    -- log backup extension
    @FileExtension NVARCHAR(3) = 'trn',
    @Retention INT = 4, -- days
    -- 0 = execute deletion of log backup,
```

```
    -- 1 = output the code without executing
    @Debug bit = 0
AS

DECLARE @DeleteDate NVARCHAR(19),
        @BakDir NVARCHAR(255),
        @Exists INT

DECLARE @FileExists TABLE (FileExists INT NOT NULL,
                           FileIsDirectory INT NOT NULL,
                           ParentDirectoryExists INT NOT NULL)

SET NOCOUNT ON

SET @DeleteDate = CONVERT(NVARCHAR(19),
                  DATEADD(DAY, -@Retention, GETDATE()), 126)

IF @DBName IS NOT NULL
  BEGIN
    IF NOT EXISTS (SELECT 1
                   FROM sys.databases
                   WHERE name = @DBName)
      BEGIN
        RAISERROR ('The specified database [%s] does not exist.
                    Please  check the name entered or do not supply
                    a database name if you want to delete  the
                    log backups for all databases.', 16, 1, @DBName);
        RETURN;
      END
  END

IF @LogBackupLocation IS NULL
  BEGIN
    EXEC xp_instance_regread
            N'HKEY_LOCAL_MACHINE',
            N'Software\Microsoft\MSSQLServer\MSSQLServer',
            N'BackupDirectory',
            @BakDir output,
            'no_output';

    IF @BakDir IS NOT NULL
      BEGIN
        INSERT INTO @FileExists
        EXEC sys.xp_fileexist @BakDir;
```

```
            SELECT @Exists = ParentDirectoryExists
            FROM @FileExists;

            IF @Exists = 1
              BEGIN
                SET @LogBackupLocation = @BakDir + ISNULL('\' + @DBName, '');
              END
          END
      END
  END

IF @LogBackupLocation IS NULL
  BEGIN
    SELECT TOP 1 @BakDir = LEFT(MF.physical_device_name,
          LEN(MF.physical_device_name) -
          CHARINDEX('\', REVERSE(MF.physical_device_name)))
    FROM msdb.dbo.backupset BS INNER JOIN
        msdb.dbo.backupmediafamily MF
          ON MF.media_set_id = BS.media_set_id
    -- log backups first, then differentials, then full backups
    ORDER BY BS.type DESC,
          BS.backup_finish_date DESC; -- newest first

    IF @BakDir IS NOT NULL
      BEGIN
        DELETE FROM @FileExists

        INSERT INTO @FileExists
        EXEC sys.xp_fileexist @BakDir;

        SELECT @Exists = ParentDirectoryExists
        FROM @FileExists

        IF @Exists = 1
          BEGIN
            SET @LogBackupLocation = @BakDir;
          END
      END
  END

IF @LogBackupLocation IS NOT NULL
  BEGIN
    IF RIGHT(@LogBackupLocation, 1) <> '\'
      SET @LogBackupLocation = @LogBackupLocation + '\';
  END
ELSE
```

```
  BEGIN
    RAISERROR ('Backup location not specified or not found.', 16, 1);
    RETURN;
  END

IF @Debug = 0
  BEGIN
    EXEC sys.xp_delete_file
          0,
          @LogBackupLocation,
          @FileExtension,
          @DeleteDate,
          1;
  END
ELSE
  BEGIN
    PRINT 'Exec sys.xp_delete_file 0, ''' + @LogBackupLocation +
          ''', ''' + @FileExtension + ''', ''' +
          @DeleteDate + ''', 1;';
  END
```

Log File Size

SQL Server 2005 had a known bug that could take both mirroring partners offline if the transaction log grew too large. During the initialization process, SQL Server scans the log files to determine the level of synchronization of the databases. If the log files are too large, the initialization process could time out. If the error occurs during mirroring setup, mirroring fails to start. If your servers reboot and the error occurs while attempting to resume the mirroring session, SQL Server takes the principal database offline because SQL cannot verify which database should be the principal. When both databases are offline, you cannot bring either database online until you drop mirroring. The first correction for this bug appeared in CU6 for SP2.

Note For more information on the error that we've described, refer to the following KB article:

http://support.microsoft.com/kb/947462.

When we first encountered this bug, it was virtually unknown. We were able to find a couple of posts online about it, but there were no posted solutions at the time. We were able to determine that the initialization process was timing out, and we created a workaround that checked the size of the log file every night and resized it if the log file was too large. We concluded that the mirroring initialization worked fine if the log file was 20 GB or smaller. However, we were not confident that 20 GB was a value that would work in all environments, so we decided to use 5 GB as the default log file size.

The procedure we wrote to correct the log size issue queries sys.master_files and sys.database_mirroring to determine which mirrored databases have log files that exceed the specified size. If a log file exceeds the specified size, it shrinks it to the specified size. Shrinking the log files is not a good practice. You should only use this procedure if you are having the log size issue and cannot upgrade or just as a workaround until you can upgrade.

Identifying Log Files to Shrink

The following query returns a list of all mirrored databases in the principal role and the sizes of their log files in MB. The results give you a list of log files to examine and to possibly shrink.

```
SELECT DBName = DB_NAME(MF.database_id),
       LogFileName = MF.[name],
       -- Size = number of 8K pages
       LogFileSize = CEILING(MF.[size] * 8 / 1024.0)
FROM sys.master_files MF INNER JOIN
     sys.database_mirroring DM
       ON DM.database_id = MF.database_id
WHERE MF.[type] = 1 -- log file
AND DM.Mirroring_Role = 1 -- Principal partner
```

When the procedure shrinks a log file, SQL Server does not duplicate the shrink file operation on the mirror partner as expected. For this reason, we perform a DBCC SHRINKFILE operation followed by an ALTER DATABASE … MODIFY FILE operation to force SQL Server to mirror the log resize operation. A knowledge base article exists for this issue, but Microsoft has not released or announced a fix for this bug.

Note See the following knowledge base article for more information on this bug:

http://support.microsoft.com/default.aspx/kb/937531.

Shrinking a Log File

This section presents a script that you can use to routinely shrink log files. However, you may not need the script. If you aren't experiencing the problem we've described, then you don't need the script. Furthermore, if you are on at least CU6 for SP2, you also do not need the procedure, as the bug that is the root cause of the problem will have been fixed. Furthermore, if you are not required to maintain the log at a specific maximum size for some other reason, then you should not use this procedure if you are using at least CU6 for SP2.

Caution If you routinely resize the log file, it will result in degraded performance if the log file has to autogrow frequently. Additionally, if you frequently shrink and expand the log file, it can result in an abnormally large number of small virtual log files (the internal units of space inside a log file), which can cause long-term performance degradation.

As you can see, you should only use the procedure described in this section if you believe it is required. You can use the procedure as is without any customization. Following are the parameters for the procedure in case you want to customize it.

@DBName: If you want to shrink the log of a single database, you can pass in the database's name, and the procedure will shrink the log of that database only. The procedure will consider all databases for log shrinkage if you do not provide a database name.

@TargetSize: This parameter has a default value of 5,120 MB or 5 GB. The parameter accepts an integer value, and the procedure makes a logical determination as to whether you intended the value entered to be KB, MB, or GB. If it believes you entered the value as KB or GB, it converts it to MB.

@Debug: We like to include a debug parameter for troubleshooting purposes. If you pass in a value of 1 for this parameter, the procedure will output the SQL to create the logins and grant the permissions without executing it. The default value of 0 will result in execution of the code.

Now that you know the parameters, following is the procedure itself.

```
CREATE PROCEDURE dbo.dba_ShrinkMirroredDatabases
    -- database to shrink; all mirrored databases if null
    @DBName sysname = NULL,
    -- target size for shrink operation. Defaults to 5 GB (5120 MB)
    @TargetSize INT = 5120,
    -- 0 = Execute it, 1 = Output SQL that would be executed
    @Debug bit = 0
AS

DECLARE @CurrID INT,
        @MaxID INT,
        @DefaultTargetSize INT,
        @FileName sysname,
        @FileSize INT,
        @NewFileSize INT,
        @SQL NVARCHAR(MAX),
        @ErrMsg NVARCHAR(500)

DECLARE @MirroredDBs TABLE
        (MirroredDBID INT IDENTITY(1, 1) NOT NULL PRIMARY KEY,
        DBName sysname NOT NULL,
        LogFileName sysname NOT NULL,
        FileSize INT NOT NULL)

SET NOCOUNT ON

-- Assume entered as GB and convert to MB
IF @TargetSize < 20
  BEGIN
    SET @TargetSize = @TargetSize * 1024
```

```
    END

-- Assume entered as MB and use 512
ELSE IF @TargetSize <= 512
  BEGIN
    SET @TargetSize = 512
  END

-- Assume entered as KB and return warning
ELSE IF @TargetSize > 19922944
  BEGIN
    SET @ErrMsg = 'Please enter a valid target size less than 20 GB. ' +
                  'Amount entered can be in GB (max size = 19), ' +
                  'MB (max size = 19456), or ' +
                  'KB (max size = 19922944).';
    GOTO ErrComplete;
  END

-- Assume entered as KB and convert to MB
ELSE IF @TargetSize > 525311
  BEGIN
    SET @TargetSize = 525311 / 1024
  END

-- Assume entered as KB and use 512 as converted MB
ELSE IF @TargetSize > 19456
  BEGIN
    SET @TargetSize = 512
  END

-- Else assume entered as MB and use as entered
INSERT INTO @MirroredDBs
          (DBName, LogFileName, FileSize)
SELECT DB_NAME(MF.database_id),
       MF.[name],
       -- Size = number of 8K pages
       CEILING(MF.[size] * 8 / 1024.0)
FROM sys.master_files MF INNER JOIN
     sys.database_mirroring DM
       ON DM.database_id = MF.database_id
WHERE MF.[type] = 1 AND -- log file
      DM.Mirroring_Role = 1 AND -- Principal partner
      -- Specified database or all databases if null
      (MF.database_id = @DBName OR
       @DBName IS NULL)
```

```
IF NOT EXISTS (SELECT 1
                FROM @MirroredDBs)
  BEGIN
    SET @ErrMsg = CASE WHEN @DBName IS NOT NULL
                       THEN
                         'Database ' + QUOTENAME(@DBName) +
                         ' was either not found or is not' +
                         ' a mirroring principal.'
                       ELSE
                         'No databases were found in the ' +
                         'mirroring principal role.'
                  END;
    GOTO ErrComplete;
  END
ELSE
  BEGIN
    SELECT @MaxID = MAX(MirroredDBID),
           @CurrID = 1
    FROM @MirroredDBs

    WHILE @CurrID <= @MaxID
      BEGIN
        SELECT @DBName = DBName,
               @FileName = LogFileName,
               @FileSize = FileSize
        FROM @MirroredDBs
        WHERE MirroredDBID = @CurrID

        IF @FileSize > @TargetSize
          BEGIN
            SET @SQL = 'Use ' + QUOTENAME(@DBName) + ';' +
                       'DBCC ShrinkFile(''' + @FileName + ''', ' +
                       CAST(@TargetSize AS NVARCHAR) + ');'

            IF @Debug = 0
              BEGIN
                EXEC sp_executesql @SQL
              END
            ELSE
              BEGIN
                PRINT @SQL
              END

            SELECT -- Size = number of 8K pages
```

```
            @NewFileSize = CEILING((([size] + 1) * 8)
        FROM sys.master_files
        WHERE [type] = 1 AND -- log file
                [name] = @FileName AND
                database_id = DB_ID(@DBName)

        IF @NewFileSize < @FileSize
          BEGIN
            SET @SQL = 'Alter Database ' + QUOTENAME(@DBName) +
                        ' Modify File (name = ' + @FileName +
                        ', size = ' +
                        CAST(@NewFileSize AS NVARCHAR) + 'KB);'

            IF @Debug = 0
              BEGIN
                EXEC sp_executesql @SQL
              END
            ELSE
              BEGIN
                PRINT @SQL
              END
          END
        END

    SET @CurrID = @CurrID + 1
    END
  END

Success:
  GOTO Complete;
ErrComplete:
  RAISERROR (@ErrMsg, 1, 1)
  RETURN
Complete:
```

Routine Patching and SQL Server Upgrades

When dealing with servers that host database mirroring, you need to make certain changes to your routine patching processes. You need to distinguish SQL Server patches and upgrades from other server patches. If a patch or upgrade will not change the databases on the server, then the patching process is simple. If it is a SQL Server patch or upgrade, you need to follow a specific upgrade path.

Installing General Patches

If you are not installing a SQL Server patch or upgrade, the only real difference is that you do one server at a time. One of our general rules of thumb is that you should never restart mirroring partners at the same time. This includes the witness server. If multiple servers are offline, then the application is offline.

We have heard arguments that failing over to the mirror for the reboot of the principal and then failing back causes a longer downtime than just rebooting both servers at the same time. It is not a good idea to reboot both servers at the same time. If the principal server fails to come back online, and the mirror server fails to come back online as well, you do not have a server that can host the application. You are now in a scramble to try to get a server up and running.

Even if the mirror server comes back online without problem, it may not be able to take over as principal. If the mirror server is not able to create a quorum with a mirroring witness or if the mirror was not in a synchronized state with the principal, it will refuse to come online and will remain offline. Likewise, if you reboot the witness and either mirroring partner, the other partner will remain offline or go offline once it fails to establish a quorum with another server.

The process is simple. Patch one server, reboot the server as needed, and confirm that it has recovered successfully and is online. If the server is a mirror partner, allow the database to synchronize to the principal before updating the principal. Then perform the same actions for the next server. If the mirroring session includes a witness server, perform the same actions for the third server. It does not really matter in which order you patch the servers; however, it is a common practice to patch the witness, then the mirror, and then the principal.

Upgrading or Patching SQL Server

When you install SQL Server patches or upgrades, you need to follow a specific upgrade path. This is a rolling upgrade. This is very similar to the process we recommended in the previous section for general patching, but this time the order is important for the mirror and principal, and you should take extra care when a witness server is involved.

If you plan to patch mirroring servers that includes a witness server, you should remove the witness server from the mirroring session before you begin. You will add the witness server back into the mirroring session at the end of the process. You can upgrade the witness server at any time while not participating in the mirroring session. You can remove a witness from a mirroring session by issuing the `ALTER DATABASE [DatabaseName] SET WITNESS OFF;` command. Take note of the witness server's full network address before you disable the witness. You will need this information when you add the witness server back in to the mirroring session. The command to add the witness server back to the session is `ALTER DATABASE [DatabaseName] SET WITNESS = 'TCP://WitnessServer.FQDN.com:Port#';`.

SQL Server Books Online recommends that you change the operating mode to high safety (synchronous) if your mirroring session is operating in high performance (asynchronous) mode before you begin the patch installation. On this point, we are in total disagreement with SQL Server Books Online. If your mirroring session is operating synchronously, we recommend that you change to asynchronous mode before you begin the patching. When you are ready to fail over the database, change the operating mode to synchronous and wait for the mirror database to synchronize. Then perform a failover and return the mirroring session to an asynchronous operating mode.

When you patch or upgrade the mirroring partners, you should patch the mirror partner first. When you are confident that the patch installation is complete and the mirror server is online and in a synchronized state, fail over to the mirror server. When the failover occurs, the database upgrade will complete, and the mirroring partners will be at different build levels. SQL Server will suspend the mirroring session because of the build number discrepancy, and you can resume mirroring as soon as you complete the upgrade of the original principal.

Fail Back to the Original Principal

With mirroring, a failure of the original database causes the mirror to become the new original. Once that happens, you can simply continue to use that new original, and you can create a new mirror to cover the next failure that might occur. However, there are various reasons why you may want to quickly fix the original database and fail back to that, essentially putting things back to the way that they were before the failure occurred. This section discusses those reasons, and then we present a script to automate the failback process.

Reasons to Fail Back to the Original

There are several reasons why you might want to fail back to the original principal as soon as possible after an automatic failover. The three most common reasons for this are to preserve your single license coverage for both servers, because a less powerful server is acting as the failover, or because the failover instance does not fully support all components of the system.

If you are using the mirror instance as a failover-only server so that you can cover both instances with a single license, you can only use the failover instance as an active server for up to 30 days before you have to purchase separate licensing for it. The goal of this licensing model is to provide a grace period for you to be able to get your original server back online and functional. Failure to fail back to the original principal in a timely manner can then be a very expensive mistake for your company. You can avoid this mistake by having SQL Server fail over the server as soon as the original principal is back online.

Note You can find information on the 30-day limit for the single licensing model for failover servers at the following URLs. For SQL Server 2005, see `www.microsoft.com/sqlserver/2005/en/us/Special-Considerations.aspx#passive`. For SQL Server 2008, see `www.microsoft.com/sqlserver/2008/en/us/licensing-faq.aspx#licensing`.

One of the benefits of using database mirroring is that it does not require high-priced, beefy hardware. It is a common practice for companies to use an older server as a failover server or to consolidate their failover servers into a single machine. We set up a system for a company that featured 17 primary/principal servers and 4 failover servers. Ultimately, each failover server hosted log shipping secondary databases and mirrors for four or more servers. The servers could handle the load of a single server failover, but it would not be able to handle the load if four or more servers failed over. In this scenario, we configured the mirrored databases to fail back to the original principal as soon as the server was ready.

If your system has applications or clients that do not support the failover partner attribute of connection strings or if there is some other limitation that prevents you from configuring certain components of your system to run on the mirror instance, you may want to automatically fail back to the principal instance as soon as possible. For example, we set up mirroring for an application that had moved into sustained engineering and had no budget for new development. The application had a C# component coded to connect to run on the local SQL Server and connect to the local instance. It would not have taken much effort to modify the component to work with mirroring, but the product team decided that the component was not critical and that if it did not run for one day the system would be okay. We set up a job to fail the database back to the original principal as soon as it was online and synchronized to reduce the chance that the component would fail to run.

The procedure that performs the failback to the original principal should only be set up on the designated mirror server. The procedure queries sys.database_mirroring to check for any mirrored databases that are serving in the principal role and are in a synchronized state. You can query for a list of databases that fit this criteria with the following query.

```
SELECT DB_NAME(database_id)
FROM sys.database_mirroring
WHERE mirroring_role = 1 AND -- Principal partner
      mirroring_state = 4    -- Synchronized
```

Procedure to Fail Back to the Original Principal

In this section, we describe a procedure that you can use to fail back to the original principal. The procedure is as straightforward and simple as you can get. If the procedure detects any databases that fit the criteria, it issues the failback command one at a time for each database. We designed the procedure to accept an optional parameter for a database name in case you want to use this for specific databases but not for others. As usual, we included a debug parameter that allows you to output the T-SQL code that you could use to perform manual failovers.

Following are the parameter descriptions.

@DBName: If you want to fail over a single database when appropriate, you can pass in the database's name, and the procedure will only consider the specified database for failover to the original principal. The procedure will consider all databases for failover if you do not provide a database name.

@Debug: We like to include a debug parameter for troubleshooting purposes. If you pass in a value of 1 for this parameter, the procedure will output the T-SQL to fail back any databases that are acting in the principal role and are in a synchronized state without executing it. The default value of 0 will result in execution of the code.

And following is the code to create the procedure itself.

```
CREATE PROCEDURE dbo.dba_FailoverMirrorToOriginalPrincipal
    -- database to fail back; all applicable databases if null
    @DBName sysname = NULL,
    -- 0 = Execute it, 1 = Output SQL that would be executed
    @Debug bit = 0
AS

DECLARE @SQL NVARCHAR(200),
        @MaxID INT,
        @CurrID INT

DECLARE @MirrDBs TABLE
                (MirrDBID INT IDENTITY(1, 1) NOT NULL PRIMARY KEY,
                 DBName sysname NOT NULL)

SET NOCOUNT ON
```

```
-- If database is in the principal role
-- and is in a synchronized state,
-- fail database back to original principal

INSERT INTO @MirrDBs (DBName)
SELECT DB_NAME(database_id)
FROM sys.database_mirroring
WHERE mirroring_role = 1 AND  -- Principal partner
      mirroring_state = 4 AND -- Synchronized
     (database_id = DB_ID(@DBName) OR
      @DBName IS NULL)

SELECT @MaxID = MAX(MirrDBID)
FROM @MirrDBs

WHILE @CurrID <= @MaxID
  BEGIN
    SELECT @DBName = DBName
    FROM @MirrDBs
    WHERE MirrDBID = @CurrID

    SET @SQL = 'Alter Database ' + QUOTENAME(@DBName) +
               ' Set Partner Failover;'

    IF @Debug = 1
      BEGIN
        EXEC sp_executesql @SQL;
      END
    ELSE
      BEGIN
        PRINT @SQL;
      END

    SET @CurrID = @CurrID + 1
  END
```

Setting Database Owner and TRUSTWORTHY Property

The database owner and the TRUSTWORTHY database property have both been areas of trouble for mirrored databases in the past. It is not always obvious to everyone that SQL Server resets these properties when you set up database mirroring. You cannot change these two properties directly on the mirror database while it is in a restoring state. You must bring the database completely online to change the properties.

When you back up a database, SQL Server resets the TRUSTWORTHY property. The TRUSTWORTHY property tells the SQL instance that it can trust the objects contained within a database. Any time you restore a database, you have to set the TRUSTWORTHY property. You cannot change this database property while the database is in a restoring state. If you must set this property on a database mirror for the system to function properly, you will have to fail over to the mirror in order to reset the TRUSTWORTHY property.

SQL Server Books Online recommends that you fail over the database after you set up mirroring, set the TRUSTWORTHY property on the database, and then fail back to the original principal. This is a great suggestion, and we definitely echo their recommendation. We strongly recommend that you fail the database over and back at least once after setting up mirroring to validate that the failover occurs as expected and to run a quick test to ensure that the application continues to function. You should occasionally schedule a test failover of the databases on a recurring basis. If you have a regular downtime window for routine maintenance, we recommend testing the failover at least once a month.

You can enable the TRUSTWORTHY property with an ALTER DATABASE command. If you want to set this property on a database named MirrorTest, the command would be:

```
ALTER DATABASE [MirrorTest] SET TRUSTWORTHY ON;
```

When you restore a database or create a new database, SQL Server sets your account as the owner of the database. The reasoning behind this is to ensure that you have full permissions in the database that you just created. The problem with this practice is that if you leave the company, your account is not a valid account and a non-existent user owns the database. If the database owner account is not a valid account, you will see unexpected failures due to permissions. If you see unusual permissions errors that you cannot readily explain, you should check the database owner account by querying sys.databases and joining it to sys.server_principals. Our recommendation is to always use the built-in sa account as the owner of all production databases. The sa account will default ownership to the SQL Server Service account. You do not need to enable SQL authentication, and the sa account can be disabled.

You should use a left join when you query the system views for the database owner. If the server login that originally owned the database no longer exists, you will not find a matching server login. The following query will tell you the name of the database owner. For consistency, we will use the name MirrorTest as the database name.

```
SELECT P.name
FROM sys.databases D LEFT JOIN
     sys.server_principals P
        ON P.sid = D.owner_sid
WHERE D.name = 'MirrorTest'
```

The built-in sa account will always have an SID (security identifier) of 0x01. If we want to programmatically change the database owner to the built-in sa account, we do not care to which account the owner maps. You will see a value in the owner_sid column in sys.databases even if the login no longer exists. You can simply check the owning SID and change the database owner if it is not the expected value. In SQL Server 2005, you change the database owner by executing the system procedure sys.sp_changedbowner in the context of the database. The command to change the database owner for a database named MirrorTest would be:

```
EXEC MirrorTest.sys.sp_changedbowner @loginame = 'sa'
```

In SQL Server 2008, you can use the same command, or you can use the `ALTER AUTHORIZATION` command to change the database owner. The new command is a server-level command, but the database still has to be online to make the change. The full command would look like the following:

```
ALTER AUTHORIZATION ON DATABASE::MirrorTest TO sa;
```

When dealing with mirrored databases, we think you should handle the database owner a little smarter than this. What if there is a requirement for the database owner to be a specific account? What if the `TRUSTWORTHY` property is off when you set up mirroring but someone enables it later? If you change the database owner or the `TRUSTWORTHY` property setting, the change will not propagate to the mirror database, and you may not think to or may not want to fail over the database to make the same changes on the mirror database. We prefer to have measures in place to check these settings and update them as needed whenever a failover occurs.

Controlled Failover of Mirrored Databases

You can expect to deal with two types of failovers, automatic failovers due to a failure and controlled failovers triggered by an administrator. When performing a controlled failover, all of the existing documentation makes it sound simple and straightforward. Sometimes it is that simple. If you only have one or two mirrored databases and all mirroring sessions are running in synchronous mode, failing over is as easy as issuing an `ALTER DATABASE [DatabaseName] SET PARTNER FAILOVER` command for each mirrored database.

Problems You Might Encounter

If conditions are not ideal, you may need to perform additional steps to execute a failover. When you issue the failover command on a mirrored database running in asynchronous mode, you will receive an error because the mirroring session is not in a synchronized state. You will need to change the operating mode to synchronous and wait for the databases to synchronize before failing over the mirrored database. You can determine the operating mode and state of synchronicity, also known as the safety level, by querying the `sys.database_mirroring` system view. You can query the columns `mirroring_safety_level` and `mirroring_safety_level_desc` to determine the operating mode and the columns `mirroring_state` and `mirroring_state_desc` to determine the safety level. After changing the operating mode to asynchronous, you need to continue checking the mirroring state until the databases enter a synchronized state, and then you can fail over the database.

We have had a few people suggest that you can simplify the failover process by executing the command to set the safety level to full for all databases because it does not return an error if you set it to the existing value. There is a major problem with this approach. All mirrored databases now have their safety level set to full regardless of the original settings. You need to set the safety level off after the failover if the safety level was off before the failover.

Rather than trying to determine which steps to perform on which databases, you should use a procedure that handles all of the logic and performs the appropriate steps accordingly. This makes the process quicker and easier for you. This will also make it possible for staff without technical expertise with database mirroring to perform a failover.

Procedure to Perform a Controlled Failover

The procedure we describe in this section queries the system databases to determine which databases are in the principal role. It checks the mirroring state and safety level and takes the appropriate steps for performing the failover. Additionally, this procedure checks the database owner account and the TRUSTWORTHY property and updates these values if they are different on the new principal. After the failover has completed, it sets the safety level off for any database with a safety level that was originally set to off.

The procedure accepts an optional parameter to allow you to specify a database name. If you provide a database name, the procedure will fail over only the database that you specified. A second optional parameter allows you to customize the maximum amount of time you want to allow for the synchronization of the databases after setting the safety level from off to full. As usual, we include a parameter for running the procedure in debug mode. The following list describes each parameter for the stored procedure.

@DBName: If you want to fail over a single database, you can pass in the database's name, and the procedure will only consider the specified database for failover to the mirroring partner. The procedure will consider all databases for failover if you do not provide a database name.

@MaxCounter: After changing the safety level to full, the procedure will check the mirroring state in a looping fashion until the databases are in a synchronized state. It waits for five seconds before making the each loop. If the databases do not synchronize by the final loop, it returns an error, and the procedure will stop processing the current database. You can customize the total amount of time to wait for each database by specifying the maximum number of loops to perform. The default value is 60 loops, which will result in a maximum wait time of five minutes.

@Debug: We like to include a debug parameter for troubleshooting purposes. If you pass in a value of 1 for this parameter, the procedure will output the SQL to fail back any databases that are acting in the principal role and are in a synchronized state without executing it. The default value of 0 will result in execution of the code.

And following is the code itself.

```
CREATE PROCEDURE dbo.dba_ControlledFailover
    -- database to fail back; all applicable databases if null
    @DBName sysname = NULL,
    -- @MaxCounter = max # of loops, each loop = 5 seconds
    -- 60 loops = 5 minutes
    @MaxCounter INT = 60,
    -- 0 = Execute it, 1 = Output SQL that would be executed
    @Debug bit = 0
AS

DECLARE @SQL NVARCHAR(1000),
        @MaxID INT,
        @CurrID INT,
        @DMState INT,
        @SafeCounter INT,
        @PartnerServer sysname,
        @SafetyLevel INT,
        @TrustWorthyOn bit,
        @DBOwner sysname,
        @Results INT,
        @ErrMsg VARCHAR(500),
```

```
        @Print NVARCHAR(1000)
DECLARE @Databases TABLE
        (DatabaseID INT IDENTITY(1, 1) NOT NULL PRIMARY KEY,
         DatabaseName sysname NOT NULL,
         PartnerServer sysname NOT NULL,
         SafetyLevel INT NOT NULL,
         TrustWorthyOn bit NOT NULL,
         DBOwner sysname NULL)

SET NOCOUNT ON

INSERT INTO @Databases
        (DatabaseName,
         PartnerServer,
         SafetyLevel,
         TrustWorthyOn,
         DBOwner)
SELECT D.name,
       DM.mirroring_partner_instance,
       DM.mirroring_safety_level,
       D.is_trustworthy_on,
       SP.name
FROM sys.database_mirroring DM INNER JOIN
     sys.databases D
       ON D.database_id = DM.database_id LEFT JOIN
     sys.server_principals SP
       ON SP.sid = D.owner_sid
WHERE DM.mirroring_role = 1 AND -- Principal role
      DM.mirroring_state IN (2, 4) AND -- Synchronizing, Synchronized
      (D.name = @DBName OR
       @DBName IS NULL)

IF NOT EXISTS (SELECT 1
               FROM @Databases) AND
               @DBName IS NULL
   BEGIN
     RAISERROR ('There were no mirroring principals found on this server.',
                1, 1);
   END

IF NOT EXISTS (SELECT 1
               FROM @Databases) AND
               @DBName IS NOT NULL
   BEGIN
```

```
    RAISERROR ('Database [%s] was not found or is not a mirroring principal
              on this server.', 1, 1, @DBName);
  END

SELECT @MaxID = MAX(DatabaseID),
       @CurrID = 1
FROM @Databases

-- Set Safety to Full on all databases first, if needed
WHILE @CurrID <= @MaxID
  BEGIN
    SELECT @DBName = DatabaseName,
           @PartnerServer = PartnerServer,
           @SafetyLevel = SafetyLevel
    FROM @Databases
    WHERE DatabaseID = @CurrID

    -- Make sure linked server to mirror exists
    EXEC @Results = dbo.dba_ManageLinkedServer
        @ServerName = @PartnerServer,
        @Action = 'create'

    IF @Results <> 0
      BEGIN
        RAISERROR ('Failed to create linked server to mirror instance
                   [%s].', 1, 1, @PartnerServer);
      END

    IF @SafetyLevel = 1
      BEGIN
        SET @SQL = 'Alter Database ' + QUOTENAME(@DBName) +
                   ' Set Partner Safety Full;'

        SET @Print = 'Setting Safety on for database ' +
                     QUOTENAME(@DBName) + '.';

        IF @Debug = 0
          BEGIN
            PRINT @Print
            EXEC sp_executesql @SQL
          END
        ELSE
          BEGIN
            PRINT '-- ' + @Print
            PRINT @SQL;
```

```
            END
          END

      SET @CurrID = @CurrID + 1
    END


-- Reset @CurrID to 1
SET @CurrID = 1

-- Pause momentarily
WAITFOR Delay '0:00:03';

-- Failover all databases
WHILE @CurrID <= @MaxID
  BEGIN
    SELECT @DBName = DatabaseName,
           @DMState = DM.mirroring_state,
           @SafeCounter = 0,
           @SafetyLevel = SafetyLevel
    FROM @Databases D INNER JOIN
        sys.database_mirroring DM
          ON DM.database_id = DB_ID(D.DatabaseName)
    WHERE DatabaseID = @CurrID

    WHILE @DMState = 2 AND -- Synchronizing
          @SafeCounter < @MaxCounter
      BEGIN
        WAITFOR Delay '0:00:05';

        SELECT @DMState = mirroring_state,
               @SafeCounter = @SafeCounter + 1
        FROM sys.database_mirroring
        WHERE database_id = DB_ID(@DBName)
      END

    IF @DMState = 2 AND @SafeCounter = @MaxCounter
      BEGIN
        RAISERROR('Synchronization timed out for database [%s].
                   Please check and fail over manually.', 1, 1, @DBName);

      IF @SafetyLevel = 1
        BEGIN
          SET @SQL = 'Alter Database ' + QUOTENAME(@DBName) +
                     ' Set Partner Safety Full;'
```

```
            SET @Print = 'Setting Safety Full for database ' +
                            QUOTENAME(@DBName) + '.';

            IF @Debug = 0
              BEGIN
                PRINT @Print
                EXEC sp_executesql @SQL
              END
            ELSE
              BEGIN
                PRINT '-- ' + @Print
                PRINT @SQL;
              END
          END
        END
      ELSE
        BEGIN
          SET @SQL = 'Alter Database ' + QUOTENAME(@DBName) +
                        ' Set Partner Failover;'

          SET @Print = 'Failing over database ' + QUOTENAME(@DBName) + '.';

          IF @Debug = 0
            BEGIN
              PRINT @Print
              EXEC sp_executesql @SQL
            END
          ELSE
            BEGIN
              PRINT '-- ' + @Print
              PRINT @SQL;
            END
        END

    SET @CurrID = @CurrID + 1
  END

-- Reset @CurrID to 1
SET @CurrID = 1

-- Pause momentarily
WAITFOR Delay '0:00:03';

-- Set safety level and db owner on failed over databases
WHILE @CurrID <= @MaxID
```

```
BEGIN
  SELECT @DBName = DatabaseName,
         @PartnerServer = PartnerServer,
         @SafetyLevel = SafetyLevel,
         @TrustWorthyOn = TrustWorthyOn,
         @DBOwner = DBOwner,
         @DMState = DM.mirroring_state,
         @SafeCounter = 0
  FROM @Databases D INNER JOIN
       sys.database_mirroring DM
         ON DM.database_id = DB_ID(D.DatabaseName)
  WHERE DatabaseID = @CurrID

  -- Make sure linked server to mirror exists
  EXEC @Results = dbo.dba_ManageLinkedServer
       @ServerName = @PartnerServer,
       @Action = 'create'

  WHILE @DMState = 2 AND -- Synchronizing
        @SafeCounter < @MaxCounter
    BEGIN
      WAITFOR Delay '0:00:05';

      SELECT @DMState = mirroring_state,
             @SafeCounter = @SafeCounter + 1
      FROM sys.database_mirroring
      WHERE database_id = DB_ID(@DBName)
    END

  IF @DMState = 2 AND
     @SafeCounter = @MaxCounter
    BEGIN
      RAISERROR('Synchronization timed out for database [%s]
                 after failover. Please check and set
                 database options manually.', 1, 1, @DBName);
    END
  ELSE
    BEGIN
      -- Turn safety off if it was originally off
      IF @SafetyLevel = 1
        BEGIN
          SET @SQL = 'Alter Database ' + QUOTENAME(@DBName) +
                     'Set Partner Safety Off;'
```

```
        SET @SQL = 'Exec ' + QUOTENAME(@PartnerServer) +
                    '.master.sys.sp_executesql N''' + @SQL + ''';';

        SET @Print = 'Setting Safety off for database ' +
                        QUOTENAME(@DBName) +
                        ' on server ' + QUOTENAME(@PartnerServer) + '.';

        IF @Debug = 0
          BEGIN
            PRINT @Print
            EXEC sp_executesql @SQL
          END
        ELSE
          BEGIN
            PRINT '-- ' + @Print
            PRINT @SQL;
          END
    END

-- Set TrustWorthy property on if it was originally on
IF @TrustWorthyOn = 1
  BEGIN
    SET @SQL = 'Alter Database ' + QUOTENAME(@DBName) +
                ' Set TrustWorthy On;'

    SET @SQL = 'EXEC ' + QUOTENAME(@PartnerServer) +
                '.master.sys.sp_executesql N''' + @SQL + ''';';

    SET @Print = 'Setting TrustWorthy On for database ' +
                    QUOTENAME(@DBName) +
                    ' on server ' + QUOTENAME(@PartnerServer) + '.';

    IF @Debug = 0
      BEGIN
        PRINT @Print
        EXEC sp_executesql @SQL
      END
    ELSE
      BEGIN
        PRINT '-- ' + @Print
        PRINT @SQL;
      END
  END

-- Change database owner if different than original
```

```
        SET @SQL = 'If Exists (Select 1 From sys.databases D' +
                    CHAR(10) + CHAR(9) +
                    'Left Join sys.server_principals P' +
                    ' On P.sid = D.owner_sid' + CHAR(10) + CHAR(9) +
                    'Where P.name Is Null' + CHAR(10) + CHAR(9) +
                    'Or P.name <> ''' + @DBOwner + ''')' + CHAR(10) +
                    CHAR(9) +
                    'Exec ' + QUOTENAME(@DBName) +
                    '..sp_changedbowner ''' + @DBOwner + ''';'

        SET @SQL = REPLACE(@SQL, '''', ''''''')
        SET @SQL = 'Exec ' + QUOTENAME(@PartnerServer) +
                    '.master.sys.sp_executesql N''' + @SQL + ''';';

        SET @Print = 'Changing Database owner to ' + QUOTENAME(@DBOwner) +
                      ' for database ' + QUOTENAME(@DBName) +
                      ' on server ' + QUOTENAME(@PartnerServer) + '.';

        IF @Debug = 0
          BEGIN
            PRINT @Print
            EXEC sp_executesql @SQL
          END
        ELSE
          BEGIN
            PRINT '-- ' + @Print
            PRINT @SQL;
          END
    END

    SET @CurrID = @CurrID + 1
  END
```

Automatic Failover of Mirrored Databases

As we mentioned previously, you will also experience automatic failovers. For the most basic database-mirroring setup, an automatic failover is no problem. If the database has no dependencies on external resources or cross-database dependencies, you can just let it run on either mirroring partner. The odds are good that you will have to deal with a system that is not this simple at some point.

If you are designing a highly available solution that supports automatic failover and has a higher degree of complexity, you may need to be able to respond to a failover event automatically. Your solution may require that you enable SQL jobs on the new principal or disable the same SQL jobs on the original principal if the server is still online. Another common task you may need to perform is failing over other dependent databases manually in the event of a single database failure.

You can monitor for database mirroring state change events and start a procedure in response to a failover or send an e-mail alert. SQL Server provides you with two easy ways to monitor for an automatic failover and take action when an automatic failover occurs. You can use the built-in SQL alert system to start a SQL job that performs some responsive actions or send an alert to a SQL operator or both. The Service Broker system also has the ability to automatically execute a stored procedure in response to event notifications.

Creating a SQL Alert to Detect Automatic Failovers

SQL Server has functionality for querying Windows Management Instrumentation (WMI) namespaces and raising alerts when a WMI query returns records. The event that you will need to monitor is the DATABASE_MIRRORING_STATE_CHANGE event. Using WMI, you can query this event the same way you would query a table.

A SQL alert is easy to set up because there is an interface you can use. After you have set up the alert using the interface, you can have the interface output the alert to a query window or a script file before you create the alert. You can also script an existing alert by right-clicking on the alert in Object Explorer and using the Script ... As options in the pop-up menu. Saving the script will allow you to recreate the alert quickly if you have a need. Also, with a little customization, you can use the script to deploy the alert to multiple servers without going through the interface every time.

You will need to formulate your WMI query before you create the alert. The simplest functional query is to check the State column of the event for an automatic failover event. If you want to monitor for a specific table, you can include the DatabaseID or DatabaseName columns in your query. The following two SELECT statements demonstrate a couple of ways to form your WMI query.

```
SELECT *
FROM DATABASE_MIRRORING_STATE_CHANGE
WHERE State = 8

SELECT *
FROM DATABASE_MIRRORING_STATE_CHANGE
WHERE DatabaseName = 'MirrorTest' AND
      State = 8
```

When an automatic failover occurs, the database mirroring state will transition through a series of state changes. The state will change to Automatic Failover when the failover begins. When the mirror database comes online, the state will change to Synchronizing Mirror. After the databases synchronize, the state will change to Synchronized Mirror with Witness. We have listed the state values in Table 6-1.

*Table 6-1. **Database Mirroring States***

State ID Number	State Name	State Description
0	Null Notification	State unknown
1	Synchronized Principal with Witness	
2	Synchronized Principal without Witness	
3	Synchronized Mirror with Witness	
4	Synchronized Mirror without Witness	
5	Connection with Principal Lost	
6	Connection with Mirror Lost	
7	Manual Failover	Manual failover started
8	Automatic Failover	Automatic failover started
9	Mirroring Suspended	Connection cannot be re-established
10	No Quorum	Disconnected from partner and witness both
11	Synchronizing Mirror	Occurs after a failover or when the mirror is not synchronized
12	Principal Running Exposed	Principal lost connection to witness, no automatic failover
13	Synchronizing Principal	Synchronizing Principal with Mirror

You can create a SQL alert with Object Explorer in SQL Server Management Studio. There are a few simple steps to follow for setting up an alert.

1. Expand the SQL Server Agent node in Object Explorer (see Figure 6-1).
2. Right-click on the Alerts folder.
3. Click on New Alert.

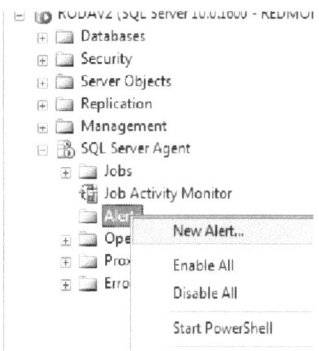

Figure 6-1. *New Alert context menu*

4. Fill in the General page of the pop-up dialog (see Figure 6-2).

- Give the alert a descriptive name.
- Select "WMI event alert" from the drop-down for the Type of alert.
- The Namespace should default to the correct namespace. The namespace is specific to the SQL instance. The last element in the namespace is the instance name.
- Enter the WMI query in the Query field.

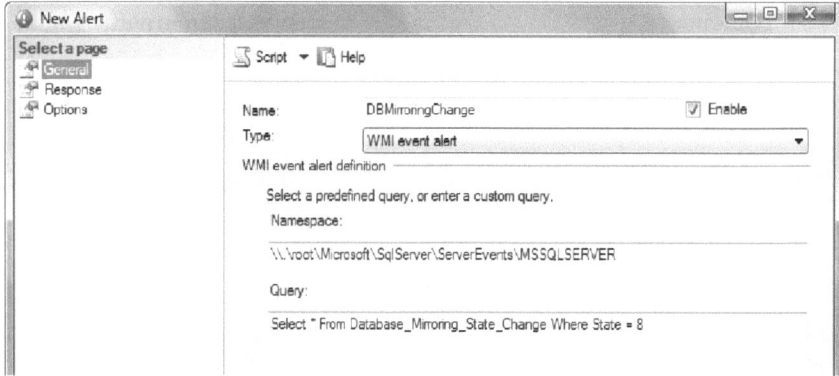

Figure 6-2. *New Alert General page*

5. Fill in the Response page (see Figure 6-3).

- Check "Execute job" if you want a job executed in response to the failover.
- Select the job from the drop-down list or click the New Job button to create a new job.
- Click the View Job button if you want to open the selected job.
- If you want to send an alert, check "Notify operators."
- Check the appropriate notification type for each SQL operator indicating the method to use to send the alert.

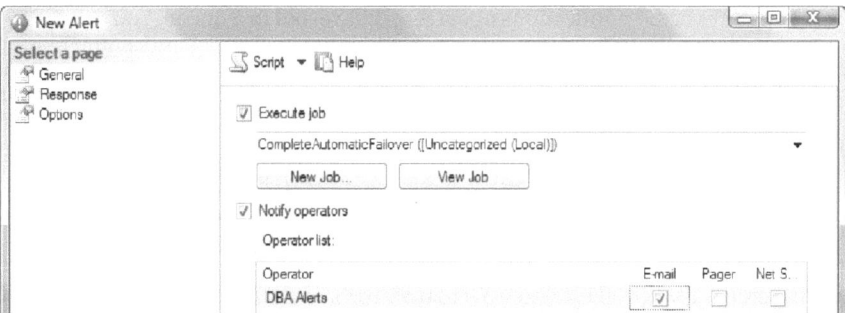

Figure 6-3. *New Alert Response page*

6. Fill in the Options page (see Figure 6-4).

- Check the appropriate notification types for which you want to send the error text, if any.
- Enter any additional information that you want sent with the alert.
- Customize the length of time that the alert system should wait before sending follow-up alerts. This will prevent the server from sending an alert e-mail if multiple automatic failovers occur very closely together.

Figure 6-4. *New Alert Options page*

7. Optionally, use the Script function to script out the alert as configured.
8. Click OK to create the alert.

Using Service Broker to Detect Automatic Failovers

You can use Service Broker to capture server events and respond to them by executing a predefined stored procedure. We commonly refer to this process as automatic activation. This is only one of the activation types that Service Broker uses, and the official name of this activation type is internal activation. The other type, external activation, is when Service Broker activates a queue reader that is external to SQL Server.

Service Broker captures event notifications about a specific event in a queue. You can configure the queue to activate a stored procedure to process the messages in the queue. The procedure reads the messages in the queue and takes action accordingly. You can capture any existing server events or you can create an event notification for any SQL trace events so you can capture the event notification. Trace events do not bubble up to the server level, and Service Broker does not detect trace events. This is where the event notification comes in handy.

The DATABASE_MIRRORING_STATE_CHANGE event is the SQL trace event that you need to capture. The message in the queue will contain an XML formatted message that you can parse out to determine all of the properties of the event. Event notifications use the XML namespace PostEventNotification for the formation of the event notification message, and so we know exactly what the XML will look like ahead of time.

You will need to create several objects external to the mirrored database. You can use the msdb database for this or you can use an operational database as a holder of these objects. Whichever database you use, you will need to enable Service Broker in the database if not already enabled. You can query sys.databases to determine whether you need to enable Service Broker. The is_broker_enabled column is a bit flag that indicates a yes or no value for Service Broker enablement.

The following query shows how you would check to see whether Service Broker is enabled in the msdb database.

```
SELECT CASE is_broker_enabled
            WHEN 1 Then 'Enabled'
            ELSE 'Disabled'
        END
FROM sys.databases
WHERE name = 'msdb'
```

If you need to enable Service Broker, you would use an ALTER DATABASE [DatabaseName] SET ENABLE_BROKER command. Enabling Service Broker requires an exclusive lock on the database. You must perform this change at a time when there is no activity in the database. If you have replication running on the database or any jobs that hit the database, you should stop and disable them before you try to enable Service Broker. If you are enabling Service Broker in the msdb database, you must stop the SQL Server Agent to gain a lock on the database.

Now that you have Service Broker enabled, you need to create the stored procedure for processing messages and the Service Broker objects. You will need to create all of the following objects in the specified order:

1. Stored procedure for processing the messages in the queue
2. Service Broker queue
3. Service Broker service
4. A route for the Service Broker service
5. An event notification for the DATABASE_MIRRORING_STATE_CHANGE event

These objects work together to raise a notification and process it. When database mirroring transitions into a different state, SQL Server raises an event notification. The Service Broker service detects the event notification and routes it to the defined Service Broker queue. The queue activates the stored procedure that receives and parses the event notification messages and takes the prescribed action.

Stored Procedure to Respond to a Failover

You will need to reference the Service Broker queue in the procedure, so you might be surprised that we suggest creating the procedure first. When you create the Service Broker queue, you define the activation procedure in the CREATE QUEUE statement. Both objects reference the other, but stored procedures utilize deferred name resolution. You can create a stored procedure that references a queue that does not exist; however, you cannot create a queue that references a procedure that does not exist.

Your procedure needs to receive messages from the Service Broker queue and parse the body of the messages. The RECEIVE statement is similar to the SELECT statement. You use it to select statements from a Service Broker queue. Select the top unread message and assign it to a variable for parsing. The example code that follows uses a queue name of DBMirrorQueue. If you use a different name, be sure to use the correct name in the procedure.

```
DECLARE @Message XML

RECEIVE TOP (1)
        @Message = Cast(message_body as XML)
FROM DBMirrorQueue;
```

The messages are in a very simple XML format. Event notifications use the XML schema definition http://schemas.microsoft.com/SQL/Notifications/PostEventNotification. The XML root node EVENT_INSTANCE has a single level of nodes with a single property per node. The message will be in the following format.

```
<EVENT_INSTANCE>
        <EventType>DATABASE_MIRRORING_STATE_CHANGE</EventType>
        <PostTime>2009-03-07T17:57:55.070</PostTime>
        <SPID>22</SPID>
        <TextData>DBM: Synchronized Principal without Witness -&gt;
                        DBM: Manual Failover</TextData>
        <DatabaseID>5</DatabaseID>
        <TransactionID />
        <StartTime>2009-06-07T17:57:55.070</StartTime>
        <IntegerData>2</IntegerData>
        <ServerName>MirrorServer</ServerName>
        <State>7</State>
        <DatabaseName>MirrorTest</DatabaseName>
        <LoginSid>ax01</LoginSid>
        <RequestID>0</RequestID>
        <EventSequence>14532</EventSequence>
        <IsSystem>1</IsSystem>
        <SessionLoginName />
</EVENT_INSTANCE>
```

Assign the message to a variable in the RECEIVE statement, and use the value() method to parse the XML message into individual variables. Once you have assigned the individual properties, you can make logical decisions as to what steps to take, if any. We like to parse all properties and then decide which ones to use, but you can parse only the properties that you care about if you prefer. The key properties that you will consider are state and database name.

The value() method accepts two arguments. The first argument is an XQuery expression that defines the element. The expression must point to a singleton element. The second argument defines the data type of the contained value. If the XQuery engine cannot convert the value contained in the element to the specified data type, it will return a conversion error. The syntax of the value() method call that you will make is .value('(/XML root node/Property node)[1]', 'data type').

For the two properties that we mentioned previously, you could parse the values using the following commands.

```
DECLARE @DBName sysname,
        @MirrorStateChange int

SET    @MirrorStateChange =
        @Message.value('(/EVENT_INSTANCE/State)[1]', 'int');

SET    @DBName =
        @Message.value('(/EVENT_INSTANCE/DatabaseName)[1]', 'sysname');
```

One example usage of this procedure would be handling the single database failover scenario. If you have multiple mirrored databases, and your applications require that all databases are live on the same server to support cross-database queries, your applications will fail if only one database fails over. The following sample procedure below will fail over all databases still in the principal role and not in the process of failing over when it detects a database failover. The procedure performs a controlled failover of the remaining databases by calling the controlled failover procedure we created earlier.

```
CREATE PROCEDURE dbo.dba_MirroringStateChanged
AS

DECLARE @Message XML,
        @DBName sysname,
        @MirrorStateChange INT,
        @ServerName sysname,
        @PostTime datetime,
        @SPID INT,
        @TextData NVARCHAR(500),
        @DatabaseID INT,
        @TransactionsID INT,
        @StartTime datetime;

SET NOCOUNT ON;

-- Receive first unread message in service broker queue
RECEIVE TOP (1)
    @Message = CAST(message_body AS XML)
FROM DBMirrorQueue;
```

```
BEGIN TRY
  -- Parse state change and database affected
  -- 7 or 8 = database failing over,
  --11 = synchronizing,
  --1 or 2 = synchronized
  SET @MirrorStateChange =
        @Message.value('(/EVENT_INSTANCE/State)[1]', 'int');

  SET @DBName =
        @Message.value('(/EVENT_INSTANCE/DatabaseName)[1]', 'sysname');

  SET @ServerName =
        @Message.value('(/EVENT_INSTANCE/ServerName)[1]', 'sysname');

  SET @PostTime =
        @Message.value('(/EVENT_INSTANCE/PostTime)[1]', 'datetime');

  SET @SPID = @Message.value('(/EVENT_INSTANCE/SPID)[1]', 'int');

  SET @TextData =
        @Message.value('(/EVENT_INSTANCE/TextData)[1]', 'nvarchar(500)');

  SET @DatabaseID =
        @Message.value('(/EVENT_INSTANCE/DatabaseID)[1]', 'int');

  SET @TransactionsID =
        @Message.value('(/EVENT_INSTANCE/TransactionsID)[1]', 'int');

  SET @StartTime =
        @Message.value('(/EVENT_INSTANCE/StartTime)[1]', 'datetime');
END TRY
BEGIN CATCH
  PRINT 'Parse of mirroring state change message failed.';
END CATCH

IF (@MirrorStateChange IN (7, 8)) -- database failing over
  BEGIN
    -- Fail over all databases still in the principal role
    IF EXISTS (SELECT 1
                FROM sys.database_mirroring
                WHERE mirroring_role = 1 AND -- Principal
                      mirroring_state <> 3)  -- Pending Failover
      BEGIN
        EXEC master.dbo.dba_ControlledFailover
      END
  END
```

Now that you have the procedure for processing the messages and taking any required action in place, you will need to create a Service Broker queue. The queue will store the messages and activate the procedure when new messages are added to the queue.

Service Broker Queue

When SQL Server fires an event notification in response to the prescribed event, it routes the notification to a Service Broker queue. A queue is similar to a table and holds the notification in the form of an XML message. You can configure the queue to activate the stored procedure you just created in the previous section. You can find metadata information for existing queues in the sys.service_queues system catalog view.

You use the CREATE QUEUE statement to create a Service Broker queue. There are a few arguments that you have to specify when you create the queue. You have to provide the activation procedure name, the maximum number of queue readers, and as whom the procedure should execute.

Use the PROCEDURE_NAME argument to define the stored procedure that the Service Broker should activate when a message arrives. If you store the procedure in the same database as the queue, you can refer to the procedure by name only. If the procedure name is unique, you do not have to specify the schema name as part of the procedure name, but we highly recommend that you do so. This will avoid invoking the wrong procedure if someone creates a procedure later with the same name and a different schema name. If the procedure is stored in a different database, you must specify the database name as part of the procedure.

You can have as many as 32,767 queue readers active at any given time. The MAZ_QUEUE_READERS argument allows you to adjust the how aggressively your procedure processes the messages in the queue. For this event, you do not want several instances of the procedure to try to manage the failover process simultaneously. You should set this the maximum number of queue readers to one.

When the stored procedure executes, you want it to have sufficient privileges to perform the failover and related processes. If you set the EXECUTE AS argument to EXECUTE AS SELF, it will execute under the context of the account creating the queue. If you set the argument to EXECUTE AS OWNER, it will execute under the context of the account that owns the queue. You also have the option to execute as a specific account. If you use this option, you must ensure that the account has the permissions required to perform all of the functions defined in the procedure. The safest choice is to execute as the queue owner.

The following command will create a queue named DBMirrorQueue that activates the procedure dbo.dba_MirroringStateChanged as a single queue reader executed under the context of the queue owner.

```
-- Create Queue if not exists

IF NOT EXISTS (SELECT 1
               FROM sys.service_queues
               WHERE name = 'DBMirrorQueue')
  BEGIN
    CREATE QUEUE DBMirrorQueue
    WITH ACTIVATION (
    PROCEDURE_NAME = dbo.dba_MirroringStateChanged,
    MAX_QUEUE_READERS = 1,
    EXECUTE AS OWNER);
  END
```

You will notice that the queue definition does not state what messages it will contain. The queue is just a container. The queue requires a Service Broker service and a Service Broker route in order to receive event notification messages. The service defines what type of service will be running for the queue, and the route determines the appropriate service to use for routing the messages.

Service Broker Service and Route

The two components that define how a Service Broker queue is used and routes the messages to the queue are the Service Broker service and the Service Broker route. These two objects work together to capture the event notification and send it to the queue. The service is bound to the queue for a specific contract. The route is in turn bound to the service.

A Service Broker service binds a contract to a Service Broker queue. You will not need to create a contract for managing event notifications, as SQL Server provides a built-in contract for that. You will need to provide the URL of the schema definition of the contract PostEventNotification. You use the CREATE SERVICE statement to create a Service Broker service. You can query for existing services in the sys.services system catalog view.

There are two arguments that you have to define for the service, the queue to which it will be bound and the contract name. The following query creates a service named DBMirrorService bound to the queue you created in the previous step for the PostEventNotification contract.

```
-- Create Service if not exists
IF NOT EXISTS (SELECT 1
               FROM sys.services
                WHERE name = 'DBMirrorService')
  BEGIN
    CREATE SERVICE DBMirrorService
         ON QUEUE DBMirrorQueue (
                [http://schemas.microsoft.com/SQL/Notifications/
PostEventNotification]
                );
  END
```

After you create the service, you need to create a route for the service. The route defines how to route messages to the prescribed service. You can create a route to a remote instance of SQL Server or to the local database. You will create a local route for the service that you created. You will find the metadata for Service Broker routes in the sys.routes system catalog view.

You will need to provide the name of the service that you just created for the SERVICE_NAME argument and Local to indicate the local database for the ADDRESS argument. The following query uses the CREATE ROUTE statement to create a Service Broker route named DBMirrorRoute.

```
-- Create Route if not exists
IF NOT EXISTS (SELECT 1
               FROM sys.routes
                WHERE name = 'DBMirrorRoute')
  BEGIN
    CREATE ROUTE DBMirrorRoute
    WITH SERVICE_NAME = 'DBMirrorService',
    ADDRESS = 'Local';
  END
```

You have a procedure, a queue, a service, and a route. All that you need to do now is to create the event notification. An event notification sends information about an event to a Service Broker service. The event can be a server-level or database-level event. Event notifications even allow you to trap SQL trace events that would otherwise only be detectable via a SQL trace. Database mirroring state change is the SQL trace event for which you want SQL Server to raise an event notification.

You create an event notification using the CREATE EVENT NOTIFICATION statement. You can query for existing event notifications in the sys.event_notifications system catalog view or for server-level event notifications in the sys.server_event_notifications system catalog view. You will need to provide several arguments for the event notification. You must define the event level, server or database as the location of the event; the name of the event; the name of the service that will handle the notification; and the location of the Service Broker instance.

For the event notification that you are creating here, the event is a server-level event. The SQL trace event for which we want a notification raised is DATABASE_MIRRORING_STATE_CHANGE. The notification will be bound to the service we created previously. You are creating the event notification in the same database as the other objects and can specify the Service Broker instance as the instance in the local database. If you were using a Service Broker instance in a different database, you would need to identify it by its GUID, which can be found in the service_broker_guid column in the sys.databases system catalog view.

The following query creates an event notification named DBMirrorStateChange on the server for the DATABASE_MIRRORING_STATE_CHANGE event for the DBMirrorService service in the current database. Since this is a server-level event notification, the query checks the sys.server_event_notifications system view to ensure that the event notification does not already exist.

```
-- Create Event Notification if not exists
IF NOT EXISTS (SELECT 1
             FROM sys.server_event_notifications
             WHERE name = 'DBMirrorStateChange')
  BEGIN
    CREATE EVENT NOTIFICATION DBMirrorStateChange
    ON SERVER
    FOR DATABASE_MIRRORING_STATE_CHANGE
    TO SERVICE 'DBMirrorService', 'current database';
  END
```

Now that you have all of the objects in place, event notifications will send messages to the queue, and the procedure you wrote will process the messages automatically and perform the prescribed actions. If you are using the procedure as written above to fail over all mirrored databases in the event of a single database failover, you can test the process by issuing the failover command for a single database. If everything works as expected, the procedure will activate and fail over all of the remaining mirrored databases to the mirror server.

Another method you can use to test the Service Broker processes is to disable the activation procedure by issuing an ALTER QUEUE statement. When a failover occurs, the event notification will send messages to the queue, but the procedure will not process the messages. You can then select directly from the queue to validate that the event notification messages are being queued. Just do not forget to enable the activation procedure when you are finished.

Summary

In this chapter, we covered many of the maintenance considerations you should be aware of when managing mirrored databases. We covered the techniques you should know to maintain a healthy transaction log, including backups, retention, and size. We also briefly touched on patching and upgrading your servers from an OS and SQL perspective. We will discuss upgrading in much greater detail in Chapter 8. Finally, we covered several techniques for managing the failover (both automatic and controlled) of mirrored databases.

Proper maintenance is crucial to any system, especially a system that is trying to achieve high availability. We hope you now understand the importance of basic maintenance such as log backups. The techniques for automating routine processes for database and server maintenance will make your task of managing servers that host mirrored databases a much simpler task. The processes defined in this chapter will allow you to simplify all of your maintenance routines that deal with mirrored databases. Automating maintenance tasks will also allow operators who are not highly knowledgeable of database mirroring to manage mirrored databases.

## CHAPTER 7

Monitoring and Alerting

Having the proper monitoring and alerting is the key to maintaining a highly available environment. The simple fact is that things go wrong; that's probably why you set up database mirroring in the first place. It's your job to make sure you know as soon as possible when something does go wrong or when undesirable events occur within database mirroring. When monitoring and alerting your database mirroring configuration, you are mainly concerned with two events. One is when the state of database mirroring changes, and the other is when database mirroring exceeds a specific warning threshold. We will cover the components that work in the background that will allow you to capture these events. We will also show you the tools you can use to monitor database mirroring, manage warning thresholds, and configure alerts based on these thresholds.

Monitoring Components

Two components work together behind the scenes to provide insight into the status of database mirroring. These components are the *database mirroring status table* and the *Database Mirroring Monitor Job*. Many of the statistics you receive about database mirroring come from the database mirroring status table, and without the Database Mirroring Monitor Job, this data could become stale, providing an inaccurate representation of the state of database mirroring.

Database Mirroring Status Table

The database mirroring status is stored in the `dbm_monitor_data` table in the `msdb` database. This is an undocumented table only referred to in SQL Server Books Online as the database mirroring status table. Either the Database Mirroring Monitor or the Database Mirroring Monitor Job creates this table automatically the first time a database mirroring status update occurs. Both the Database Mirroring Monitor and the Database Mirroring Monitor Job call the `sp_dbmmonitorupdate` system stored procedure that creates and updates the database mirroring status table. The database mirroring status table will generally contain one row for each database that is being mirrored each time it is updated. How frequently the database mirroring status table is updated depends on the method used and the configuration settings. We will discuss how and when the database mirroring status table is updated throughout the chapter. This table is automatically purged by the same system stored procedure that is used to create and update the table. The default retention period is seven days. You can see some sample data from the database mirroring status table in Figure 7-1.

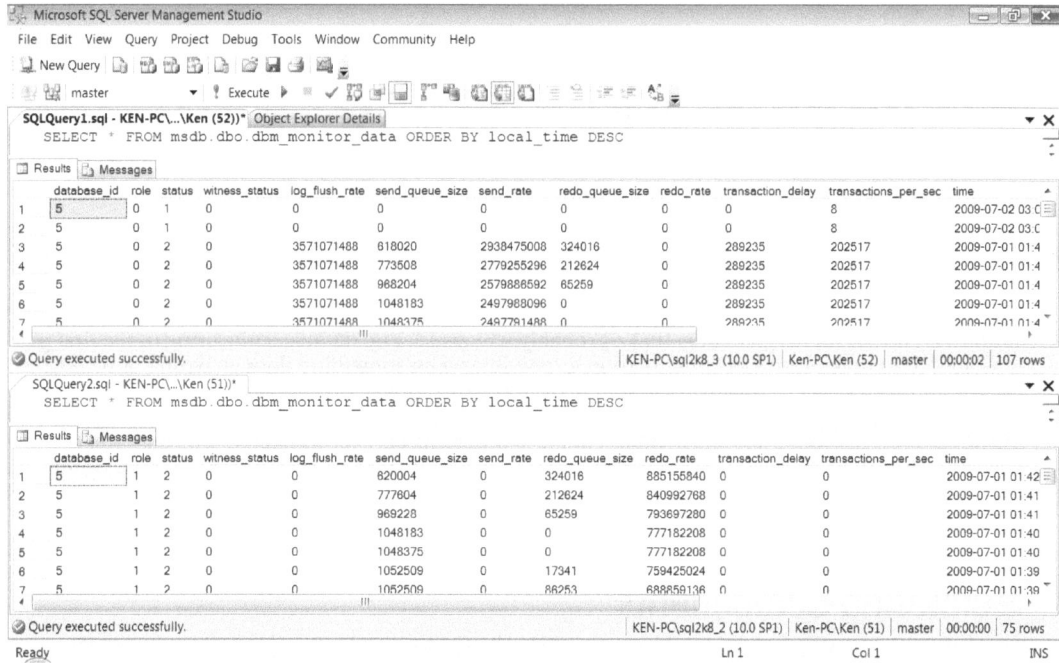

Figure 7-1. Database mirroring status table sample data

We have split the screen so you can see that the database mirroring status table on the principal and the mirror has the same structure; however, they store different values depending on the role of the database. For example, you can see that the `redo_rate` is always 0 on the principal server since the principal server does not redo transactions. Therefore, in order to get a total view of the database mirroring status, you have to query the database mirroring status table on both the principal server and the mirror server.

Database Mirroring Monitor Job

The Database Mirroring Monitor Job, which by the way is the actual name of the job, runs periodically in SQL Server Agent to update the database mirroring monitor table. The default schedule is to run once a minute, but you can change it to run anywhere from 1 to 120 minutes. The only step in the job is a T-SQL step that calls the `sp_dbmmonitorupdate` system stored procedure. If SQL Server Agent is disabled, the Database Mirroring Monitor Job cannot run, and you could end up with stale data in your database mirroring status table. The Database Mirroring Monitor Job is created automatically when you start a database mirroring session using SQL Server Management Studio; however, you can create and manage the job using the following system stored procedures if you set up database mirroring using T-SQL commands.

- `sp_dbmmonitoraddmonitoring`: Creates the Database Mirroring Monitor Job with a default schedule to run every minute. You can pass an optional parameter, `update_period`, to this stored procedure to override the default schedule of every minute. For example, the following code will create a new Database Mirroring Monitor Job that runs every 10 minutes.

```
EXEC sp_dbmmonitoraddmonitoring 10
```

- `sp_dbmmonitorchangemonitoring`: You can use this stored procedure to update the interval in which an existing Database Mirroring Monitor Job will run. There are actually two parameters you will need to pass to this stored procedure. The first is called `parameter`, and the second is called `value`. The only value you can use for the `parameter` argument is 1, which means update period, followed by the new update interval for the `value` argument. The way Microsoft configured this stored procedure tells us that they plan to implement additional functionality in a future release. Valid values for the update interval are between 1 and 120. You can run the following code to change the Database Mirroring Monitor Job to run every 15 minutes.

```
EXEC sp_dbmmonitorchangemonitoring 1, 15
```

- `sp_dbmmonitordropmonitoring`: You can use this stored procedure to drop the Database Mirroring Monitor Job. This stored procedure does not accept any parameters. To drop the Database Mirroring Monitor Job, you execute the stored procedure as follows.

```
EXEC sp_dbmmonitordropmonitoring
```

Understanding Warning Thresholds

Once you have configured database mirroring, you can set up warning thresholds that will trigger *performance threshold events* that are written to the Windows Event Log whenever the threshold you have defined has been exceeded. You can then configure alerts to fire based on the error numbers for these events, so SQL Server can notify you if a certain threshold is exceeded. SQL Server only evaluates these thresholds whenever a new value is written to the database mirroring status table. Since the Database Mirroring Monitor Job automatically updates the database mirroring status table, you want to make sure SQL Server Agent is running and the Database Mirroring Monitor Job is running frequently enough to meet your monitoring and alerting needs. The following is a list of warning thresholds you can configure along with their respective error numbers.

- *Unsent log (error number 32042)*: You can configure the number of kilobytes in unsent logs that can accumulate on the principal server before this event is raised. This is especially important in the high-performance mode but can also be useful in high-safety mode if database mirroring has been paused. You may accumulate excess unsent logs if you have a communication issue between partners preventing the principal server from sending logs to the mirror server.
- *Unrestored log (error number 32043)*: You can configure the number of kilobytes in unrestored logs that can accumulate on the mirror server before this event is raised. This is useful in determining the amount of time it will take to roll forward the log on the mirror server in the event of a failover. Excess unrestored log is generally because the I/O subsystem on the mirror server cannot keep up with the logs coming from the principal server.
- *Oldest Unsent transaction (error number 32040)*: You can configure the number of minutes worth of transactions that can accumulate in the send queue on the principal server before this event is raised. This is especially important in the high-performance mode but can also be useful in high-safety mode if database mirroring has been paused.
- *Mirror commit overhead (error number 32044)*: You can configure the number of milliseconds in the average transaction delay that can be tolerated on the principal server before this event is raised. This delay is the time the principal server waits for the mirror server to write a transaction to the redo queue. Therefore, this is only relevant in high-safety mode since the principal server does not wait for the mirror server in high-performance mode.

You will see how to manage these thresholds using both the Database Mirroring Monitor and system stored procedures in the sections "Using the Database Mirroring Monitor" and "Using System

Stored Procedures." We will also show you how to create alerts for these events in the "Creating Alerts" section later in this chapter.

Using the Database Mirroring Monitor

The Database Mirroring Monitor was introduced in SQL Server 2005 SP1 and provides a user-friendly interface that allows you to monitor the status of database mirroring and configure warning thresholds. To open the Database Mirroring Monitor, right-click on a database in the SQL Server Management Studio Object Explorer and select Tasks ➤ Launch Database Mirroring Monitor. You will then see the Database Mirroring Monitor home screen shown in Figure 7-2.

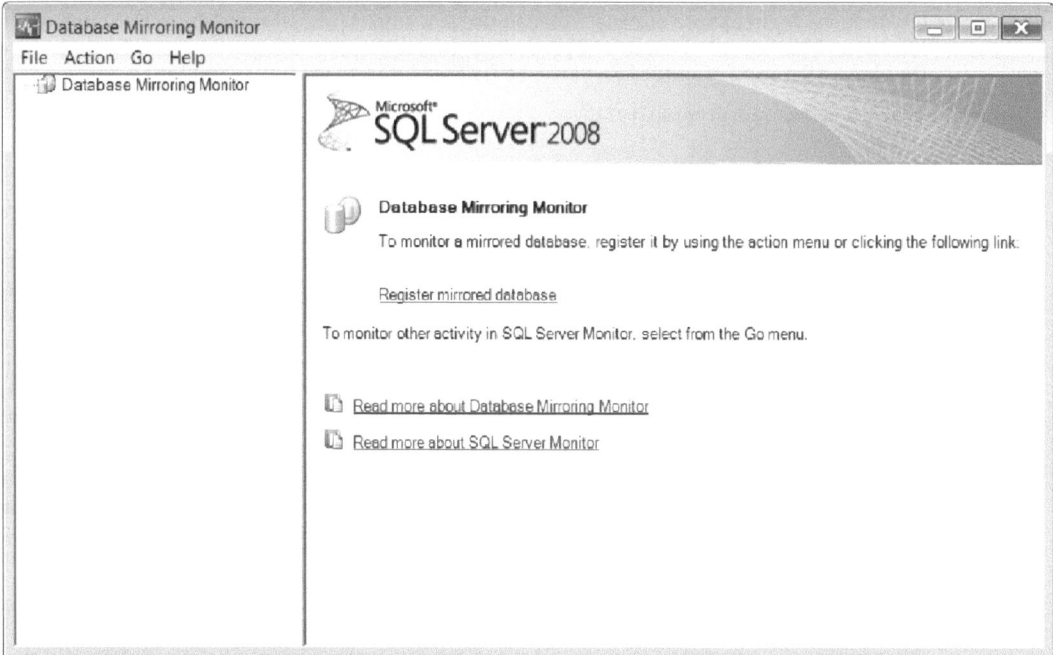

Figure 7-2. Database Mirroring Monitor home screen

Registering Mirrored Databases

From the screen in Figure 7-2 you can register a mirrored database by clicking the "Register mirrored database" hyperlink or by right-clicking the Database Mirroring Monitor in the left pane and selecting "Register mirrored database" from the context menu. You can see the Register Mirrored Database dialog box in Figure 7-3.

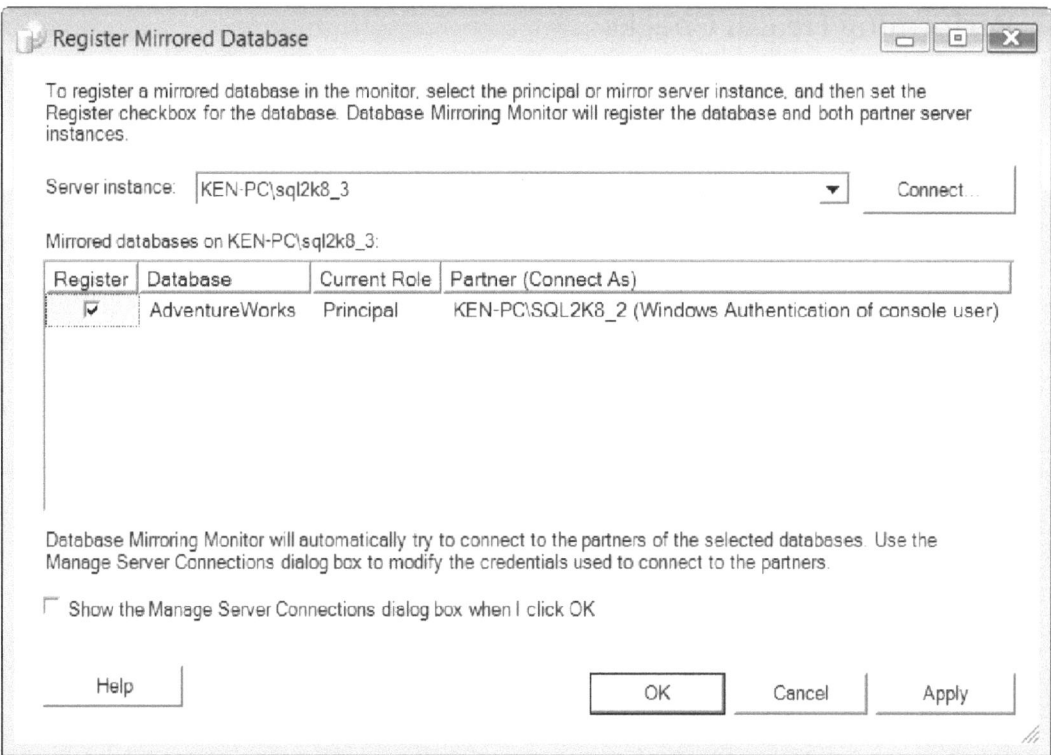

Figure 7-3. Register Mirrored Database dialog box

Click the Connect button to connect to a mirrored SQL Server instance. Once you have established a connection, you can select the mirrored databases you would like to register. By default, SQL Server will try to connect to the partner servers using Windows Authentication. You can select the "Show the manage Server Connections dialog box when I click OK" check box to open the Manage Server Connections dialog box where you can change the credentials used to connect to each mirroring partner. Select the appropriate options and click OK to return to the Database Mirroring Monitor home screen. You can now see the registered databases in the tree menu in the left pane under the Database Mirroring Monitor node.

Note The `dbm_monitor` role is automatically created in the `msdb` database as soon as you have registered the first database. You can now add users to the `dbm_monitor` role that will allow them limited rights to use the Database Mirroring Monitor. For example, a user in the `dbm_monitor` role will not be able to refresh the mirroring status; they will only have access to the most recent rows inserted into the database mirroring monitor table.

Performing Health Checks

Once you have registered one or more databases, you can get a general idea on the health of database mirroring based on the icon and text next to the name of each database. If your database is SYNCHRONIZED, you will see a standard database icon. If the status of your database is UNKNOWN, SYNCHRONIZING, or SUSPENDED, you will see a warning icon. Lastly, if your database is DISCONNECTED, you will see an error icon. Select a database to display the Database Mirroring Monitor status page shown in Figure 7-4.

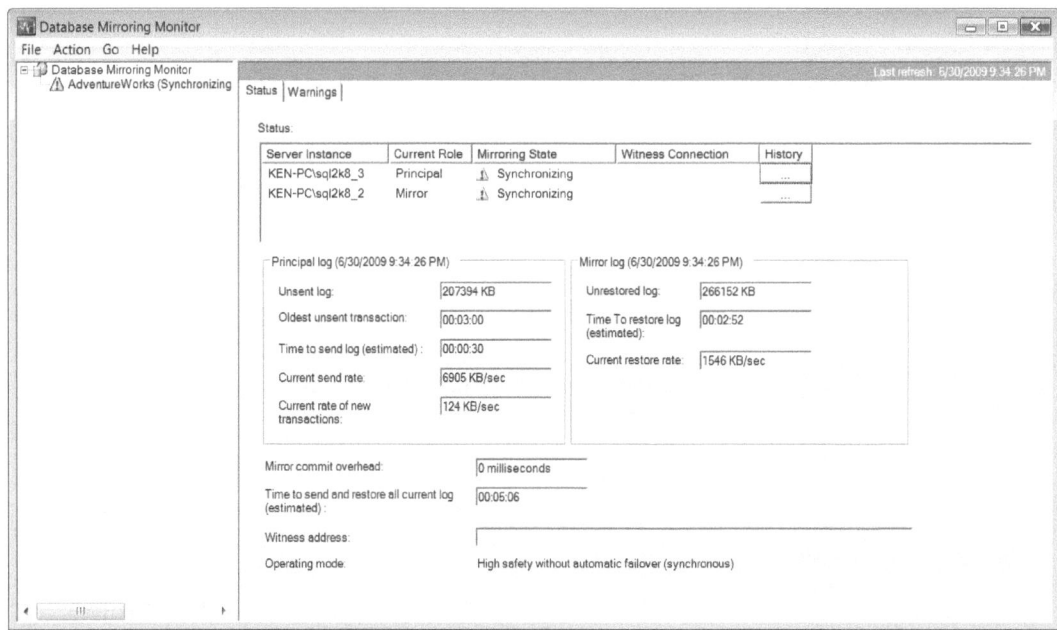

Figure 7-4. *Database Mirroring Monitor status page*

The Database Mirroring Monitor status page displays a read-only view of most of the monitoring information you need to be concerned with on the principal and the mirror servers. You will need to be able to connect to both the principal and the mirror servers in order to receive the information pertaining to each server. The Database Mirroring Monitor refreshes the status information every 30 seconds through asynchronous connections to the principal and mirror servers. However, if you are a member of the `dbm_monitor` database role instead of the `sysadmin` server role, you will have to wait for the data to be updated by the Database Mirroring Monitor Job.

The Database Mirroring Monitor status page is broken into four sections: one that provides a quick status of database mirroring, one that is relevant only to the principal server, one that is only relevant to the mirror server, and finally a general section towards the bottom that is relevant to the overall mirroring configuration. The following list provides a brief explanation of the information you see on the Database Mirroring Monitor status page.

Status: The status section contains a grid view that provides the latest state for the principal and the mirror servers, including the state of each server as it relates to the witness.

Principal log: This section contains the log status on the principal server as of the time displayed in parentheses following the label. This section contains the following information.

- *Unsent log*: This is the number of kilobytes waiting in the send queue.
- *Oldest unsent transaction*: This is the age of the oldest transaction in the send queue waiting to be sent to the mirror server. This will help you determine the amount of potential data loss (in time) in the event of a failure.
- *Time to send log (estimated)*: This is a rough estimate for the amount of time it will take for the principal server to transmit the transactions in the send queue to the mirror server.
- *Current send rate*: This is the rate in kilobytes that transactions are being sent to the mirror server.
- *Current rate of new transactions*: This is the rate in kilobytes that new transactions are being written to the log on the principal server.

Mirror log: This section contains the log status on the mirror server as of the time displayed in parentheses following the label. This section contains the following information.

- *Unrestored log*: This is the number of kilobytes waiting in the redo queue.
- *Time to restore log (estimated)*: This is a rough estimate for the amount of time it will take for the mirror server to apply the transactions waiting in the redo queue to the mirror database.
- *Current restore rate*: This is the rate in kilobytes that transactions are being restored to the mirror database.

Mirror commit overhead: This only applies when you are using high-safety mode. This is the number of milliseconds of average delay per transaction that you can accept while the principal server waits for a transaction to write to the redo queue on the mirror server before a warning is generated on the principal server.

Time to send and restore all current log (estimated): This is the estimated time it should take to send and restore all of the transactions that have currently been committed on the principal server to the mirror server. This can be less than the combined values of the "Time to send log (estimated)" and the "Time to restore log (estimated)" text boxes, because these are parallel operations.

Witness address: This is the network address of the witness server in the form of `TCP://<Address>:<Port>`.

Operating mode: This displays one of three possible operating modes you have configured for the database mirroring session.

You can click the ellipsis button in the History column of the status grid to display the Database Mirroring History dialog box shown in Figure 7-5.

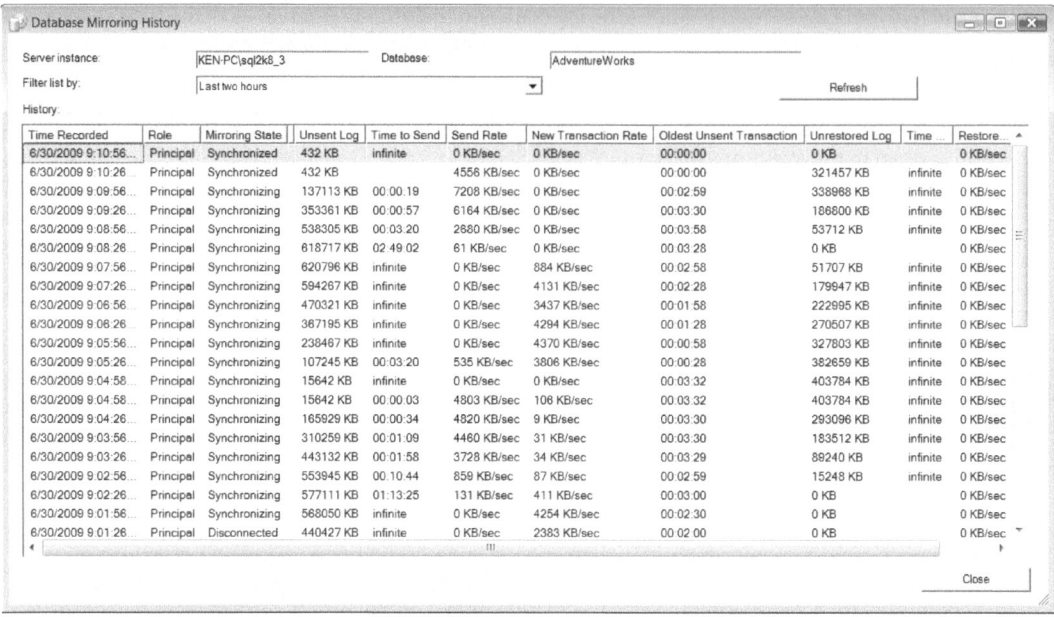

Figure 7-5. *Database Mirroring History dialog box*

The history is essentially a view of the database mirroring status table that resides in the `msdb` database on each partner. In order to refresh the data you can either select a new filter by list option or click the Refresh button.

Managing Warning Thresholds

You can select the Warnings tab to display the Database Mirroring Monitor warnings page shown in Figure 7-6 in order to manage the warning thresholds discussed in the section "Understanding Warning Thresholds" earlier in the chapter.

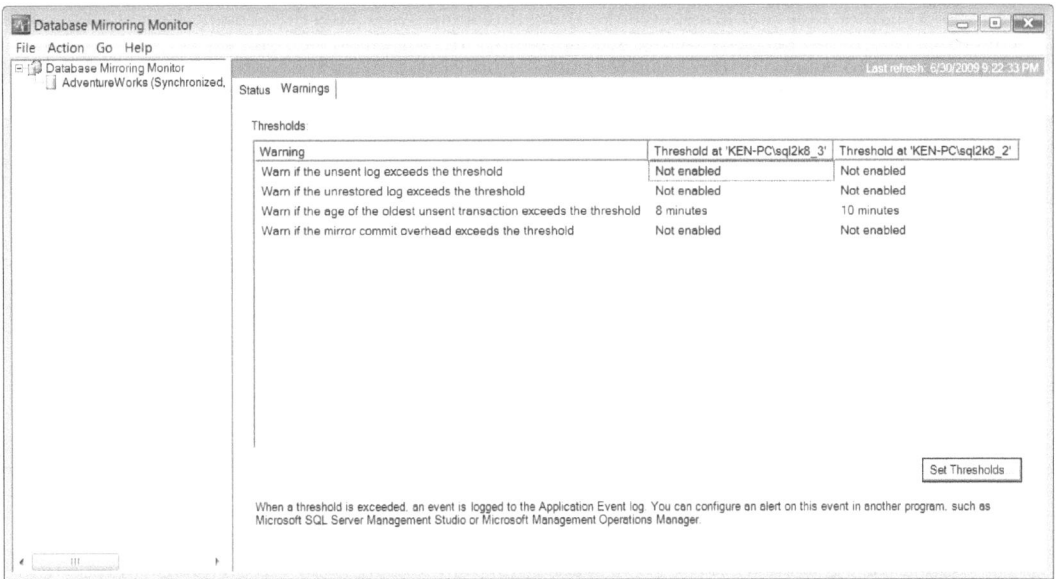

Figure 7-6. Database Mirroring Monitor Warnings page

The Warnings tab only displays a list of available thresholds and their current values. In order to manage the thresholds, you need to click the Set Thresholds button to display the Set Warning Thresholds dialog box shown in Figure 7-7.

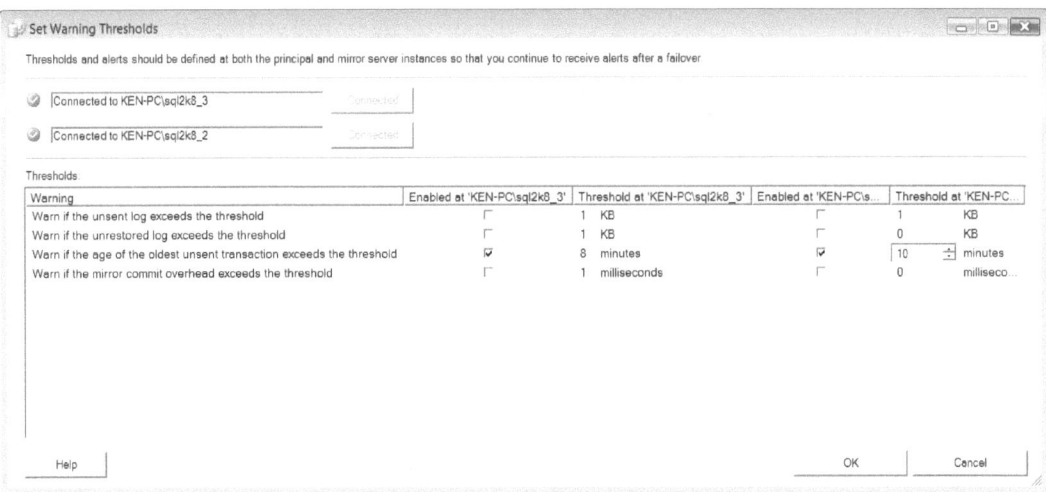

Figure 7-7. Set Warning Thresholds dialog box

You must first enable a specific warning threshold by clicking the "Enabled at <ServerName>" check box column for each row before you can change the threshold value for the server. You should also make sure to enable the threshold for both the principal and the mirror servers so your thresholds will still be effective in the event of a failover. You can configure separate thresholds for each server based on the capacity each server can handle. However, if you cannot connect to a server, you will not be able to configure the warning thresholds for that particular server. Select the appropriate thresholds and click OK.

Using System Stored Procedures

Just as with most things in SQL Server, there are multiple ways you can manage monitoring and alerting depending on your preferred method of choice. Instead of using the GUI provided by the Database Mirroring Monitor, you may want to use system stored procedures. One advantage when using system stored procedures over the GUI is that you can use the system stored procedures in T-SQL scripts. For example, you may want to generate a warning threshold script you can apply to all of your mirrored databases to ensure consistency within your environment. However, you must be a member of the sysadmin server role in order to use the system stored procedures for database mirroring.

Monitoring

You can use the sp_dbmmonitorresults system stored procedure to monitor database mirroring by directly returning rows from the database mirroring status table. You are required to supply the database name as a parameter, but there are also two optional parameters you can use change the behavior of the stored procedure. The following list describes each of the parameters you can specify when executing the sp_dbmmonitorresults system stored procedure.

@database_name: This is a required parameter that limits the result set to a single database. There is no way to return the data for all databases.

@mode: This is an optional parameter that specifies the number of rows returned by the result set. If this parameter is omitted, the default behavior is to only return the last row entered into the database mirroring status table. The required input is an integer value between 0 and 9. The following list describes each value.

- 0: Last row
- 1: Last 2 hours
- 2: Last 4 hours
- 3: Last 8 hours
- 4: Last 24 hours
- 5: Last 48 hours
- 6: Last 100 rows
- 7: Last 500 rows
- 8: Last 1,000 rows
- 9: Last 1,000,000 rows or essentially all rows

@update_table: This is an optional parameter of 1 or 0 that determines whether the database mirroring status table is updated before returning the result set. If this parameter is omitted, the default is 0 which, means the database mirroring status table is not updated prior to returning the result set.

The following code in Listing 7-1 will return the last 100 in the database mirroring status table for the AdventureWorks database and insert one row containing the most recent data before returning the result set.

Listing 7-1. *Sample Code Used to Execute the sp_dbmmonitorresults System Stored Procedure*

```
USE msdb
GO

EXEC sp_dbmmonitorresults
     @database_name = N'AdventureWorks',
     @mode = 6,
     @update_table = 1
```

You can view in Figure 7-8 the result set returned from Listing 7-1.

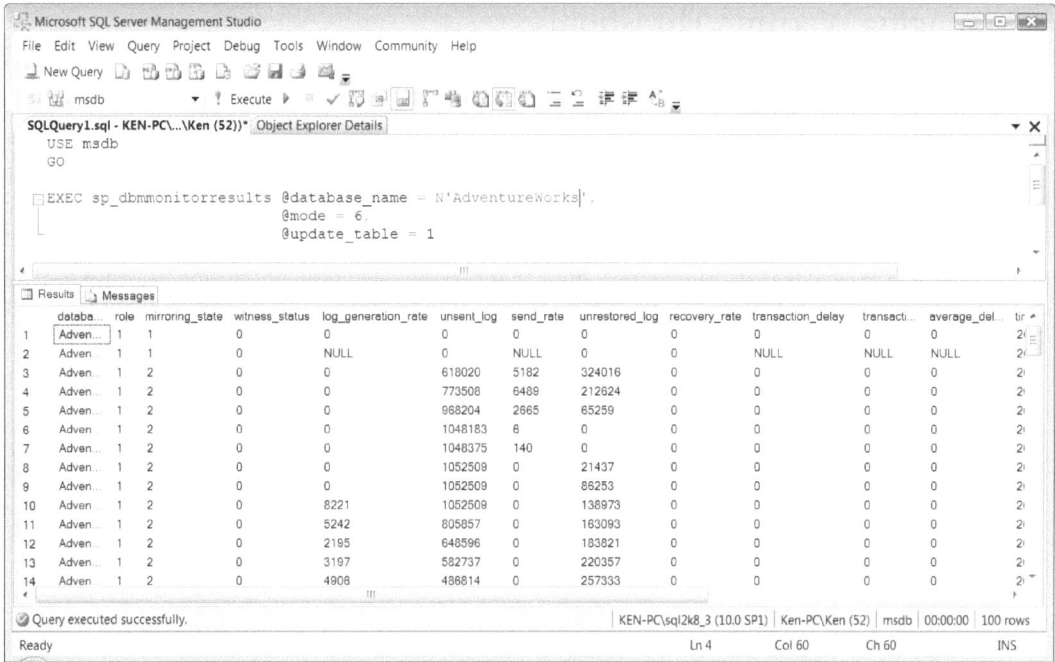

Figure 7-8. *Sample result set returned from the sp_dbmmonitorresults system stored procedure*

As you can see from the result set in Figure 7-8, the stored procedure returns a few columns with a meaningless integer value. You will need to know what each of these values represent before you can make any sense of the data. You can use the following list to see a description for each column that contains such a value. All of the remaining values returned by the `sp_dbmmonitorresults` system stored procedure correlate to the same values we discussed in the "Using the Database Mirroring Monitor" section earlier in this chapter.

role

- 1: Principal
- 2: Mirror

mirroring_state

- 0: Suspended
- 1: Disconnected
- 2: Synchronizing
- 3: Pending Failover
- 4: Synchronized

witness_state

- 0: Unknown
- 1: Connected
- 2: Disconnected

Managing Warning Thresholds

You can also manage warning thresholds using system stored procedures instead of the Database Mirroring Monitor. There are three system stored procedures you can use to configure, view, and remove warning thresholds: `sp_dbmmonitorchangealert`, `sp_dbmmonitorhelpalert`, and `sp_dbmmonitordropalert`.

You can use the `sp_dbmmonitorchangealert` system stored procedure to add or change values for a specific warning threshold. You need to supply the name of the database for the warning, an integer value that correlates to a specific warning, the threshold value for the warning, and a value indicating whether the warning is enabled or disabled. You must supply all of the parameters when using the `sp_dbmmonitorchangealert` stored procedure; there are no default values. The following list describes each of the parameters you can specify when executing the `sp_dbmmonitorchangealert` stored procedure.

`@database_name`: This is the name of the database for which you wish to configure the warning threshold.

`@alert_id`: This is an integer value between 1 and 5 representing the warning you wish to configure. You can use the following list to correlate warning descriptions with their respective values.

- 1: Oldest unsent transaction
- 2: Unsent log
- 3: Unrestored log
- 4: Mirror commit overhead
- 5: Retention period

`@threshold`: This is the value that represents the new warning threshold. This value is measured in kilobytes, minutes, or milliseconds, depending on the particular warning. To determine what metric a specific warning threshold uses, see the "Understanding Warning Thresholds" section earlier in this chapter.

`@enabled`: This is a bit value (1 meaning enabled, 0 meaning disabled) indicating whether the warning threshold is enabled. The Retention period warning threshold ignores this value.

The following code in Listing 7-2 will set the warning threshold in the AdventureWorks database to 20 minutes for the oldest unsent transaction.

Listing 7-2. Sample Code Used to Execute the sp_dbmmonitorchangealert System Stored Procedure

```
USE msdb
GO

EXEC sp_dbmmonitorchangealert
     @database_name = N'AdventureWorks',
     @alert_id = 1,
     @threshold = 20,
     @enabled = 1
```

You can use the `sp_dbmmonitorhelpalert` system stored procedure to return information about one or all of the warning thresholds for a specific database. You need to supply the name of the database, and an optional integer value that correlates to a specific warning. The following list describes each of the parameters you can specify when executing the `sp_dbmmonitorhelpalert` system stored procedure.

- `@database_name`: This is the name of the database for which you wish to view the warning threshold.
- `@alert_id`: This is an optional integer value between 1 and 5 representing the warning you wish to view. If you do not supply this parameter, all warning thresholds will be returned for the specific database supplied in the `@database_name` parameter. The values for this parameter are the same values we described for the `@alert_id` parameter for the `sp_dbmmonitorchangealert` system stored procedure earlier in this section.

The code in Listing 7-3 will show the warning threshold we configured in the `AdventureWorks` database for the oldest unsent transaction in Listing 7-2.

Listing 7-3. Sample Code Used to Execute the sp_dbmmonitorhelpalert System Stored Procedure

```
USE msdb
GO

EXEC sp_dbmmonitorhelpalert
     @database_name = N'AdventureWorks',
     @alert_id = 1
```

You can see in Figure 7-9 the result set returned by running the code in Listing 7-3.

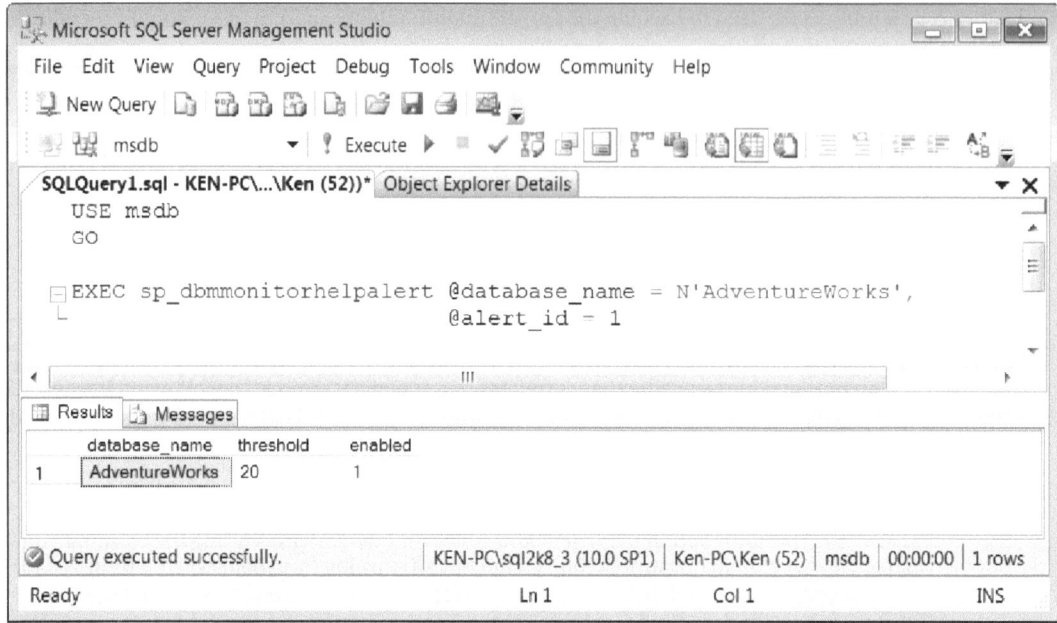

Figure 7-9. *Sample result set returned from the sp_dbmmonitorhelpalert system stored procedure*

Finally, you can use the `sp_dbmmonitordropalert` stored procedure to remove a warning threshold by setting the threshold value to NULL. You need to supply the name of the database and an optional integer value that correlates to a specific warning. The following list describes each of the parameters you can specify when executing the `sp_dbmmonitordropalert` system stored procedure.

- `@database_name`: This is the name of the database for which you wish to remove the warning threshold.
- `@alert_id`: This is an optional integer value between 1 and 5 representing the warning you wish to remove. If you do not supply this parameter, all warning thresholds will be removed for the specific database supplied in the `@database_name` parameter. The values for this parameter are the same values we described for the `@alert_id` parameter for the `sp_dbmmonitorchangealert` system stored procedure earlier in this section.

The code in Listing 7-4 will remove the warning threshold we configured in the AdventureWorks database for the oldest unsent transaction in Listing 7-2.

Listing 7-4. Sample Code Used to Execute the sp_dbmmonitordropalert System Stored Procedure

```
USE msdb
GO

EXEC sp_dbmmonitordropalert
     @database_name = N'AdventureWorks',
     @alert_id = 1
```

Understanding Performance Counters

You can use performance counters to monitor database mirroring by using Performance Monitor (PerfMon), or you can automatically respond to certain events based on the value of these counters using SQL Server Agent alerts. The database mirroring performance counters are located in the `SQLServer:Database Mirroring` performance object for the default instance of SQL Server. If you have a named instance of SQL, the name of the performance object will be `MSSQL$InstanceName:Database Mirroring`. The following list describes each counter in the `SQLServer:Database Mirroring` performance object.

- *Bytes Received/sec*: This is the number of bytes received per second by either partner.
- *Bytes Sent/sec*: This is the number of bytes sent per second by either partner.
- *Log Bytes Received/sec*: This is the number of log bytes received per second by the mirror server.
- *Log Bytes Redone from Cache/sec*: This is the number of log bytes acquired from the mirroring log cache within the last second on the mirror server.
- *Log Bytes Sent from Cache/sec*: This is the number of log bytes acquired from the mirroring log cache within the last second on the principal server.
- *Log Bytes Sent/sec*: This is the number of log bytes sent per second from the principal server to the mirror server.
- *Log Compressed Bytes Rcvd/sec*: This is the number of compressed log bytes received in the last second on the mirror server.
- *Log Compressed Bytes Sent/sec*: This is the number of bytes of compressed logs sent by the principal server in the last second.
- *Log Harden Time (ms)*: This is the number of milliseconds that the log blocks waited to be hardened to disk within the last second.
- *Log Remaining for Undo KB*: This is the total number of kilobytes of log on the mirror server remaining to be scanned after failover during the undo phase.
- *Log Scanned for Undo KB*: This is the total number of kilobytes of log on the mirror server that have been scanned after failover during the undo phase.
- *Log Send Flow Control Time (ms)*: This is the number of milliseconds that log stream messages waited for send flow control within the last second by either partner.
- *Log Send Queue KB*: This is the total number of kilobytes of log on the principal server that have not been sent to the mirror server.
- *Mirrored Write Transactions/sec*: This is the number of transactions that have been written to the mirror database that waited for the log to be sent to the mirror server in order to commit within the last second.
- *Pages Sent/sec*: This is the number of pages sent per second from the principal server to the mirror server.
- *Receives/sec*: This is the number of mirroring messages received per second by either partner.
- *Redo Bytes/sec*: This is the number of bytes of log rolled forward on the mirror database per second.
- *Redo Queue KB*: This is the total number of kilobytes of hardened log that need to be applied to the mirror database.
- *Send/Receive Ack Time*: This is the number of milliseconds that messages waited for acknowledgement from either partner within in the last second. This counter is useful when trying to determine if you are experiencing database mirroring issues due to network latency.
- *Sends/sec*: This is the number of mirroring messages sent per second from either partner.
- *Transaction Delay*: This is the number of milliseconds the principal server has waited for commit acknowledgement from the mirror server. This is only relevant when you are using high-safety mode.

In addition to using these counters with PerfMon and SQL Server Agent alerts, you can also query the `sys.dm_os_performance_counters` dynamic management view (DMV), as shown in Listing

7-5, for the `SQLServer:Database Mirroring` performance object to view each counter maintained by SQL Server.

Listing 7-5. Query to Return the Counters for the SQLServer:Database Mirroring Prformance Object

```
SELECT object_name,
       counter_name,
       instance_name,
       cntr_value
FROM sys.dm_os_performance_counters
WHERE object_name like '%mirror%'
```

You can see in Figure 7-10 the sample result set returned by running the query in Listing 7-5. We ran the query on the principal server, so the values pertaining to the mirror server contain a 0 for the value.

	object_name	counter_name	instance_name	cntr_value
1	MSSQL$SQL2K8_3:Database Mirroring	Bytes Sent/sec	AdventureWorks	239890
2	MSSQL$SQL2K8_3:Database Mirroring	Pages Sent/sec	AdventureWorks	2
3	MSSQL$SQL2K8_3:Database Mirroring	Sends/sec	AdventureWorks	822
4	MSSQL$SQL2K8_3:Database Mirroring	Transaction Delay	AdventureWorks	413
5	MSSQL$SQL2K8_3:Database Mirroring	Redo Queue KB	AdventureWorks	0
6	MSSQL$SQL2K8_3:Database Mirroring	Redo Bytes/sec	AdventureWorks	0
7	MSSQL$SQL2K8_3:Database Mirroring	Log Send Queue KB	AdventureWorks	0
8	MSSQL$SQL2K8_3:Database Mirroring	Bytes Received/sec	AdventureWorks	54692
9	MSSQL$SQL2K8_3:Database Mirroring	Receives/sec	AdventureWorks	850
10	MSSQL$SQL2K8_3:Database Mirroring	Log Bytes Received/sec	AdventureWorks	0
11	MSSQL$SQL2K8_3:Database Mirroring	Log Bytes Sent/sec	AdventureWorks	417792
12	MSSQL$SQL2K8_3:Database Mirroring	Send/Receive Ack Time	AdventureWorks	45946
13	MSSQL$SQL2K8_3:Database Mirroring	Log Compressed Bytes Rcvd/sec	AdventureWorks	0
14	MSSQL$SQL2K8_3:Database Mirroring	Log Compressed Bytes Sent/sec	AdventureWorks	22538
15	MSSQL$SQL2K8_3:Database Mirroring	Mirrored Write Transactions/sec	AdventureWorks	48
16	MSSQL$SQL2K8_3:Database Mirroring	Log Scanned for Undo KB	AdventureWorks	0
17	MSSQL$SQL2K8_3:Database Mirroring	Log Remaining for Undo KB	AdventureWorks	0
18	MSSQL$SQL2K8_3:Database Mirroring	Log Bytes Sent from Cache/sec	AdventureWorks	417792
19	MSSQL$SQL2K8_3:Database Mirroring	Log Bytes Redone from Cache/sec	AdventureWorks	0
20	MSSQL$SQL2K8_3:Database Mirroring	Log Send Flow Control Time (ms)	AdventureWorks	5
21	MSSQL$SQL2K8_3:Database Mirroring	Log Harden Time (ms)	AdventureWorks	0

Figure 7-10. *Sample result set returned from the sys.dm_os_performance_counters DMV for the SQLServer:Database Mirroring object*

Configuring Database Mail

In order to get all of the benefits of using alerts in SQL Server Agent, you first need to configure Database Mail. You also need to create an operator and enable SQL Server Agent to use Database Mail. You can use the GUI to do all of this, but it is easier just to create a T-SQL script you can have on hand whenever you need to configure Database Mail. The next few sections will walk you through the prerequisites needed for the "Creating Alerts" section later in this chapter. The first thing you need to do is make sure you have Database Mail enabled. You can do this by using the `sp_configure` stored procedure as follows.

```
sp_configure 'show advanced options', 1;
GO
RECONFIGURE;
GO
sp_configure 'Database Mail XPs', 1;
GO
RECONFIGURE
GO
```

You also need to make sure Service Broker is enabled for the `msdb`. Database Mail depends on Service Broker to deliver e-mail messages. If Service Broker is not enabled, your mail messages will queue, but they will not be delivered. You can run the following query to determine whether Service Broker is enabled.

```
SELECT is_broker_enabled FROM sys.databases WHERE name = 'msdb'
```

If Service Broker is disabled, you can enable it by running the following `ALTER DATABASE` command. Enabling Service Broker requires a database lock. You will need to stop SQL Server Agent before running the `ALTER DATABASE` command so that Service Broker can acquire the appropriate lock.

```
ALTER DATABASE msdb SET ENABLE_BROKER
```

Now you need to add a Database Mail profile. You can do this using the `sysmail_add_profile_sp` stored procedure. The following code adds a profile named DBA Mail Profile.

```
EXEC msdb.dbo.sysmail_add_profile_sp
     @profile_name = 'DBA Mail Profile',
     @description = 'Profile used by the database administrator to send email.'
```

You can use the `sysmail_add_account_sp` to create the mail accounts. The following code will create a mail account named DBA Mail Account.

```
EXEC msdb.dbo.sysmail_add_account_sp
     @account_name = 'DBA Mail Account',
     @description = 'Profile used by the database administrator to send email.',
     @email_address = 'DBA@somecompany.com',
     @display_name = 'KEN-PC\SQL2K8',
     @mailserver_name = 'KEN-PC'
```

Once you have created a profile and an account, you need to associate the account with the profile by using the `sysmail_add_profileaccount_sp` stored procedure. The following code binds the DBA Mail Account to the DBA Mail Profile with a priority (sequence number) of 1. If you add multiple accounts with the same priority, Database Mail will randomly choose the account that sends the mail.

```
EXEC msdb.dbo.sysmail_add_profileaccount_sp
     @profile_name = 'DBA Mail Profile',
     @account_name = 'DBA Mail Account',
     @sequence_number = 1
```

The final script is shown in Listing 7-6. You can change the script to fit your organization by adding multiple accounts or changing parameters to the correct values. By using the @@ServerName function in the display name, each server will be able to send e-mail using its own name. As you can see, creating a Database Mail script is a far more efficient way to set up Database Mail across multiple servers.

Listing 7-6. Database Mail Setup Script

```
--MAKE SURE TO STOP SQL SERVER AGENT BEFORE RUNNING THIS SCRIPT!
USE msdb
GO

--Enable Database Mail
sp_configure 'show advanced options', 1;
GO
RECONFIGURE;
GO
sp_configure 'Database Mail XPs', 1;
GO
RECONFIGURE
GO

--Enable Service Broker
ALTER DATABASE msdb SET ENABLE_BROKER

--Add the profile
EXEC msdb.dbo.sysmail_add_profile_sp
     @profile_name = 'DBA Mail Profile',
     @description = 'Profile used by the database administrator to send email.'

--Add the account
EXEC msdb.dbo.sysmail_add_account_sp
     @account_name = 'DBA Mail Account',
     @description = 'Profile used by the database administrator to send email.',
     @email_address = 'DBA@somecompany.com',
     @display_name =  (Select @@ServerName),
```

```
        @mailserver_name =  'KEN-PC'

--Associate the account with the profile
EXEC msdb.dbo.sysmail_add_profileaccount_sp
        @profile_name = 'DBA Mail Profile',
        @account_name = 'DBA Mail Account',
        @sequence_number = 1


Print 'Don't Forget To Restart SQL Server Agent!'
```

Creating an Operator

Now that you have configured Database Mail, you need to define an operator that will receive alert notifications. An operator consists of two basic pieces of information: a name used to identify the operator and the contact information used to notify the operator. You can add an operator using the sp_add_operator procedure located in the msdb. The following statement adds an operator named DBA Support and supplies an e-mail address as the contact information. You just need to change the e-mail address for your configuration.

```
EXEC msdb.dbo.sp_add_operator
    @name='DBA Support',
    @email_address='DBASupport@somecompany.com'
```

Enabling SQL Server Agent Notifications

You have to enable the alert system in SQL Server Agent before you can start receiving notifications. Once you have configured Database Mail and added an operator, the next thing you should do is enable the alert system and designate a fail-safe operator. This is a designated operator that will receive notifications in the event that the primary operator is unreachable. SQL Server stores the fail-safe operator information in the registry in case the operator tables in the msdb are unavailable. You can use the following script in Listing 7-7 to enable Database Mail in SQL Server Agent and set the fail-safe operator.

Listing 7-7. Script to Enable Database Mail in SQL Server Agent

```
--MAKE SURE TO **START** SQL SERVER AGENT
--BEFORE RUNNING THIS SCRIPT!!!!!!!

--Enable SQL Server Agent to use Database Mail
-- and set fail-safe operator


EXEC master.dbo.sp_MSsetalertinfo
        @failsafeoperator=N'DBASupport', --Failsafe Operator
            @notificationmethod=1,
            @failsafeemailaddress = N'DBA@Somecompany.com'
```

```
EXEC msdb.dbo.sp_set_sqlagent_properties
            @email_save_in_sent_folder=1


EXEC master.dbo.xp_instance_regwrite
        N'HKEY_LOCAL_MACHINE',
        N'SOFTWARE\Microsoft\MSSQLServer\SQLServerAgent',
        N'UseDatabaseMail',
        N'REG_DWORD', 1


EXEC master.dbo.xp_instance_regwrite
        N'HKEY_LOCAL_MACHINE',
        N'SOFTWARE\Microsoft\MSSQLServer\SQLServerAgent',
        N'DatabaseMailProfile',
        N'REG_SZ',
        N'DBMailProfile'


 PRINT '**********Please Restart SQL Server Agent!************'
```

Creating Alerts

Now that you know how to create warning thresholds and have a good understanding of the performance counters you can use with database mirroring, you can create alerts to perform certain actions based on these events. An alert is essentially an automatic response to a predefined event. You can create alerts based on error number raised by warning thresholds, performance events, and Windows Management Instrumentation (WMI) events. You have already seen how to create an alert based on WMI events in Chapter 6 in the section "Creating a SQL Alert to Detect Automatic Failovers," so we will cover the remaining two options here.

Warning Thresholds

You have seen how to configure warning thresholds using both the Database Mirroring Monitor and system stored procedures. Configuring these warning thresholds is kind of a prerequisite for creating alerts based on these thresholds. Technically, you can create an alert without setting these thresholds, but the alert will never fire, so you will essentially have a useless alert. Once you have properly configured the appropriate warning thresholds, you are just a few simple steps away from creating an alert to perform a predefined action that will occur when these thresholds are exceeded. Expand the SQL Server Agent node in the SQL Server Management Studio Object Explorer, right-click the Alerts folder and select New Alert from the context menu to display the New Alert dialog box shown in Figure 7-11.

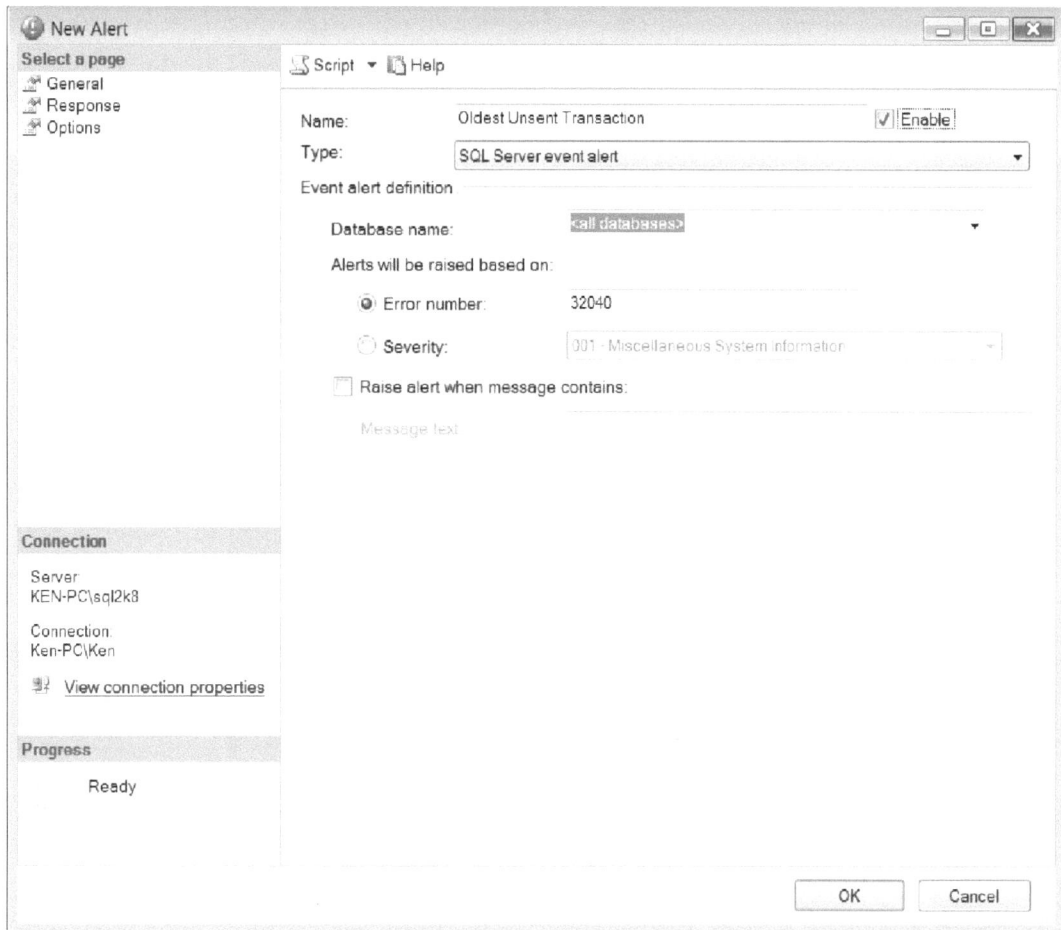

Figure 7-11. *New Alert dialog box General page*

Give the alert a descriptive name such as **Oldest Unsent Transaction** and make sure the Enable check box is selected. You will leave the Type drop-down set to SQL Server event alert. You can also create the alert for all databases or only a specific database by selecting a single database from the "Database name" drop-down. For this example, we will leave the default selection of all databases. In the "Alerts will be raised based on" section, you need to select the "Error number" radio button and enter **32040** in the text box. You can find each error number for its respective warning threshold in the "Understanding Warning Thresholds" section earlier in this chapter. Now you need to determine what action you want to occur in the event that this warning threshold is exceeded. Select the Response page as shown in Figure 7-12 to configure this action.

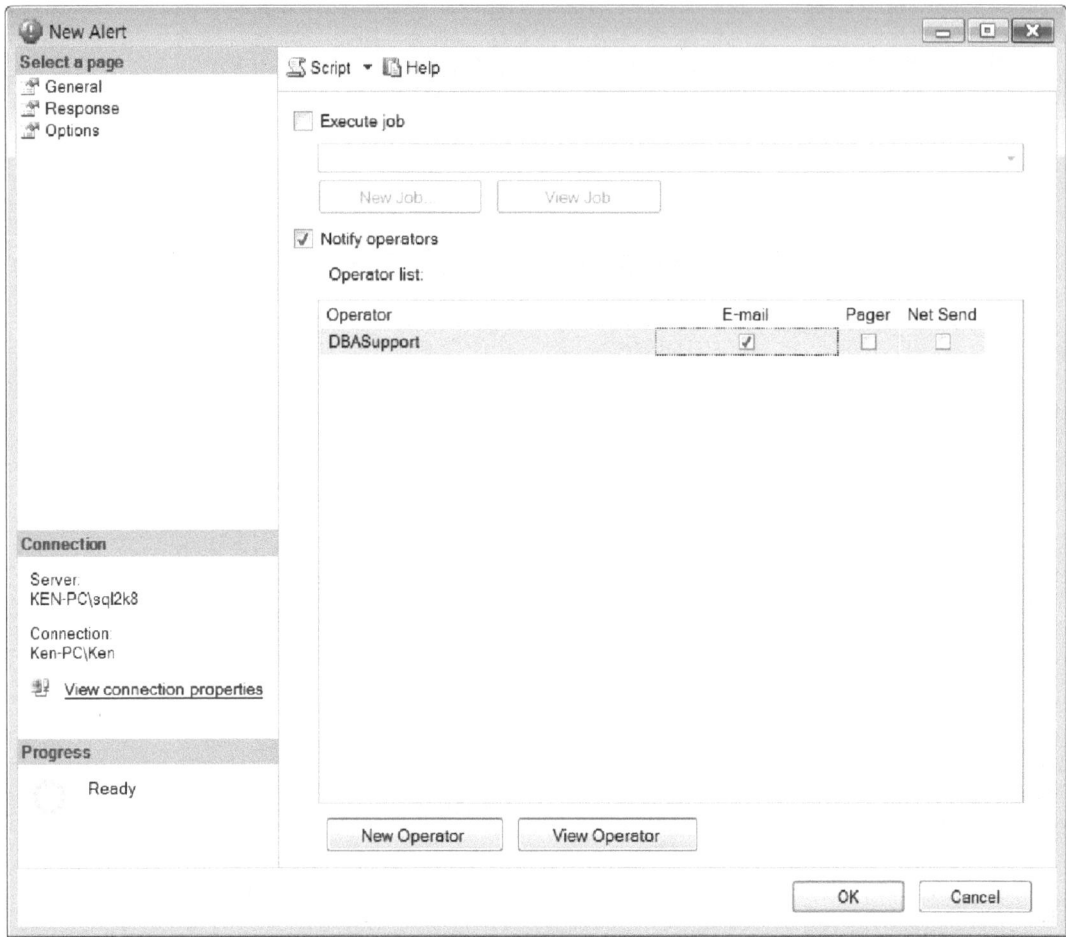

Figure 7-12. New Alert dialog box Response page

If you recall, we set this threshold to 20 minutes in the "Using System Stored Procedures" section. We have configured the alert to e-mail an existing operator called DBASupport whenever this threshold has been exceeded. Alternatively, you could have configured this alert to start a SQL Server Agent Job, which in turn could perform any number of actions you could imagine using SQL Server. Finally, select the Options page shown in Figure 7-13 to make a few final adjustments.

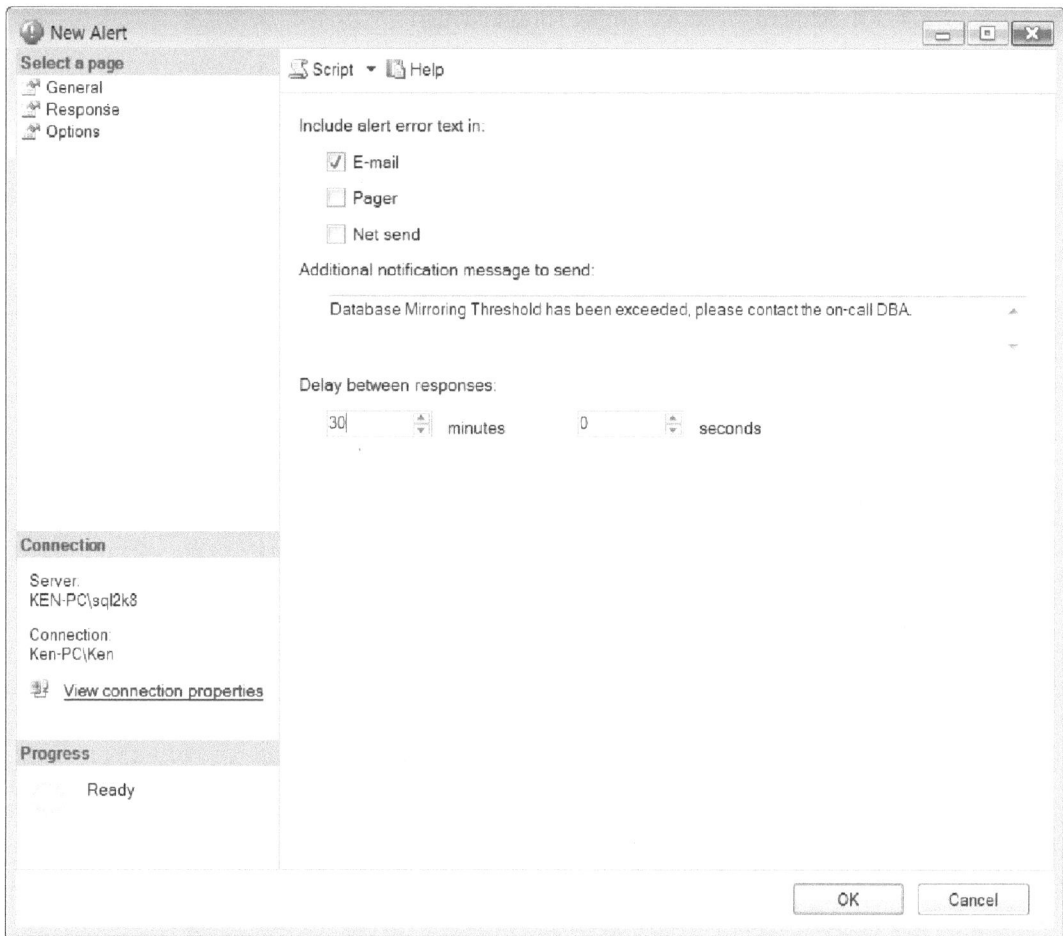

Figure 7-13. *New Alert dialog box Options page*

From the Options page, you can add a couple of nice features. For example, let's say all of your e-mails go to a support desk or network operations center (NOC). You can add additional text to the e-mail providing specific instructions for these external groups. You can also set the "Delay between responses" field so you aren't spammed when an error does occur.

You can use the following script in Listing 7-8 to create the same alert we configured using the GUI in this section. All you need to do is change the error number and the alert name in the T-SQL script to create the alerts for the remaining warning thresholds.

Listing 7-8. T-SQL Script to Create a Warning Threshold Alert

```
USE msdb
GO

EXEC msdb.dbo.sp_add_alert
     @name=N'Oldest Unsent Transaction',
     @message_id=32040,
     @severity=0,
     @enabled=1,
     @delay_between_responses=1800,
     @include_event_description_in=1,
     @notification_message=
       N'Database Mirroring Threshold has been exceeded,
         please contact the on-call DBA.'
GO

EXEC msdb.dbo.sp_add_notification
     @alert_name=N'Oldest Unsent Transaction',
     @operator_name=N'DBASupport',
     @notification_method = 1
GO
```

Performance Events

You can create an alert based on performance events by selecting **SQL Server performance condition alert** from the Type drop-down and following a similar process used to create an alert based on warning thresholds. The only difference between these two alerts is the information you need to enter on the General page of the New Alert dialog box. You can see the New Alert Dialog box for a SQL Server performance condition alert in Figure 7-14.

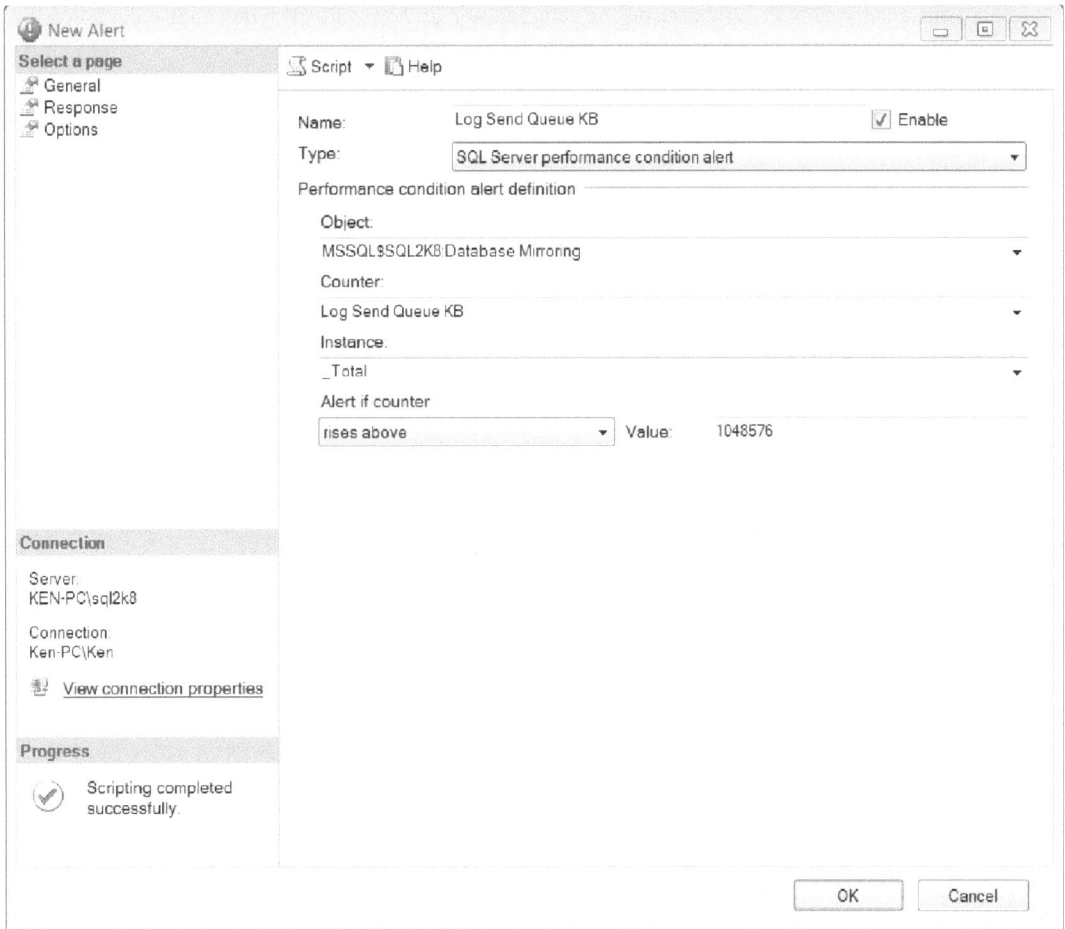

Figure 7-14. New Alert dialog box General page

Give the alert a descriptive name such as **Log Send Queue KB** and make sure the Enable check box is selected. You will need to change the Type drop-down to "SQL Server performance condition alert." Once you change the type, you will see the "Performance condition alert definition" section change to allow you to configure the remaining alert options. Select the `SQLServer:Database Mirroring` performance object from the Object drop-down, where SQLServer is specific to your instance. Select the counter you want to configure. As indicated by the alert name, we have selected the Log Send Queue KB counter. Now select the instance in which you would like to configure the alert. An instance is either an individual database name or _Total for all databases.

Unlike the warning thresholds that need to be preconfigured, you can define the thresholds for performance events directly within the alert. You can choose from one of three options from the "Alert if counter" drop-down: falls below, becomes equal to, and rises above. Finally, enter the value the counter is checked against. This value is specific to each counter, which can be kilobytes, minutes, and so on, depending on the counter. We have configured the alert to fire if the log send queue reaches a combined total of one gigabyte for all databases on the principal server. Alternatively, you can use the following T-SQL script in Listing 7-9 to create the same alert.

Listing 7-9. T-SQL Code to Create a Performance Condition Alert

```
USE msdb
GO

EXEC msdb.dbo.sp_add_alert
     @name=N'Log Send Queue KB',
     @enabled=1,
     @delay_between_responses=1800,
     @include_event_description_in=1,
     @notification_message=
      N'Database Mirroring Threshold has been exceeded,
        please contact the on-call DBA.',
     @performance_condition=
N'MSSQL$SQL2K8:Database Mirroring|Log Send Queue KB|_Total|>|1048576 '
GO

EXEC msdb.dbo.sp_add_notification
     @alert_name=N'Log Send Queue KB',
     @operator_name=N'DBASupport',
     @notification_method = 1
```

Useful Views

There are several ways to gain insight into your database mirroring configuration, but sometimes the easiest way is to simply run a query. There are some useful views available in SQL Server that expose many of the details you need to know about your database mirroring configuration. You can use the following catalog and dynamic management views to provide a quick look at your current database mirroring configuration.

- sys.database_mirroring: This catalog view contains information such as the state of the mirroring session, the role of the database, the safety level, the partner name, the witness name and state, the log sequence number (LSN) of the latest committed transaction, and information about the redo queue. This view returns one row for each database on the SQL Server instance. If you are not mirroring a database, all of the mirroring columns will return NULL values.

- sys.database_mirroring_endpoints: This catalog view contains information about the database mirroring endpoint used by the SQL Server instance. This view inherits information from the sys.endpoints catalog view. The sys.database_mirroring_endpoints catalog view is limited to only the database mirroring endpoint, whereas the sys.endpoints catalog view contains all endpoints for the SQL Server instance. The sys.database_mirroring_endpoints catalog view also contains information specific to database mirroring such as the state and the role of the server as well.

- `sys.database_mirroring_witnesses`: This catalog view contains one row for each witness role that the SQL Server instance plays in a database mirroring configuration. This catalog view contains information such as the partner names and roles, safety level, and the database mirroring states.
- `sys.dm_db_mirroring_connections`: This DMV returns one row for each database mirroring connection. This view returns information such as the connection state and time, user name and authentication method, and the number of bytes sent and received by the connection.
- `sys.dm_db_mirroring_auto_page_repair`: This DMV contains a rolling history of the last 100 automatic page repair attempts for any mirrored database on the SQL Server instance. This view contains information such as the ID of the file and page where the error occurred, the type of error that occurred, and the status of the page repair attempt.

Using the State Change Trace Event

You can monitor the `Database Mirroring State Change` event class using a SQL trace or directly from SQL Server Profiler. This event will fire whenever the state of a mirrored database changes. The overhead of monitoring the `Database Mirroring State Change` event class is relatively low. In other words, it's not something you need to worry about like some of the more expensive events you can capture such as the `Showplan XML` event class. The `Database Mirroring State Change` event class is located in the Database Event Category shown in Figure 7-15. You can capture the prior state, the new state, whether the state change was due to a system change or a user change, along with a lot of other useful information about the state change.

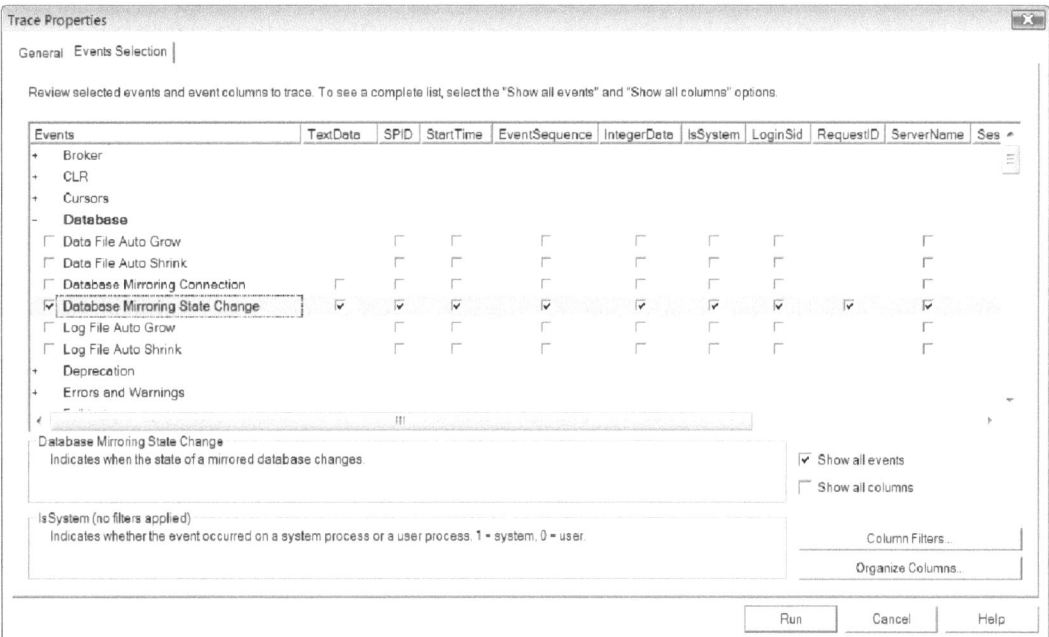

Figure 7-15. Database Mirroring State Change Events Selection dialog box

You can see an example of the `Database Mirroring State Change` event in Figure 7-16. The state changes in Figure 7-16 caused by the SQL Server service on the mirror server being recycled. One interesting thing to note is that the `IntegerData` column is actually the previous state, and the State column is the new state. You can easily follow the flow of state changes that have occurred during the process of recycling the mirror server using SQL Server Profiler.

EventClass	TextData	IntegerData	State
Trace Start			
Database Mirroring State Change	DBM: Synchronized Principal without Witness -> DBM: Connection with Mirror Lost	2	6
Database Mirroring State Change	DBM: Connection with Mirror Lost -> DBM: Synchronized Principal without Witness	6	2
Database Mirroring State Change	DBM: Synchronized Principal without Witness -> DBM: Principal Running Exposed	2	12
Database Mirroring State Change	DBM: Principal Running Exposed -> DBM: Synchronizing Principal	12	13
Database Mirroring State Change	DBM: Synchronizing Principal -> DBM: Synchronized Principal without Witness	13	2

Figure 7-16. *Database Mirroring State Change event captured in SQL Server Profiler*

You can view a listing of the State IDs and their descriptions in Table 6-1 in the previous chapter. Most of the other columns in the `Database Mirroring State Change` event class are pretty self-explanatory, but you can find out more about each one in SQL Server Books Online at `http://msdn.microsoft.com/en-us/library/ms191502.aspx`. You can also hover over a column in the Events Selection tab in SQL Server Profiler to get a brief description of the column. For example, you can see the description of the `IsSystem` column in Figure 7-15.

Summary

We have covered several monitoring techniques in this chapter to help you proactively manage your server. We started out with the basic monitoring components used in database mirroring such as the database mirroring status table and the Database Mirroring Monitor Job. Then we discussed the various warning thresholds and performance counters along with ways to configure them, including using the database mirroring monitor and system stored procedures. We also explained how to receive automatic notifications by configuring Database Mail and SQL Server Agent alerts. Finally, we covered some ways to gather useful information using views and SQL Server Profiler.

As you can see, there are several tools available for monitoring and alerting for your data database mirroring configuration. You can use these tools for everything from just keeping an eye on the status of database mirroring to automatically alerting you of predefined events. If you take a little extra time up front to properly configure monitoring and alerting for your database mirroring configuration, you will see that it will save you a lot of time in the end. Proper monitoring and alerting could possibly even save you from an unrecoverable disaster situation. After all the time and money you have spent on setting up database mirroring, it is definitely worth a little extra effort to make sure database mirroring is running as expected.

## CHAPTER 8

Upgrading to SQL Server 2008

When it comes to upgrading, there are two basic strategies: an in-place upgrade and a side-by-side upgrade. In many cases, you will be better off taking advantage of the upgrade process to buy new hardware, upgrade the OS, and perform a fresh install of SQL Server 2008. This is known as a side-by-side upgrade. However, in some cases, you may want to upgrade SQL Server as if you were applying a service pack. This is known as an in-place upgrade. Database mirroring can help you minimize downtime during an upgrade with either strategy as long as you know the proper procedures. We will walk you through some of the steps you should take before, during, and after upgrading to Microsoft SQL Server 2008. We will explain the considerations you should be aware of when upgrading existing mirroring configurations to SQL Server 2008. We will also show you how database mirroring can help you minimize downtime while upgrading to SQL Server 2008 even if you aren't currently using database mirroring.

Using the Upgrade Advisor

The first thing you need to do before you upgrade a mirrored database, or any database for that matter, is to make sure the database is compatible with SQL Server 2008. You can use the Microsoft SQL Server 2008 Upgrade Advisor to analyze your SQL Server instances to identify configuration items that may interfere with your upgrade process. The Upgrade Advisor will provide links to web pages that will present you with the information you need to resolve the conflicts before the upgrade.

You can install the Upgrade Advisor from the first page of the SQL Server 2008 install screen, or you can download it from the following URL: `www.microsoft.com/downloads/details.aspx?familyid=F5A6C5E9-4CD9-4E42-A21C-7291E7F0F852&displaylang=en`.

The install is pretty straightforward; you should be able to accept all the defaults and just keep clicking Next. Once you have completed the install, you can use the following steps to produce your analysis report:

1. Open the application and select Launch Upgrade Advisor Analysis Wizard.
2. This brings you to the welcome screen, as shown in Figure 8-1. Click Next to continue.

Figure 8-1. *Upgrade Advisor Analysis Wizard welcome screen*

3. Enter the server name and select the components you would like to analyze, as shown in Figure 8-2. Click Next to continue.

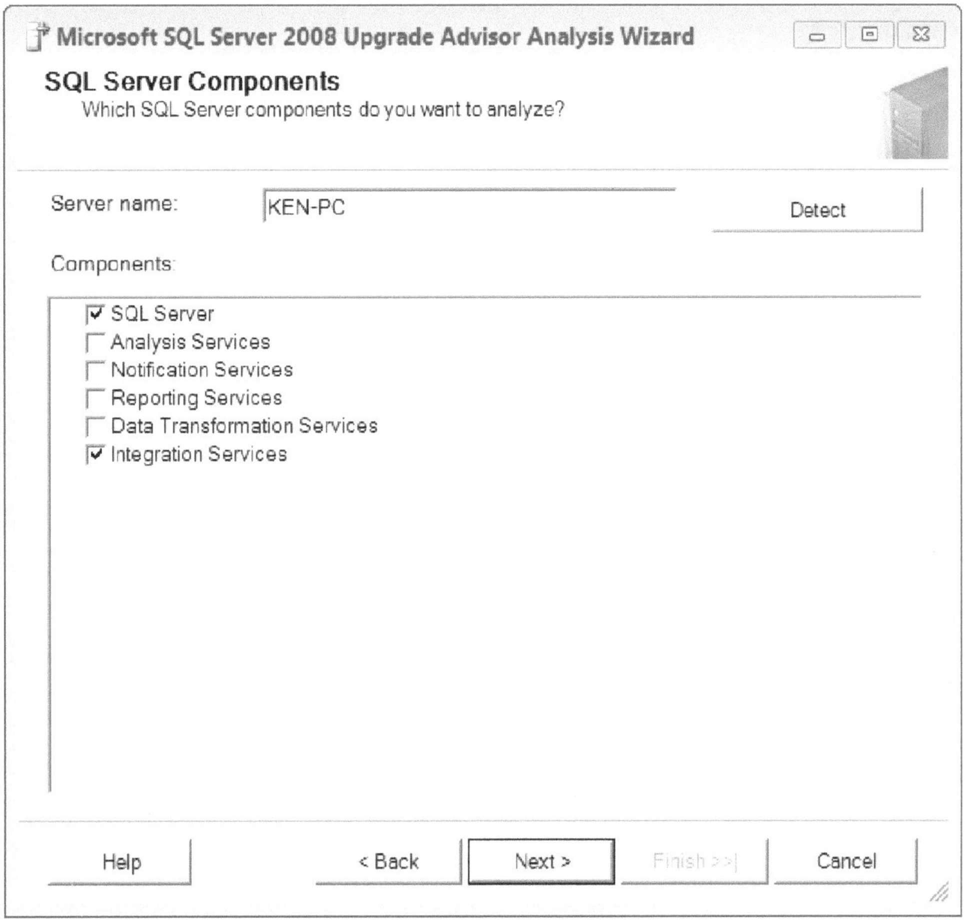

Figure 8-2. Upgrade Advisor server and components selection

4. This brings you to the authentication page, shown in Figure 8-3, from where you can select the instance name and enter your credentials. Click Next to continue.

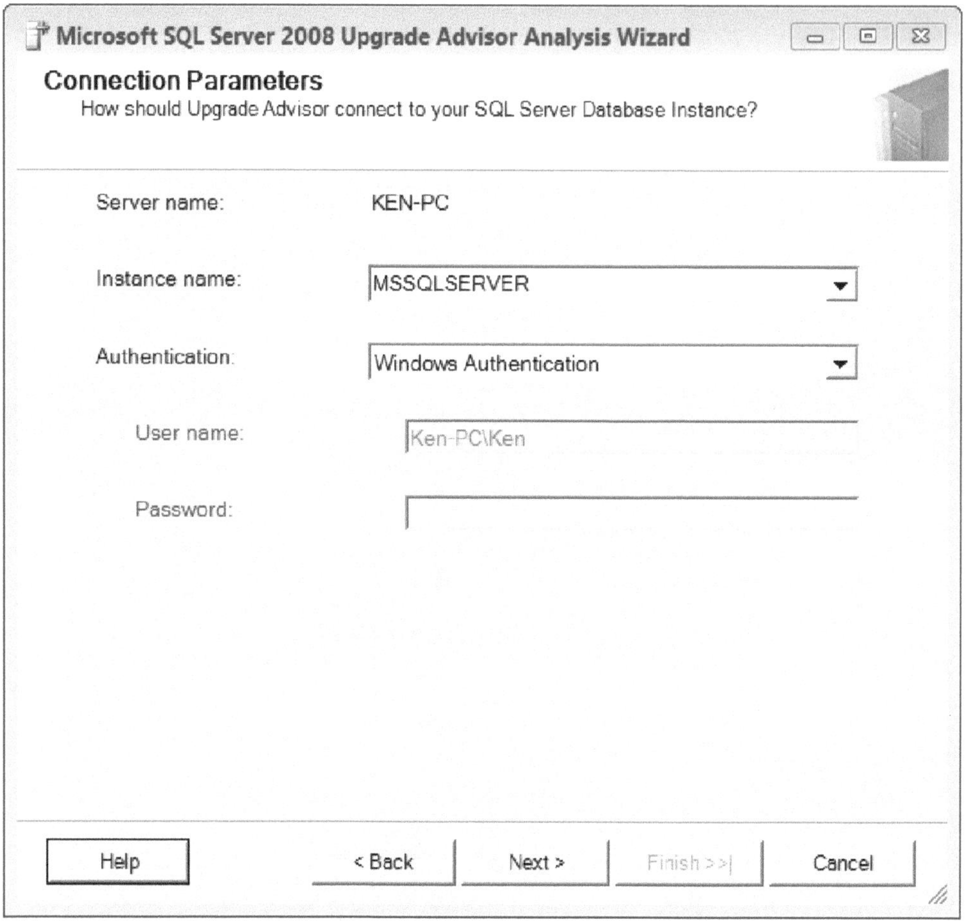

Figure 8-3. Upgrade Advisor authentication

5. After authenticating, you can select the databases you would like to analyze. Figure 8-4 shows all databases selected. You may also choose to analyze trace or batch files. Click Next to continue. If you have selected other components (refer to Figure 8-2), such as Analysis Services or Reporting Services, there will be authentication screens for each of those as well. Also, if you have selected Data Transformation Services (DTS) packages or SQL Server Integration Services (SSIS), you will be given the option to analyze packages for the server or select a path containing package files on subsequent screens.

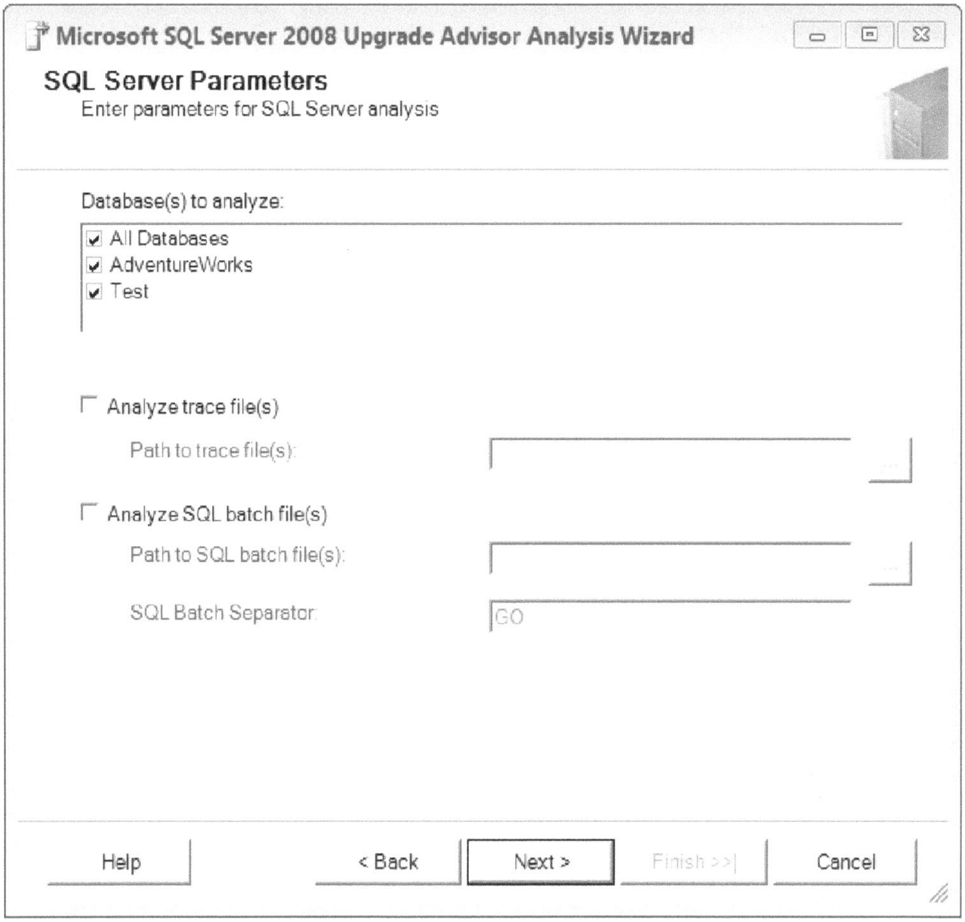

Figure 8-4. *Upgrade Advisor SQL Server parameters*

6. The confirmation screen in Figure 8-5 is then displayed. Confirm the options and click Run to begin the analysis.

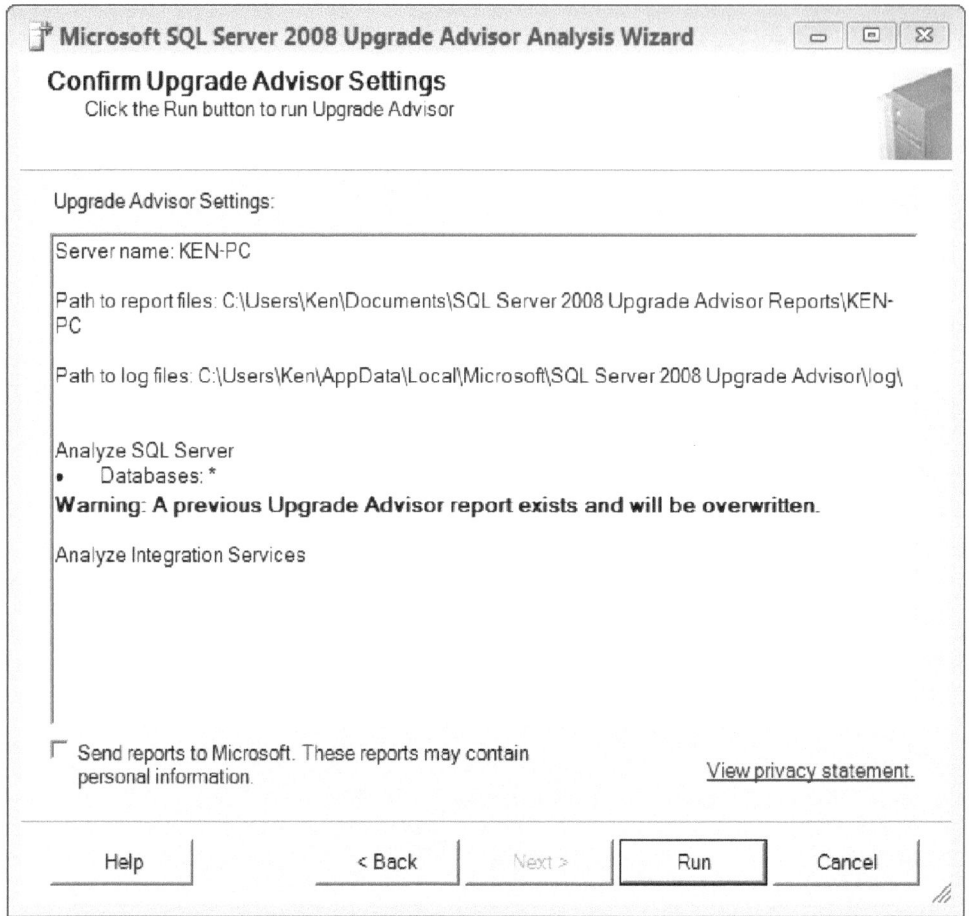

Figure 8-5. Upgrade Advisor confirmation screen

7.   Figure 8-6 shows the analysis in progress. As you can see, certain rules are analyzed for each selected component.

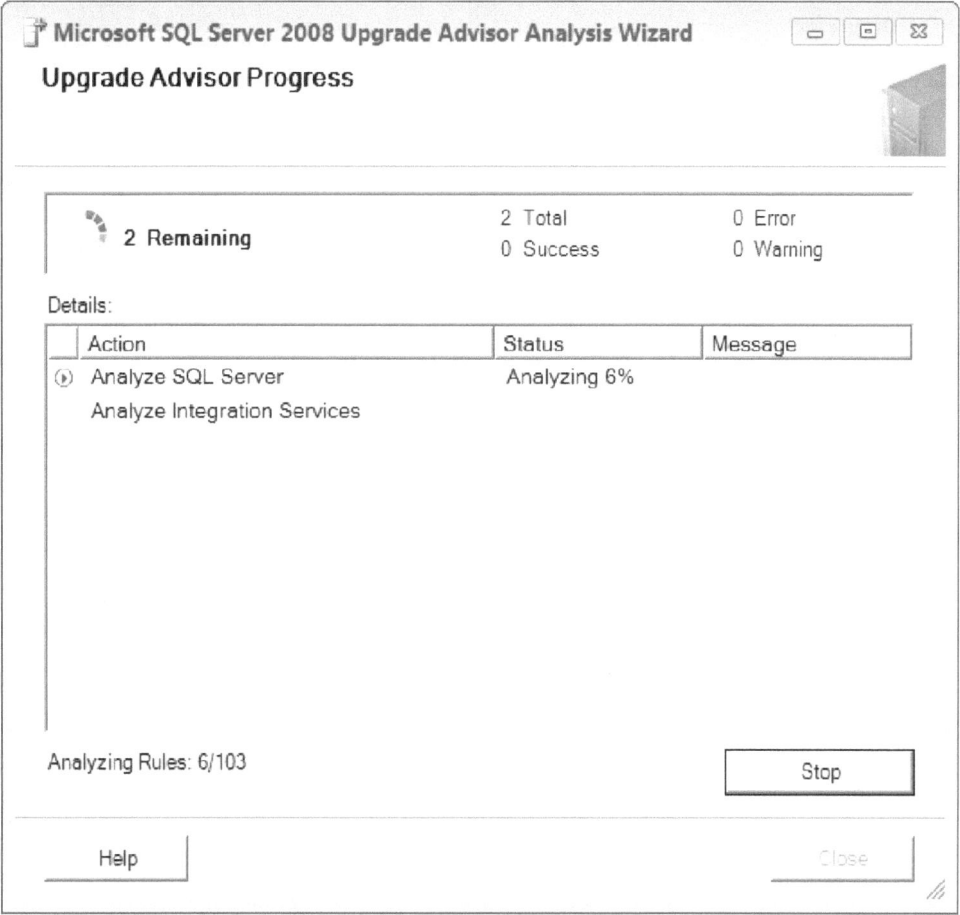

Figure 8-6. Upgrade Advisor rule analysis

8. After the analysis has completed, warnings will be displayed for those components needing attention. Figure 8-7, for example, shows a warning pertaining to SQL Server itself. Click Launch Report to display an analysis showing the details behind the warning.

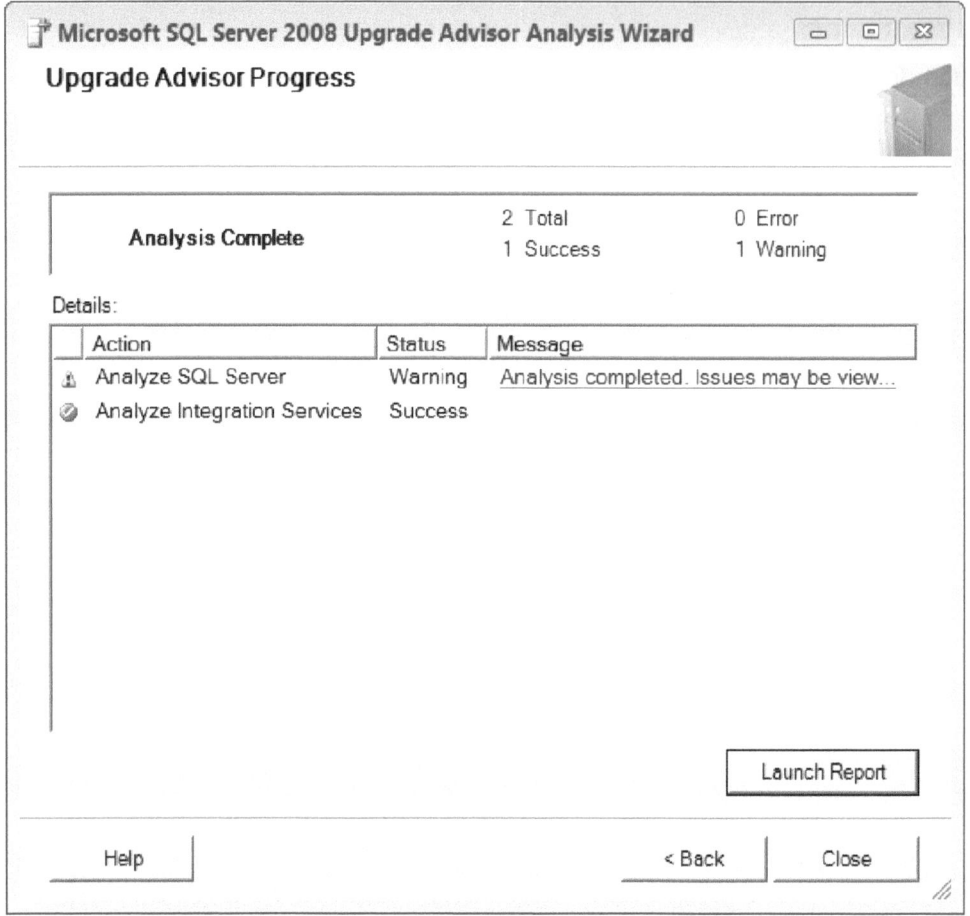

Figure 8-7. *Upgrade Advisor rule analysis completed*

9. Figure 8-8 shows a detailed analysis report. Notice the red circles with X marks in the Importance column. This report is showing that you will encounter a problem relating to a change in storage format for types xs:dateTime, xs:date, and xs:time. Three objects are affected. Click the Show Affected Objects link, and you'll get the screen shown in Figure 8-9, which lists those objects. Click the "Tell me more about this issue and how to resolve it" link if you want to see the Upgrade Advisor help page explaining how to resolve the problem.

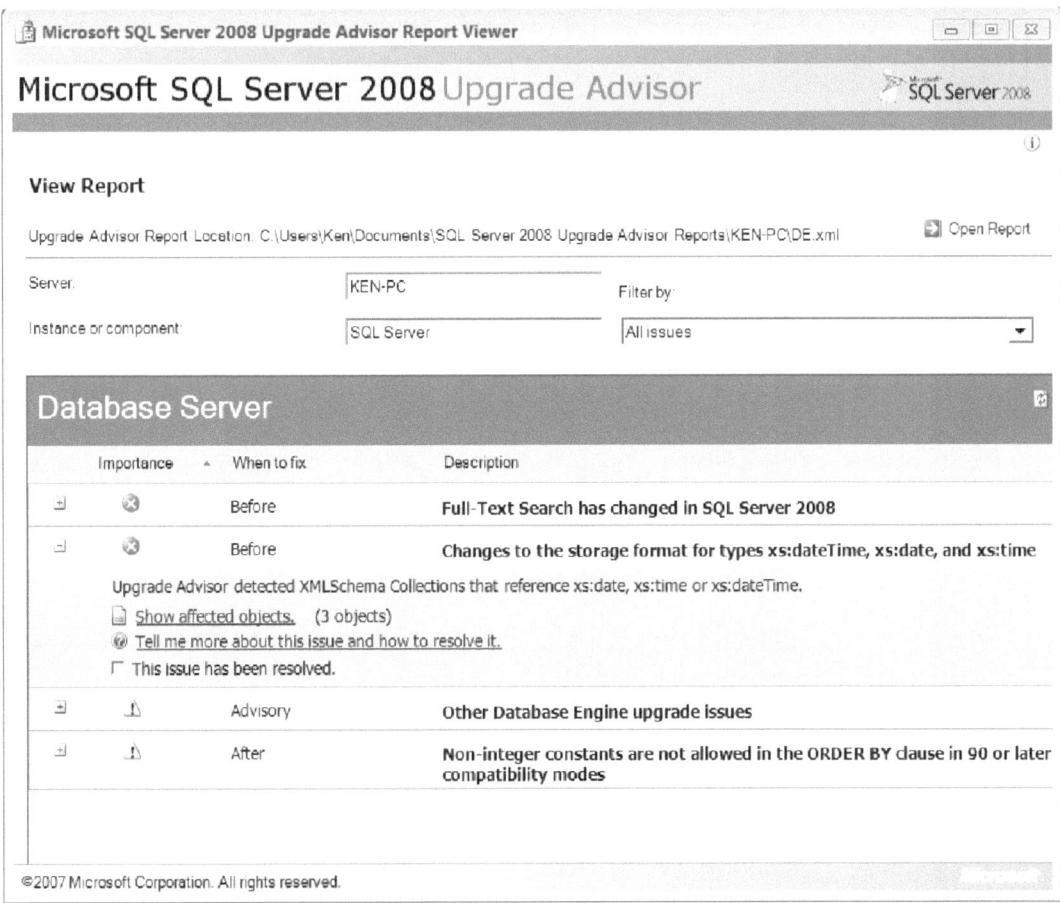

Figure 8-8. Upgrade Advisor analysis report

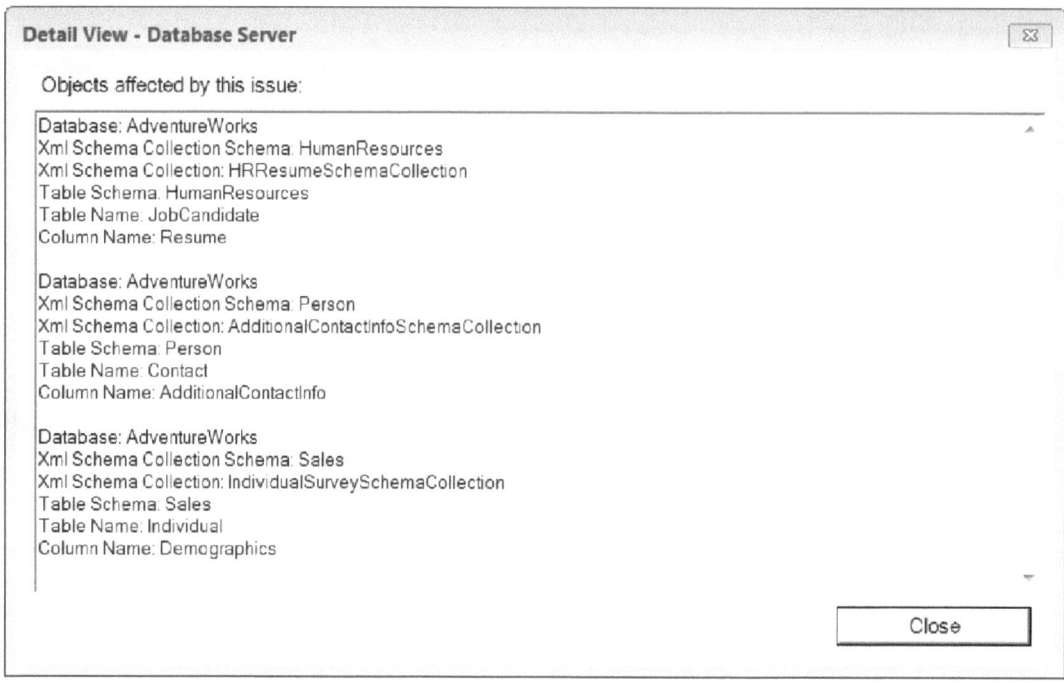

Figure 8-9. *Upgrade Advisor affected objects*

Upgrade Advisor is helpful in planning an upgrade, and you should definitely take the time to make sure you resolve all of the conflicts. Once you have run Upgrade Advisor, you don't have to rerun the analysis every time you want to view the reports. You can review the reports again without rerunning the analysis by selecting Launch Upgrade Advisor Report Viewer from the application home screen.

Upgrade Strategies

Once you have determined that your databases are compatible with SQL Server 2008, you are ready to perform an upgrade. There are two ways to perform an upgrade. The first is known as an in-place upgrade, and as the name implies, it upgrades an entire instance "in place" by converting the data files to the new format. The second approach is known as a side-by-side upgrade, which consists of installing a second instance of SQL Server and moving the data files to the new version. Both methods have their pros and cons, and the best method for one application may not be the best method for another. An in-place upgrade provides simplicity but lacks the flexibility offered by a side-by-side upgrade.

One of the benefits of performing an in-place upgrade is that you can use the same server and instance names. This may save you from having to track down all the connections to the database and point them to a new server or instance name. It is a fairly simple process, much like performing an installation or a service pack. You do not need extra disk space to make a copy of the data files because they will be converted to the new format during the upgrade. The downside is that at any point during the upgrade process, there is no turning back. The only back out is to reinstall the prior version of SQL Server and restore the databases from a backup that was made prior to the upgrade. You cannot restore a backup of a database that has been converted to SQL Server 2008 on a previous version. If you determine that a problem has been caused a week later by the upgrade, you will have to restore the database from a backup prior to the upgrade and hope you have a way to recover the transactions that have occurred since the upgrade.

A side-by-side upgrade consists of installing SQL Server 2008 and moving the databases from the old instance to the new instance. The side-by-side method gives you a chance to test the effects SQL Server 2008 will have on an application before severing the ties with the old version. You can install the new instance on a second server, or you can use the same server provided it meets the install requirements. Generally, you should take advantage of the upgrade process to upgrade the hardware as well. If the same server is used, you will need sufficient disk space to store a duplicate copy of the databases during the upgrade.

Performing an In-Place Upgrade

Upgrading your current SQL Server 2005 mirrored instances to SQL Server 2008 is very similar to patching your SQL Server instances, which we briefly discussed in the "Upgrading or Patching SQL Server" section in Chapter 6. Both patching and upgrading involve a rolling upgrade process; however, upgrading is a more intrusive process that actually takes your databases to a level at which they will no longer be compatible with SQL Server 2005. Since your databases will no longer work with SQL Server 2005 once they have been converted to SQL Server 2008, you should be a little more careful when performing an upgrade instead of just applying a patch. For example, you should make sure you have a good backup prior to the upgrade as well as that you fully understand the upgrade process. In the next few sections, we will cover the topics you need to know in order to successfully upgrade your current database mirroring environment from SQL Server 2005 to SQL Server 2008.

Considerations Prior to Performing an Upgrade

Before performing an upgrade, you should be extremely familiar with the failover and the upgrade processes. This means you need to practice, and by practice, we mean you need to actually fail over database mirroring on a test system to become familiar with the process. The upgrade process is not the time to realize you don't know how to do something. You should also look for issues that other people have encountered when upgrading and either be aware of those issues or avoid the same mistakes. For example, there is a known issue when performing a rolling upgrade from SQL Server 2005 to SQL Server 2008 on a database that contains a full-text index. There is a simple fix at http://support.microsoft.com/kb/956017 that involves enabling a trace flag, but if you were not aware of this issue, it may cause you a little extra anxiety during the upgrade.

Make sure you have a good backup. You should always plan for the worst and hope for the best. If you absolutely had to restore your database from a backup, how comfortable are you with the process? Are you sure you have current backups? Are you sure they are not corrupt? Are you comfortable with the restore process? Do you have to call someone else to pull them from tape? As we stated earlier, once your database has been converted to SQL Server 2008, your only back-out option may be to reinstall SQL Server 2005 and restore the database prior to the upgrade. There is no way to move a SQL Server 2008 database to SQL Server 2005; you can't backup and restore or detach and attach a database to a previous version. Without a good backup prior to the upgrade, your only option to restore the database to SQL Server 2005 would be to script the data in SQL 2005 compatibility mode using the Generate Scripts Wizard. Using the Generate Scripts Wizard would require a lot of downtime, and it is not really something we would suggest as a back-out plan.

Another thing you should do is check the integrity of your database before trying to upgrade it to SQL Server 2008. You should run the DBCC CHECKDB ([DatabaseName]) command against all of your databases and fix any errors prior to the upgrade. In SQL Server 2005, you can have corruption on your principal database and not on your mirror database since mirroring copies only the transactions and not the actual pages. That's why SQL Server 2008 can take advantage of automatically copying corrupt pages from either partner. If you do find corruption in SQL Server 2005, you may be able to use the mirror database to recover the data instead of having to resort to possible data loss.

Upgrading High-Performance Mode

This section will walk you through the steps required to perform a successful upgrade when using high-performance mode. The steps are a little different than the steps in the chart located at http://msdn.microsoft.com/en-us/library/bb677181.aspx in SQL Server Books Online. This is because the first thing SQL Server Books Online suggests is changing the operating mode to high-safety and then performing the upgrade. You really don't need to do this until after you have upgraded the mirror server. If there are any changes in the principal database, it will slow down the upgrade while it waits for the changes to be committed on the mirror. You can use the following steps to upgrade your SQL Server 2005 high-performance mode mirroring instances to SQL Server 2008.

1. Run the SQL Server 2008 installation to upgrade the mirror server.
2. Change the operating mode to high-safety mode without a witness and wait for the mirror database to synchronize. You can change the database to high-safety mode by running the following command from the master database on the principal server.

   ```
   ALTER DATABASE [DatabaseName] SET SAFETY FULL
   ```

3. Fail over the principal database to the new SQL Server 2008 instance. SQL Server will now suspend mirroring because the servers are at two different build levels. You will be able to resume mirroring once you have completed the upgrade on the original principal server. To fail over to the database to the mirror server, issue the following command from the master database on the principal server.

   ```
   ALTER DATABASE [DatabaseName] SET PARTNER FAILOVER
   ```

4. Change the operating mode back to high-performance. You can change the database to high-performance mode by running the following command from the master database on the principal server.

   ```
   ALTER DATABASE [DatabaseName] SET SAFETY OFF
   ```

5. Run the SQL Server 2008 installation to upgrade the original principal server (now acting as the mirror).
6. Resume the database mirroring session. To resume database mirroring run the following command on either partner.

   ```
   ALTER DATABASE [DatabaseName] SET PARTNER RESUME
   ```

Upgrading High-Safety Mode Without a Witness

This section will walk you through the steps required to perform a successful upgrade when using high-safety mode without a witness server. Again, the reference in SQL Server Books Online says to run the upgrade directly from this mode. However, if you are running SQL Server Enterprise Edition, we recommend changing to high-performance mode, upgrading the mirror server and then switching back. You can use the following steps to upgrade your SQL Server 2005 high-safety mode mirroring instances without a witness to SQL Server 2008.

1. Change the operating mode to high-performance mode. This is only applicable if you are running SQL Server Enterprise Edition. You can change the database to high-performance mode by running the following command from the master database on the principal server.

   ```
   ALTER DATABASE [DatabaseName] SET SAFETY OFF
   ```

2. Run the SQL Server 2008 installation to upgrade the mirror server.

3. Change the operating mode back to high-safety mode without a witness and wait for the mirror database to synchronize. You will only need to do this if you changed the operating mode in step 1. You can change the database to high-safety mode by running the following command from the master database on the principal server.

```
ALTER DATABASE [DatabaseName] SET SAFETY FULL
```

4. Fail over the principal database to the new SQL Server 2008 instance. SQL Server will now suspend mirroring because the servers are at two different build levels. You will be able to resume mirroring once you have completed the upgrade on the original principal server. To fail over to the database to the mirror server, issue the following command from the master database on the principal server.

```
ALTER DATABASE [DatabaseName] SET PARTNER FAILOVER
```

5. Run the SQL Server 2008 installation to upgrade the original principal server (now acting as the mirror).
6. Resume the database mirroring session. To resume database mirroring run the following command on either partner.

```
ALTER DATABASE [DatabaseName] SET PARTNER RESUME
```

Upgrading High-Safety Mode with a Witness

This section will walk you through the steps required to perform a successful upgrade when using high-safety mode with a witness server. Upgrading database mirroring running in high-safety mode with a witness is very similar to upgrading high-safety mode without a witness except for the fact that you need to remove the witness server prior to the upgrade. You can upgrade the witness server at any time during the upgrade process as long as you have removed it from the mirroring session. You can use the following steps to upgrade your SQL Server 2005 high-safety mode mirroring instances with a witness to SQL Server 2008.

1. Take note of the witness server's full network address. You will need this information when you add the witness server back in to the mirroring session. You can get the full network address of the witness server by running the following command on either partner.

```
SELECT mirroring_witness_name
FROM sys.database_mirroring
WHERE database_id = DB_ID('DatabaseName')
```

2. Remove the witness server to disable automatic failover. To remove the witness issue the following command on either partner.

```
ALTER DATABASE [DatabaseName] SET WITNESS OFF
```

3. Change the operating mode to high-performance mode. This is only applicable if you are running SQL Server Enterprise Edition. You can change the database to high-performance mode by running the following command from the master database on the principal server.

```
ALTER DATABASE [DatabaseName] SET SAFETY OFF
```

4. Run the SQL Server 2008 installation to upgrade the mirror server.
5. Change the operating mode back to high-safety mode without a witness and wait for the mirror database to synchronize. You will only need to do this if you changed the operating mode in step 3. You can change the database to high-safety mode by running the following command from the master database on the principal server.

```
ALTER DATABASE [DatabaseName] SET SAFETY FULL
```

6. Fail over the principal database to the new SQL Server 2008 instance. SQL Server will now suspend mirroring because the servers are at two different build levels. You will be able to resume mirroring once you have completed the upgrade on the original principal server. To fail over to the database to the mirror server, issue the following command from the master database on the principal server.

```
ALTER DATABASE [DatabaseName] SET PARTNER FAILOVER
```

7. Run the SQL Server 2008 installation to upgrade the original principal server (now acting as the mirror).

8. Resume the database mirroring session. To resume database mirroring run the following command on either partner.

```
ALTER DATABASE [DatabaseName] SET PARTNER RESUME
```

9. Run the SQL Server 2008 installation to upgrade the witness server. You can do this step at any time after you have removed the witness server from the mirroring session in step 2.

10. Add the witness server back to database mirroring session to enable automatic failover. To add the witness server back issue the following command on the principal server with the appropriate network address for the witness server.

```
ALTER DATABASE [DatabaseName] SET WITNESS = 'TCP://<Server>:<Port>'
```

Minimizing the Downtime of a Side-by-Side Upgrade

A side-by-side upgrade generally consists of buying a new server, installing SQL Server 2008 on the new server, moving the production databases to the new server, and then directing users to the new server. The part where database mirroring can help is moving the production database to the new server. Many times companies want as little downtime as possible when upgrading to new systems. If your databases are fairly large, copying them to a new server could take quite a while, which may or may not be acceptable depending on the terms agreed upon in the Service Level Agreement (SLA).

If you have tested your databases with SQL Server 2008 and are ready to proceed with the upgrade, you can configure database mirroring between the old and new servers to drastically reduce the downtime and overall impact to the users. You can use the following steps to minimize the downtime when performing a side-by-side upgrade from SQL Server 2005 to SQL Server 2008.

■ **Note** You must be running SQL Server 2005 Build 3215 (SP2 Cumulative Update 5) or later in order to establish a database mirroring session between SQL Server 2005 and SQL Server 2008.

---

1. Install SQL Server 2008 along with the most recent service packs on the new SQL Server.
2. Prepare the new SQL Server instance by creating any jobs, logins, and any other external objects needed by your production database.
3. Establish database mirroring between the old server and the new server using high-performance mode.
4. Right before you are ready to failover, change the mirroring configuration to high-safety mode and wait for the databases to enter the synchronized state.
5. Manually fail over the production databases to the new server.

At this point, the new principal SQL Server 2008 instance cannot synchronize with the old SQL Server 2005 instance, and SQL Server will suspend the database mirroring session. You can either upgrade the old server to SQL Server 2008 or remove database mirroring altogether by running `ALTER DATABASE [DatabaseName] SET PARNTER OFF`. Remember, don't leave database mirroring in a suspended state, or the transactions will remain active and your transaction log will fill up on the new server, which wouldn't make for a very good upgrade experience.

Post-Upgrade Procedures

In order to take advantage of everything that SQL Server 2008 has to offer, you need to take a few steps after the upgrade has occurred. Some of these procedures do not apply if your database was created in SQL Server 2005; however, we still see many changes that need to be made because a database has been migrated from SQL Server 2000 without implementing any of the following post-upgrade procedures. We will discuss each change you should make and explain how it benefits you after the upgrade. Following are the steps that you should perform after any upgrade:

- Change the compatibility level.
- Check the integrity of the objects in your database.
- Correct inaccurate row and page counts for tables and indexes.
- Set your page verification method to `CHECKSUM`.
- Update statistics.

Changing Compatibility Level

The first thing you should do after the upgrade is change the compatibility level of the database, assuming it is supported by the application. We have had some vendors allow us to upgrade the database as long as we left the compatibility level set to the prior version. When upgrading a database to SQL Server 2008, the database maintains the current compatibility level. In order to take advantage of the new features offered in SQL Server 2008, you should change the compatibility level to SQL Server 2008 (100).

■ **Note** If the database compatibility level is below SQL Server 2000 (80), it will be changed automatically to SQL Server 2000 (80) during the upgrade, which is the minimum level supported in SQL Server 2008.

To view the current compatibility level, you can query the `sys.databases` catalog view.

```
SELECT name, compatibility_level FROM sys.databases
```

The `ALTER DATABASE` command replaces the `sp_dbcmptlevel` procedure that was previously used to change the compatibility level. You can also change the compatibility level in the Options tab of the Database Properties dialog box that is displayed by right-clicking the database and selecting Properties.

Run the following statement to change the compatibility level to SQL Server 2008.

```
ALTER DATABASE [DatabaseName] SET COMPATIBILITY_LEVEL = 100
```

■ **Caution** Changing the compatibility level while the database is currently in use could result in the generation of an incorrect query plan and unpredictable queries. The faulty query plan may also be stored in the cache and used for multiple queries. It is recommended that you change the compatibility level when the database is in single-user mode.

Checking Object Integrity

The next thing you should do is run DBCC commands to test for object integrity. The DBCC CHECKDB command checks the integrity of the objects in a database and should be run on a regular basis. One thing that this command does not check in databases created in versions prior to SQL Server 2005 is the integrity of the data in the columns. Adding the DATA_PURITY option causes the CHECKDB command to look for column values that are invalid or out of range. Any database that was created in SQL Server 2005 or later will include the DATA_PURITY check by default; but if the database was created in an earlier version, you must run the command with the DATA_PURITY option at least once and fix any issues. Once the command has executed successfully and the issues have been resolved, an entry is made in the database header, and the DATA_PURITY option will be included by default as a part of the normal CHECKDB operation. If you do not know if your database was created in SQL Server 2005 or if the header contains the entry to include DATA_PURITY when running CHECKDB, it's better to be safe and go ahead and run CHECKDB with the DATA_PURITY option.

You can execute the following command to perform a CHECKDB with DATA_PURITY.

```
DBCC CHECKDB ([DatabaseName]) WITH DATA_PURITY
```

Correct Row and Page Counts

The DBCC UPDATEUSAGE command corrects inaccurate row and page counts for tables and indexes. Invalid counts are common in previous versions of SQL Server and can skew the results of certain commands such as sp_spaceused. You should always run the UPDATEUSAGE command on databases that have been upgraded from SQL Server 2000. You do not need to run the command on a regular basis unless frequent Data Definition Language (DDL) modifications are made in the database.

You can run the following command to update the usage counts for a given database.

```
DBCC UPDATEUSAGE ([DatabaseName])
```

Setting the Page Verification Method

When upgrading a database, the PAGE_VERIFY option will remain the same as it was in the prior version. You should make sure this option is set to CHECKSUM after the upgrade. The CHECKSUM option was introduced in SQL Server 2005 and provides the highest level of integrity for the data files. When the CHECKSUM option is enabled, a checksum of the whole page is computed and stored in the page header when the page is written to disk. When the page is read from disk, the checksum is recalculated and compared with the value in the header.

To view the current PAGE_VERIFY option you can query the sys.databases catalog view.

```
SELECT name, page_verify_option_desc FROM sys.databases
```

Use the `ALTER DATABASE` command to change the `PAGE_VERIFY` option to `CHECKSUM`.

```
ALTER DATABASE [DatabaseName] SET PAGE_VERIFY CHECKSUM WITH NO_WAIT
```

Updating Statistics

Updating the statistics after the upgrade allows the database engine to take advantage of the enhancements made in SQL Server 2008 to optimize query performance. The statistics that reside in the database were created with an earlier version of SQL Server. By recreating them with SQL Server 2008, you are allowing SQL Server to create more intelligent statistics to work with. This ultimately results in a better execution plan and faster, more efficient queries. You can run the following script to perform a full scan of all the statistics in a single database. Performing a full scan can be time consuming, so you should run the script during non-peak hours or before you have turned the database back over to production.

To update statistics, run the following script against each of the databases that have been upgraded.

```
USE [DatabaseName]
GO
sp_msforeachtable 'UPDATE STATISTICS ON ? WITH FULLSCAN;'
```

Summary

In this chapter, we covered many of the steps you should take in order to upgrade your mirrored instances to SQL Server 2008. First, we walked you through the steps to use the Upgrade Advisor so you can make sure your database is compatible with SQL Server 2008. Next, we covered the different upgrade strategies and the steps required to upgrade using each strategy. Last, we covered the steps you need to take after upgrading in order to take advantage of all the new features in SQL Server 2008.

Upgrading to SQL Server 2008 should be a painless process as long as you know the proper steps to take. If you have properly tested your upgrade procedures, you will be more comfortable during the actual upgrade because you will know exactly what to expect. Database mirroring does add a little complexity to the upgrade process, but if you learn to use it to your advantage, you will have far less downtime when compared to a normal stand-alone SQL Server upgrade. If you use the Upgrade Advisor to make sure your databases are compatible with SQL Server 2008, follow the steps required to upgrade your mirroring configuration, and make the appropriate changes after the upgrade, your new SQL Server environment should be running better than ever.

CHAPTER 9

Reporting Considerations

One of the first questions we always hear when discussing database mirroring is how it can be used for reporting. You cannot directly query the mirror database since it is constantly restoring transactions. However, there are a few techniques you can use with database mirroring so you do not have to use the principal database for reporting. You can create a database snapshot on the mirror server that will allow you to query a static copy of the mirror database at the time the snapshot was taken. You will need a process to maintain current database snapshots in order to provide recent data and prevent excessive disk usage. Log shipping is another way to offload reporting to another server; and when properly configured, log shipping will continue work seamlessly even when the principal database fails over. Mirroring also works with replication. Mirroring the publication database is fully supported, and you can configure the replication agents to automatically connect to the new principal database in the event of a failover. We will review each of these techniques and discuss the pros and cons of using each one as a reporting solution with database mirroring.

Using Database Snapshots

In order to use a mirrored database as a reporting solution, you must also use the database snapshot feature, which requires the Enterprise Edition of SQL Server. You can use database snapshots in conjunction with database mirroring in order to provide a static reporting solution by taking regular snapshots of the mirror database. Users are unable to connect directly to the mirror database to perform queries, but you can create a snapshot of the mirror database at any given time, which will allow users to connect to the snapshot database.

A database snapshot only contains a copy of the original data pages that have changed in the source database since the snapshot was created. It contains the original copies of those pages in order to give the effect of a read-only view of the database at the time the snapshot was created. The file that is created to hold the changed data pages when the snapshot is created is known as a *sparse file*. A database snapshot sparse file will start out very small and will grow larger as changes are made to the source database. This also means that in databases that have several transactions or bulk inserts, the snapshot can grow rather large fairly quickly. Any transactions that are uncommitted at the time you create a snapshot will not be included in the database snapshot. You can create multiple snapshots of a source database, which for the purposes of this chapter will be your mirror database, but those snapshots must reside on the same instance as the source database.

A database snapshot can never be any bigger than the size of the source database at the time the snapshot was created. Since the snapshot only contains changed pages, it relies on the source database to provide the pages that have not changed; if the source database is unavailable, then so is the snapshot. A source database that contains a snapshot cannot be dropped, detached, or restored until all of the snapshots have been dropped.

In order to keep the data current and the size of the snapshot to a minimum, you should refresh the snapshot periodically by creating a new snapshot and directing the traffic there. Then you can delete the old snapshot as soon as all the open transactions have completed. The snapshot database will continue to function after a failover has occurred; you will just lose connectivity during the failover while the databases are restarted. A failover could, however, place an additional load on the production system. Since it is now being used for processing the data for the application and serving up reporting requests, you may need to drop the snapshots and suspend reporting until another server is brought online.

Note You can create a database snapshot on all the database recovery models; however, your database must be using the Full Recovery model in order to participate in a database mirroring session.

Creating a Database Snapshot

To create a database snapshot, you must issue the CREATE DATABASE command with the AS SNAPSHOT OF clause; you cannot create a database snapshot using the SQL Server Management Studio GUI. Any user who has the right to create a database can create a database snapshot.

Before you create a database snapshot, you need to know the logical files names for every data file in the source database. You can get the logical file names by executing the following query against the source database. You will need to run the following query against the principal database since you cannot directly query the mirror database.

```
SELECT name FROM sys.database_files WHERE type <> 1
```

Listing 9-1 shows the syntax for creating a new database snapshot against the AdventureWorks database. Following are the parameters used in that script:

Test_Snapshot_1 is the name of the new database snapshot.

AdventureWorks_Data is the logical file name of the data file in the AdventureWorks database.

FileName is the name of the snapshot file that will hold the changed data files. You can use any file name, extension, and location that you like for the snapshot file.

AdventureWorks is the source database name following the AS SNAPSHOT OF clause.

Listing 9-1. Syntax Used to Generate a Database Snapshot

```
CREATE DATABASE Test_Snapshot_1
 ON
(Name = AdventureWorks_Data,
 FileName = 'C:\Test_Data.ss')
 AS SNAPSHOT OF AdventureWorks
```

To create a database snapshot with multiple filegroups, you need to supply the Name and FileName parameters for each filegroup, as shown in Listing 9-2.

Listing 9-2. *Syntax Used to Generate a Database Snapshot Using Multiple Filegroups*

```
CREATE DATABASE <Snapshot Name>
 ON
(Name = <Logical_FileName_1>,
 FileName =<Snapshot File Location 1>),
(Name =<Logical_FileName_2>,
 FileName =<Snapshot File Location 2>)
 AS SNAPSHOT OF <DatabaseName>
```

Working with Database Snapshots

Once you have created a snapshot, you can view it in the Database Snapshots folder under the Databases node in the SQL Server Management Studio Object Explorer, as shown in Figure 9-1. As you can see, the database snapshot contains all of the objects you would expect to see in a normal database. It's really just that simple; you can now query the snapshot as if it were any other database.

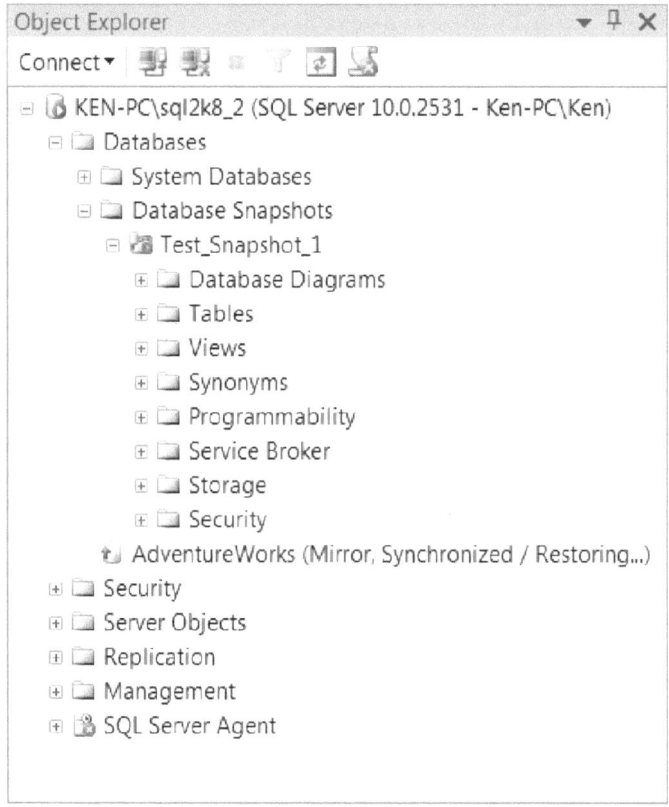

Figure 9-1. Database snapshot location in SQL Server Management Studio

Notice that if you query `sys.database_files` as shown in Figure 9-2, the physical file names are actually the source database file names and not the snapshot file names created in Listing 9-1. Querying the snapshot gives the effect of querying an exact copy of the source database at the time you created the snapshot.

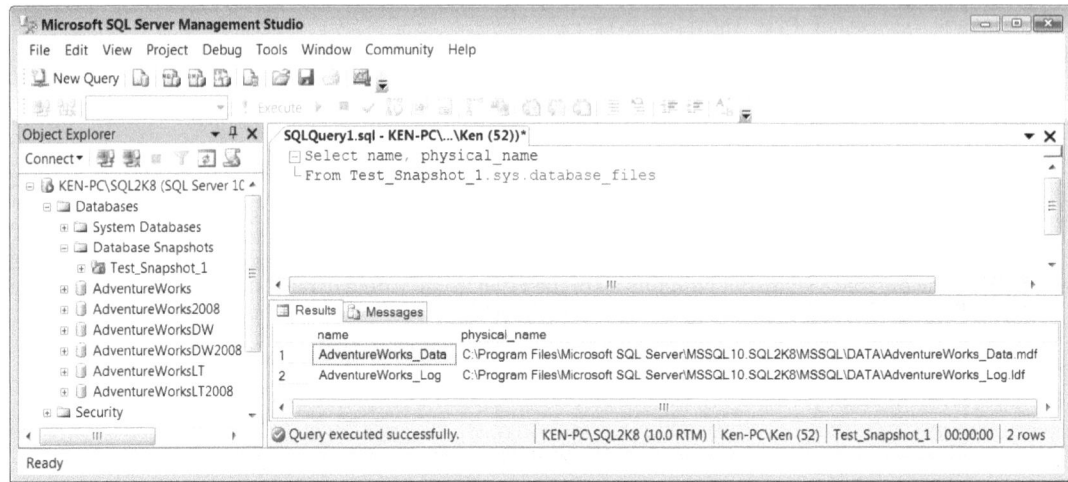

Figure 9-2. Querying sys.database_files from the snapshot returning the source database's metadata

Since querying the snapshot returns metadata about the source database, you have to query the master database by using the query shown in Listing 9-3 to return the metadata for the snapshot.

Listing 9-3. Query to View the Snapshot Metadata

```
SELECT B.name DatabaseName,
            A.name LogicalName,
            B.database_id,
            B.source_database_id,
            A.physical_name
 FROM master.sys.master_files A
           JOIN master.sys.databases B
         ON    A.database_id = B.database_id
```

You can see in Figure 9-3 the result set of Listing 9-3. Notice that the snapshot database name `Test_Snapshot_1` has a value of 6 for the `source_database_id`, which references the `database_id` of the `AdventureWorks` database.

	DatabaseName	LogicalName	database_id	source_database_id	physical_name
1	master	master	1	NULL	C:\Program Files\Microsoft SQL Server\MSSQL10.SQL2K8\MSSQL\DATA\master.mdf
2	master	mastlog	1	NULL	C:\Program Files\Microsoft SQL Server\MSSQL10.SQL2K8\MSSQL\DATA\mastlog.ldf
3	tempdb	tempdev	2	NULL	C:\Program Files\Microsoft SQL Server\MSSQL10.SQL2K8\MSSQL\DATA\tempdb.mdf
4	tempdb	templog	2	NULL	C:\Program Files\Microsoft SQL Server\MSSQL10.SQL2K8\MSSQL\DATA\templog.ldf
5	model	modeldev	3	NULL	C:\Program Files\Microsoft SQL Server\MSSQL10.SQL2K8\MSSQL\DATA\model.mdf
6	model	modellog	3	NULL	C:\Program Files\Microsoft SQL Server\MSSQL10.SQL2K8\MSSQL\DATA\modellog.ldf
7	msdb	MSDBData	4	NULL	C:\Program Files\Microsoft SQL Server\MSSQL10.SQL2K8\MSSQL\DATA\MSDBData.mdf
8	msdb	MSDBLog	4	NULL	C:\Program Files\Microsoft SQL Server\MSSQL10.SQL2K8\MSSQL\DATA\MSDBLog.ldf
9	Test_Snapshot_1	AdventureWorks_Data	5	6	C:\Test_Data.ss
10	AdventureWorks	AdventureWorks_Data	6	NULL	C:\Program Files\Microsoft SQL Server\MSSQL10.SQL2K8\MSSQL\DATA\AdventureWorks_Data.mdf
11	AdventureWorks	AdventureWorks_Log	6	NULL	C:\Program Files\Microsoft SQL Server\MSSQL10.SQL2K8\MSSQL\DATA\AdventureWorks_Log.ldf

Figure 9-3. The result set from querying metadata for a snapshot database

Dropping a Snapshot

To drop a snapshot, all you need to do is issue the `DROP DATABASE` command using the same syntax you would use to drop any database. Run the following statement to drop the `Test_Snapshot_1` database snapshot used in this section:

```
DROP DATABASE  Test_Snapshot_1
```

Rolling Snapshots

Now that you know how to create and drop a database snapshot, let's discuss how you can automate the process so you can use the mirror server for reporting. In order to maintain the most recent data and to keep the snapshots relatively small, you need a way to periodically drop old snapshots and create new ones. The problem with dropping an old snapshot and creating a new one is that everyone connected to the snapshot will be kicked out of the database while you refresh the data. Randomly losing database connectivity every so often will not make for a very good user experience with your reporting environment.

One way to avoid the users losing connectivity is to create rolling snapshots and use application logic to connect to the appropriate snapshot. You can leave the old snapshot available so the users can finish their existing queries and have the application direct new queries to the latest snapshot. You can use the script in Listing 9-4 to create a rolling database snapshot. If you create a job and schedule the script to run once an hour five minutes before the hour, it will create a new database snapshot and append the next hour to the end of the snapshot name. It will also drop any database snapshots that are older than 130 minutes, essentially leaving you with two database snapshots at all times. All you have to do then is code your application so that it always connects to the database snapshot that has the appendix name with current hour.

Listing 9-4. Script to Create Rolling Database Snapshots of the AdventureWorks Database

```
--***Run this script every hour 5 minutes before the hour***

--Set the @NextHour variable to the number of the next hour
DECLARE @NextHour VARCHAR(2) = DATEPART(HOUR,DATEADD(HOUR,1,GETDATE()))

DECLARE @SQL VARCHAR(MAX)

--***Remove any snapshots older than 130 minutes***
```

```
--       ***for the AdventureWorks database***

--Create a string of DROP DATABASE statements
--using the sys.databases table
SELECT @SQL = ISNULL(@SQL,'') + 'DROP DATABASE ' + name + ';'
FROM sys.databases
WHERE source_database_id = DB_ID('AdventureWorks') AND
      create_date < DATEADD(MINUTE,-130,GETDATE())

--Print the DROP DATABASE statements
PRINT @SQL
--Execute the DROP DATABASE statements
EXEC (@SQL)


--***Create a snapshot for the next hour***
SET @SQL =
    'CREATE DATABASE AW_SS_' + @NextHour +
    ' ON
    (NAME = AdventureWorks_Data,
     FILENAME = ''C:\AW_data_' + @NextHour + '.ss'')
     AS SNAPSHOT OF AdventureWorks;'

--Print the CREATE DATABASE statement
PRINT @SQL
--Execute the CREATE DATABASE statement
EXEC (@SQL)
```

You can see in Figure 9-4 output of the PRINT statements from Listing 9-4 in the Messages window. Since we created the Test_Snapshot_1 snapshot against the AdventureWorks database more than 130 minutes ago, it is dropped before a new snapshot AW_SS_15 is created.

Figure 9-4. Results from manually executing the script in Listing 9-4

You can see in Figure 9-5 the final configuration after it has been running a few hours. We have placed the script from Listing 9-4 in a job called Rolling Snapshots and scheduled the job to run every hour of every day between 12:55:00 a.m. and 11:59:59 p.m. As you can see, we only have two snapshots:

AW_SS_17 and AW_SS_18. You can change the settings of the script in Listing 9-4 and the job schedule to meet the needs of your environment. As long as you have some control over the application logic used to connect to SQL Server, using rolling snapshots is a great way to use the mirror server for reporting instead of only having it around for the purposes of high availability and disaster recovery.

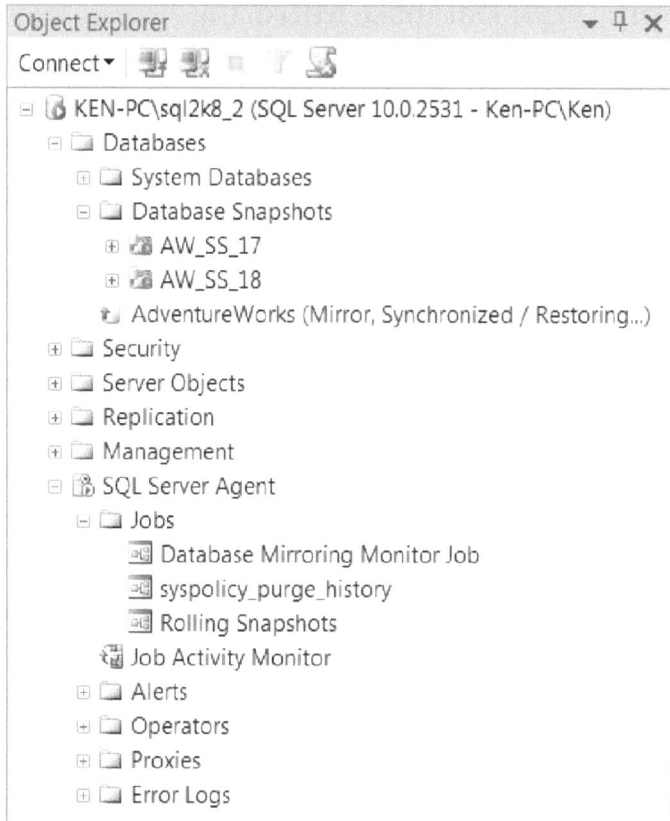

Figure 9-5. Final configuration of rolling snapshot reporting solution

Using Log Shipping

You can use log shipping in conjunction with database mirroring in order to offload reporting to a third server. While log shipping isn't always the best reporting solution, it does provide access to the database as long as you restore the log-shipped database in STANDBY mode. The only time a user cannot access a log-shipped database is when you are actually restoring the logs. You can configure when the logs are restored by setting the restore delay for the log-shipped database. Log shipping works well as a reporting solution when you only need to query day-old data. You can copy the logs to the server during business hours and then apply the logs during off-hours.

You can configure log shipping to work uninterrupted in the event of a database mirroring failover. One benefit log shipping has over database snapshots is that you can run log shipping on the Enterprise, Standard, Workgroup and Web editions of SQL Server, and it does not have to be running the same edition as the mirror servers. Another benefit of using log shipping as a reporting solution is that it provides a third site that can be used as a warm backup in the event of a major disaster. However, with both database snapshots and log shipping, users will lose connectivity while the data is being refreshed.

Implementing Log Shipping with Database Mirroring

Log shipping uses the terms *primary server* for the source database server and *secondary server* for the destination database server. Your principal and mirror servers share the responsibilities of the primary server, and a third server is configured as the secondary server. Both the principal and mirror servers contain the job required to back up the transaction logs to a shared location. The secondary server contains the jobs required to copy and restore the logs from the shared location. In the event that database mirroring fails over, the mirror server (now the new principal) starts sending backups of the transaction logs to the same shared location, and the secondary server is not even aware that a failover occurred. You can see in Figure 9-6 how log shipping works in conjunction with database mirroring.

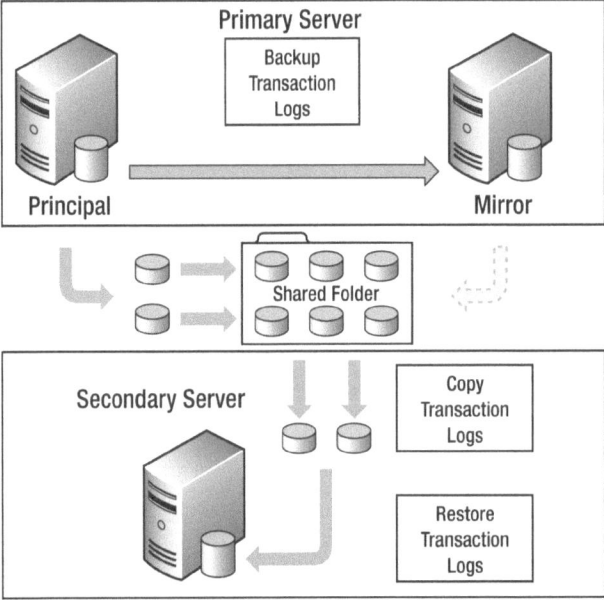

*Figure 9-6. **Log shipping configuration with database mirroring***

Let's walk through the steps required to configure log shipping to work with database mirroring. We are using the same drive for demonstration purposes. You should place your data and log files on separate drives on in a true production environment.

1. Take a Full backup of the principal database. You can use either the GUI or the following BACKUP command.

```
BACKUP DATABASE AdventureWorks TO DISK = N'C:\AWFull.bak'
```

2. Restore the backup on the secondary server WITH STANDBY. It is important that you restore the database WITH STANDBY in order to allow you to query the database between restores. You can use either the GUI or the following RESTORE command.

```
RESTORE DATABASE AdventureWorks
FROM DISK = N'C:\AWFull.bak'
WITH
  MOVE N'AdventureWorks_Data' TO N'C:\SQLData\AdventureWorks.mdf',
  MOVE N'AdventureWorks_Log' TO N'C:\SQLData\AdventureWorks_1.ldf',
  STANDBY = N'C:\SQLData\ROLLBACK_UNDO_AdventureWorks.BAK',
  STATS = 10
```

3. Right-click the principal database and select Properties from the context menu. Select the Transaction Log Shipping page shown in Figure 9-7.

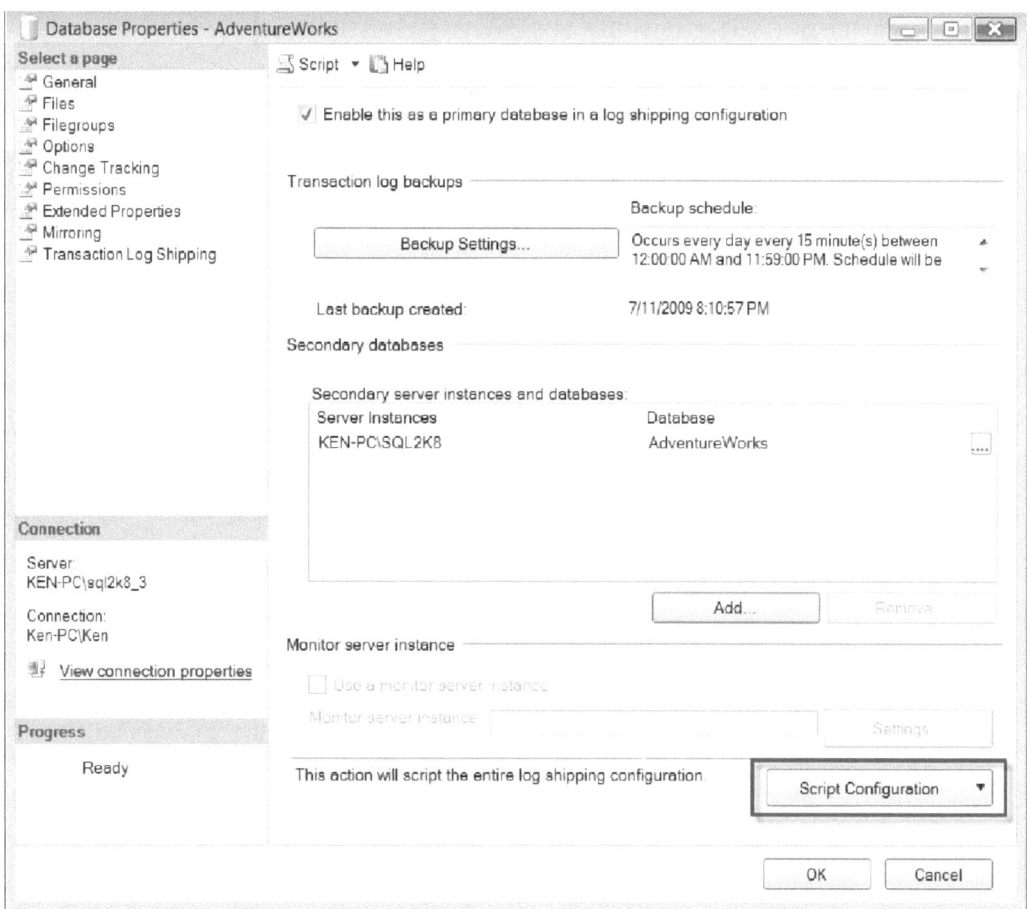

Figure 9-7. Transaction Log Shipping page of the Database Properties dialog box

4. Configure log shipping as you normally would, but before clicking OK, make sure to click Script Configuration (highlighted in Figure 9-7) and select Script Configuration to File from the drop-down to save the configuration script. For more information on configuring log shipping see the topic "How to: Enable Log Shipping (SQL Server Management Studio)" in SQL Server Books Online.

5. Click OK to complete log shipping setup between the principal mirroring server and the secondary log shipping server. Make sure log shipping is working before completing the remaining steps.

6. Change your mirroring configuration to high-safety mode if it is not already. Make sure the partners are synchronized, and then perform a manual failover.

7. Open the script you saved in step 4 and run the code between the following lines on the new principal server against the msdb database. Make sure you do not run the "Script to be run at Secondary" section, because you have already configured the secondary server.

```
-- ****** Begin: Script to be run at Primary: [Server\Instance] ******
...<Code>
-- ****** End: Script to be run at Primary: [Server\Instance]  ******
```

8. Make sure log shipping is working between the two severs, and then you can perform a manual failover to the original principal server.

The backup job will continue to run on the mirror server. You do not need to disable the backup job on the mirror server because it will realize the database cannot be backed up, and it will successfully exit the job as shown in Figure 9-8. Once a failover occurs, the database will be in a state where backups can occur, and the job will take over sending the transaction logs to the shared backup folder.

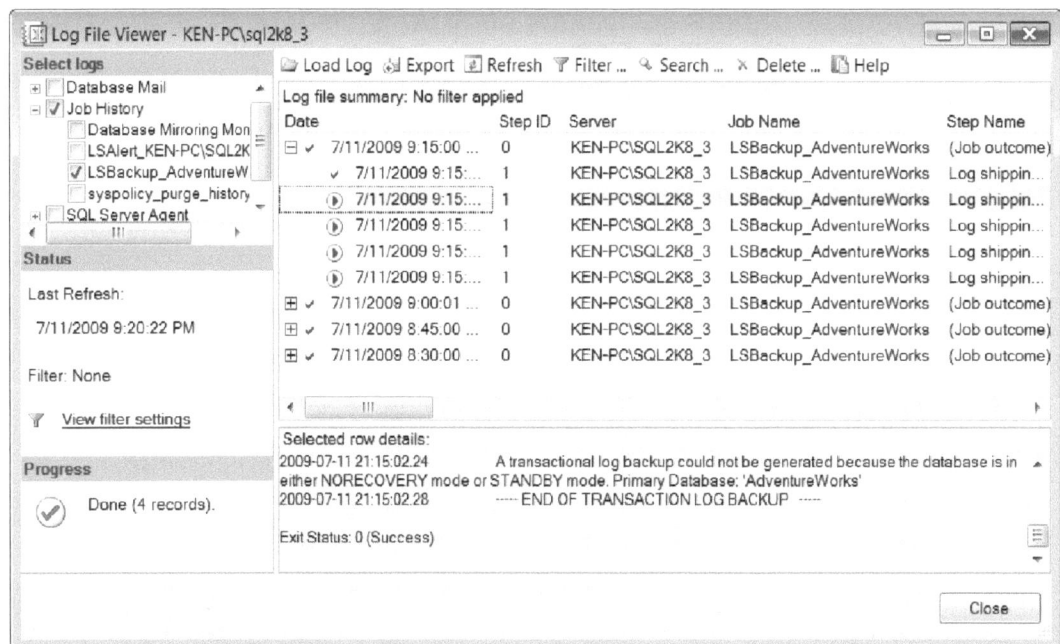

Figure 9-8. *Log shipping backup job on mirror server*

Configuring Log Shipping for Reporting

Now that you have set up log shipping on your mirrored database, you need to make a few additional changes before you are ready to use the log-shipped database for reporting. Every time you restore a transaction log to the log-shipped database, users will lose connectivity with the database. If you are restoring transaction logs every 15 minutes, this would not make for a very user-friendly reporting environment. We said earlier that log shipping makes for a better reporting solution if you can report off day-old data. When this is the case, you can configure the restore delay so that no transaction logs are restored during the day. However, the transaction logs are still copied to the secondary server. During off-hours, you can change the restore delay so that all of the copied transaction logs are continuously restored. Let's take a look at the code in Listing 9-5.

Listing 9-5. Code to Change the Restore Delay for Log Shipping

```
--Set the restore delay to 24 hours
UPDATE msdb.dbo.log_shipping_secondary_databases
SET restore_delay = 1440
WHERE secondary_database = 'AdventureWorks'

--Set the restore delay to 0 minutes
UPDATE msdb.dbo.log_shipping_secondary_databases
SET restore_delay = 0
WHERE secondary_database = 'AdventureWorks'
```

You can create a job on the secondary server that runs the first UPDATE statement in Listing 9-5 right before business hours that sets the restore delay to 1,440 minutes, or 24 hours. This will allow the users uninterrupted access to the database throughout business hours. You can then create a job to run the second UPDATE statement in Listing 9-5 as soon as business hours are over that changes the load delay to 0, which means all of the logs that have been copied to the secondary server throughout the day will immediately begin to be restored. Once log shipping has finished restoring all of the logs built up throughout the day, it will continue to restore any new logs until the job runs again to set the restore delay to 24 hours. You can change the settings in Listing 9-5 to meet your business requirements. For example, you may be able to define reporting hours that will allow you to restore transaction logs during lunch with the expectation that users will not be able to run reports during this time.

Using Replication

Replication refers to the technology behind creating and maintaining duplicate copies of database objects such as tables. For example, you can create a copy of a key table—say, a customer table—in several reporting databases located at different regional offices of your company. You can synchronize those copies manually or automatically. If automatically, you can schedule synchronizations to occur at specific times of day. You can even go so far as to force all replicated copies to be kept fully up to date as transactions against the master copy occur. Replication is best thought of as a way to make business data available in different databases or at different locations. The idea is to give different applications access to the same data or to make data conveniently available for reporting.

Type of Replication Database to Use

The only replication database you can configure to be aware of a database mirroring failover is the publication database. Luckily, this happens to be the principal database in database mirroring, or in other words, the database you need for reporting purposes. One benefit of using replication over database snapshots and log shipping is that replication provides an almost real-time reporting solution because users can access the database while transactions are being applied from the publication database. Another nice benefit of using replication is that you do not have to replicate the entire database. For example, you may only have a few tables you use for reporting purposes and you can replicate just those. You can use snapshot, transactional, and merge replication with database mirroring. However, you must use read-only subscribers or queued updated subscribers, and you cannot use peer-to-peer transactional replication because this allows updates in both databases and requires the database to be both a publisher and a subscriber.

Understanding the Terminology

Replication has its own way of referring to the participating servers and objects. Following is a list of key terms that you should be familiar with while reading this section and when talking about replication in SQL Server:

- *Publisher*: Source server containing the primary database
- *Subscriber*: Target server receiving the publication
- *Distributor*: Server used to keep track of the subscriptions and manage the activity between the publisher and the subscriber
- *Articles*: Database objects being replicated
- *Publications*: Collection of articles
- *Agents*: Executables used to help perform replications tasks

The principal and the mirror database share the same distributor similar to the way they share the same backup folder with log shipping. You should use a separate server as the distributor so that replication will continue to work if the principal server has a failure. The subscription database synchronizes with the publisher using a push or pull subscription. In a *push* subscription, the distributor pushes the data to the subscriber; in a *pull* subscription, the subscriber pulls the data. Replication supports the distribution of publications to many subscribers. The replicated data is first sent from the publisher and then stored on the distributor until the transactions are sent to the subscriber. Replication uses executables called *replication agents* to support certain replication actions that are performed. Different replication agents are used depending on the type of replication that is implemented. The three basic types of replication are known as *snapshot*, *transactional*, and *merge*.

Design Considerations

Replication is supported in all editions of SQL Server with the exception that publishing is not allowed in SQL Server Express or SQL Server Compact 3.5 SP1. Unfortunately, replication requires several up-front design considerations that may prevent you from deploying it in your environment, especially if you are supporting a vendor-supplied application. For example, each table that is published using transactional replication must have a primary key. You can see in Figure 9-9 how transactional replication works in conjunction with database mirroring.

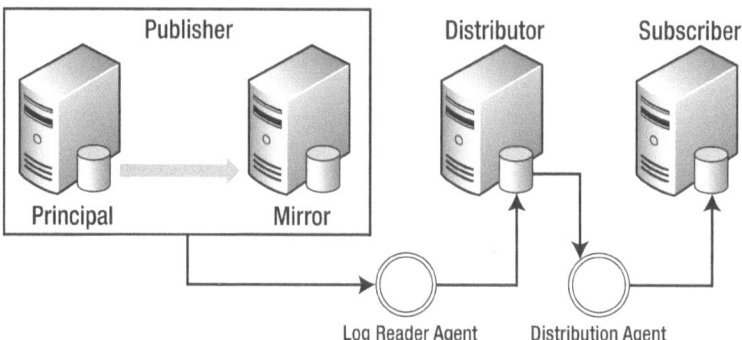

Figure 9-9. *Transactional replication configuration with database mirroring*

The log reader agent only replicates transaction to the distribution databases that have been hardened on both the principal and the mirror server in order to ensure the accuracy of the subscriber in the event of a failover. This means that latency or connection issues between the principal and the mirror affect how recent the data is at the subscriber.

Implementing Replication with Database Mirroring

You can use the following steps to configure replication with database mirroring.

1. Set up a distributor server.

The easiest way to set up a distributor is through the Configure Distribution Wizard. Connect to the SQL Server you will be using as a distributor, right-click the Replication folder, and select Configure Distribution from the context menu. Just like any wizard in SQL Server, the Configure Distribution Wizard easily walks you through the processes of configuring your server as a distributor.

2. Add both the principal and mirror servers as publishers on the distributor.

You can open the Distributor Properties dialog box by right-clicking the Replication folder and selecting "Distributor properties" from the context menu. Select the Publishers page shown in Figure 9-10 and select the Add drop-down to add both the principal and the mirror servers.

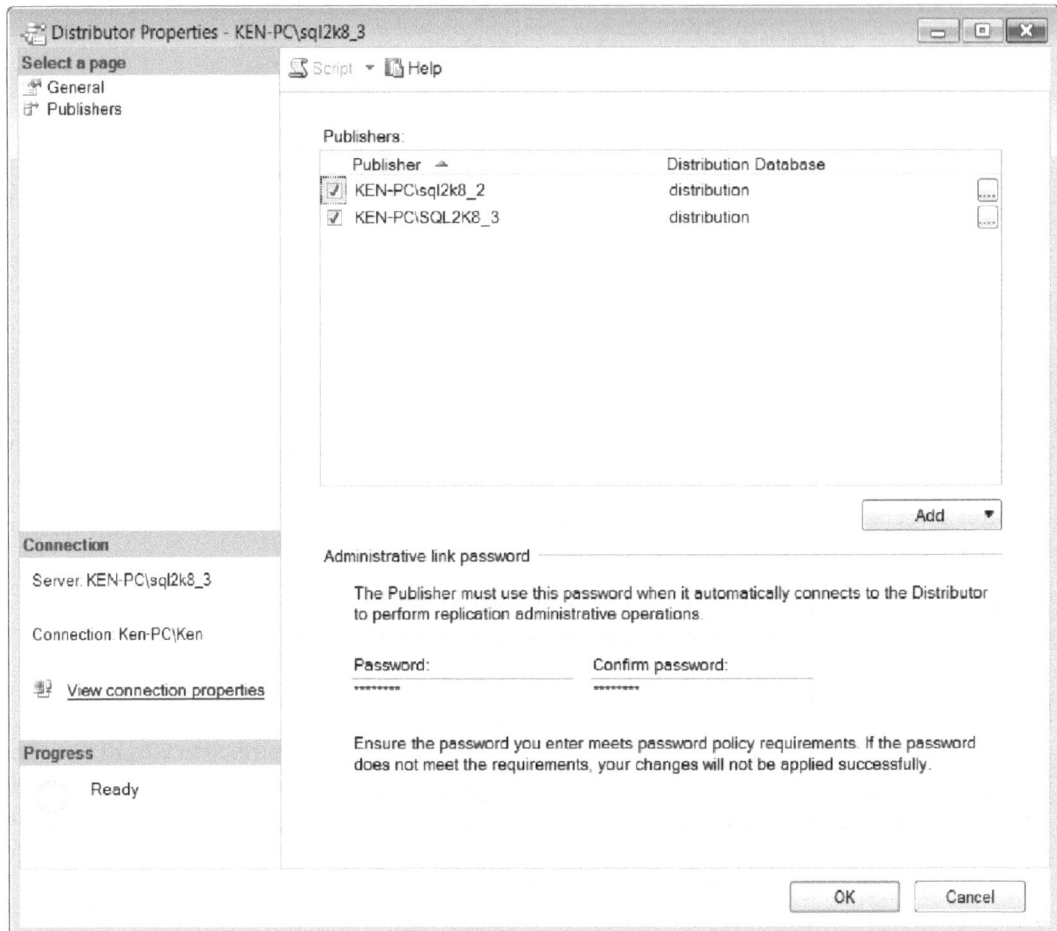

Figure 9-10. Distributor Properties Publishers page

Make sure the principal and the mirror have the same settings. You can open the Publisher Properties dialog box shown in Figure 9-11 by clicking on the ellipsis button on the line with the publisher in the Distributor Properties dialog box.

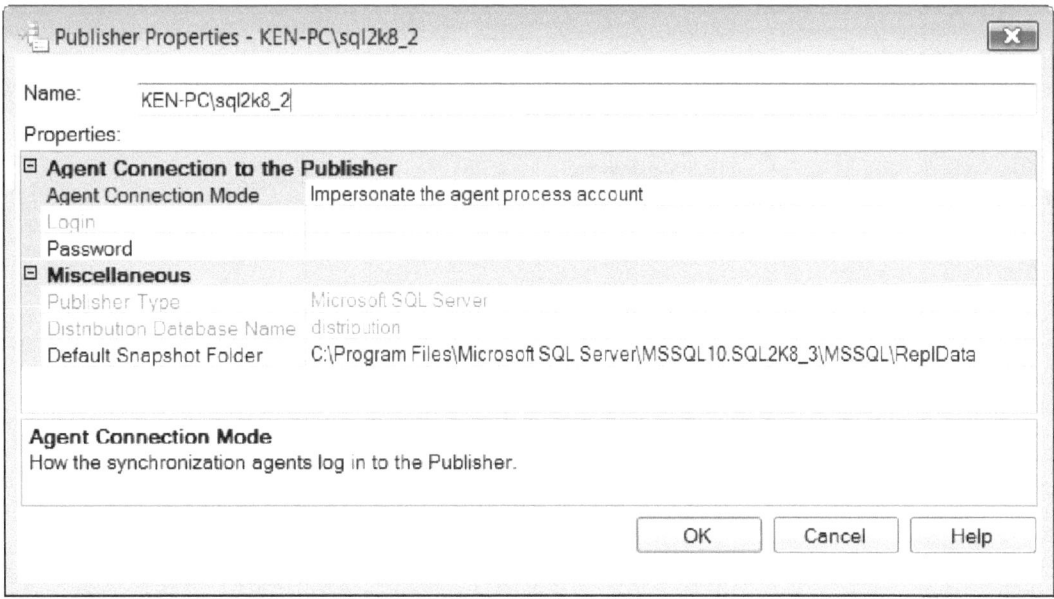

Figure 9-11. Publisher Properties dialog box

3. Create a publication on the principal server.

You can open the New Publication Wizard by right-clicking the Replication folder and selecting New ➤ Publication from the context menu.

4. Create a subscription (push or pull) on the subscriber.

You can open the New Subscription Wizard by right-clicking the Replication folder and selecting New ➤ Subscription from the context menu.

5. Configure replication agents for failover.

You need to configure the –PublisherFailoverPartner parameter for any of the following replication agents.
- Snapshot Agent
- Log Reader Agent
- Queue Reader
- Merge Agent
- SQL Server replication listener
- SQL Merge ActiveX Control

To configure the –PublisherFailoverPartner parameter, open the Distributor Properties dialog box shown in Figure 9-12 by right-clicking the Replication folder and selecting "Distributor properties" from the context menu.

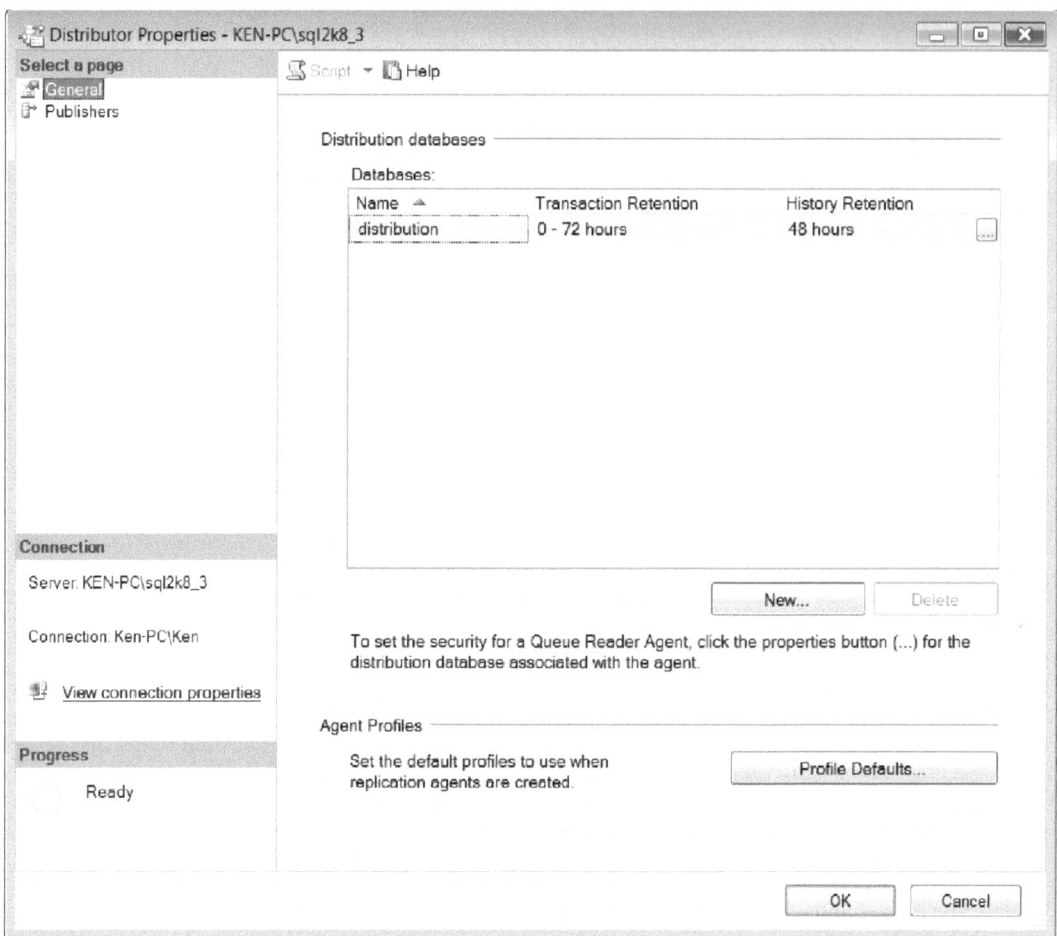

Figure 9-12. Distributor Properties General page

Select Profile Defaults to open the Agent Profiles dialog box shown in Figure 9-13.

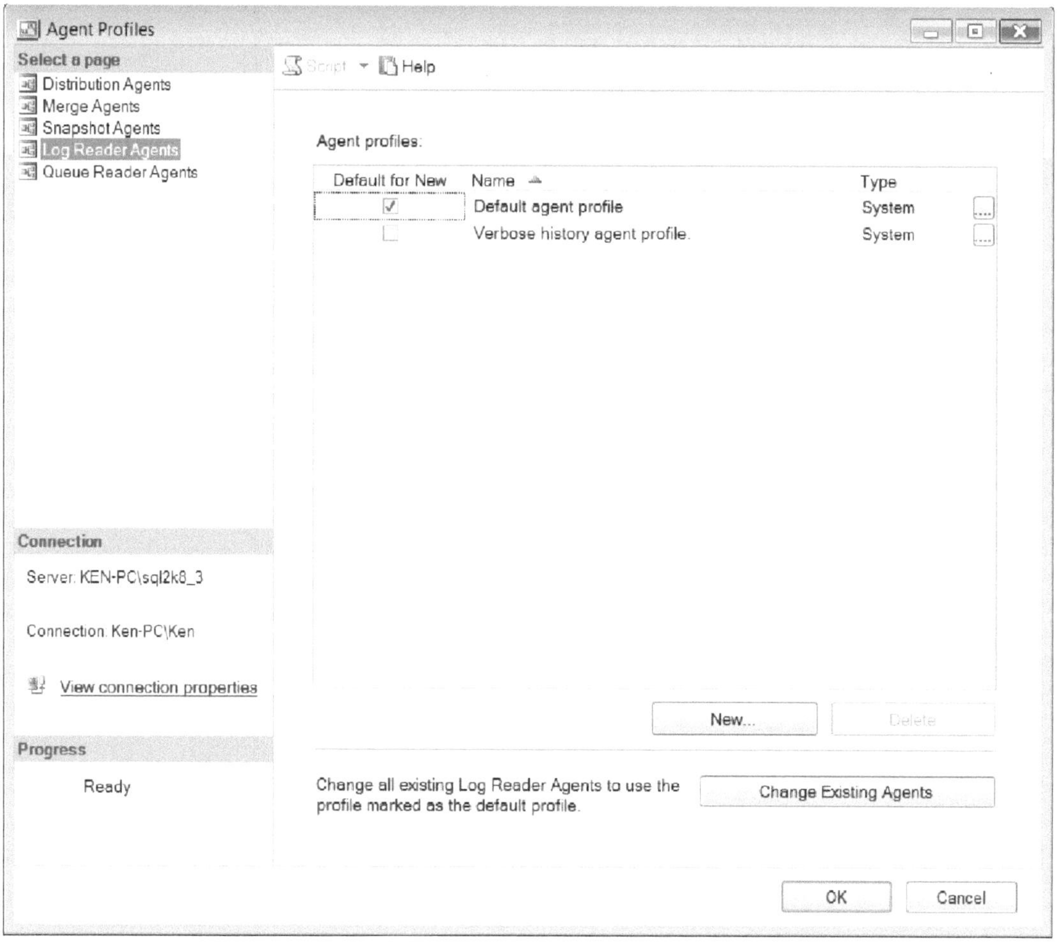

Figure 9-13. Agent Profiles dialog box

You need to create a custom profile in order to set the -PublisherFailoverPartner parameter for any of the existing agent profiles. To create a custom agent profile, select an existing profile and then click the New button to display the New Agent Profile dialog box shown in Figure 9-14.

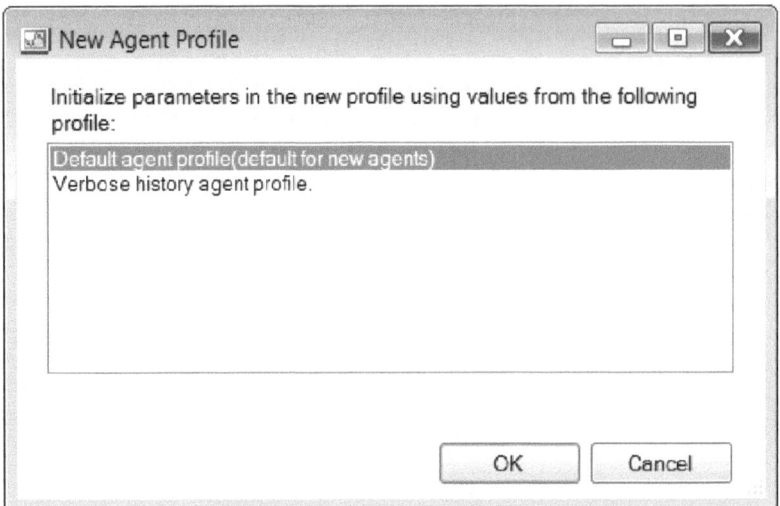

Figure 9-14. New Agent Profile dialog box for parameter initialization

Highlight an existing profile to use as a template and click OK, which will display a second New Agent Profile dialog box shown in Figure 9-15 that allows you to name the profile and set the appropriate parameter.

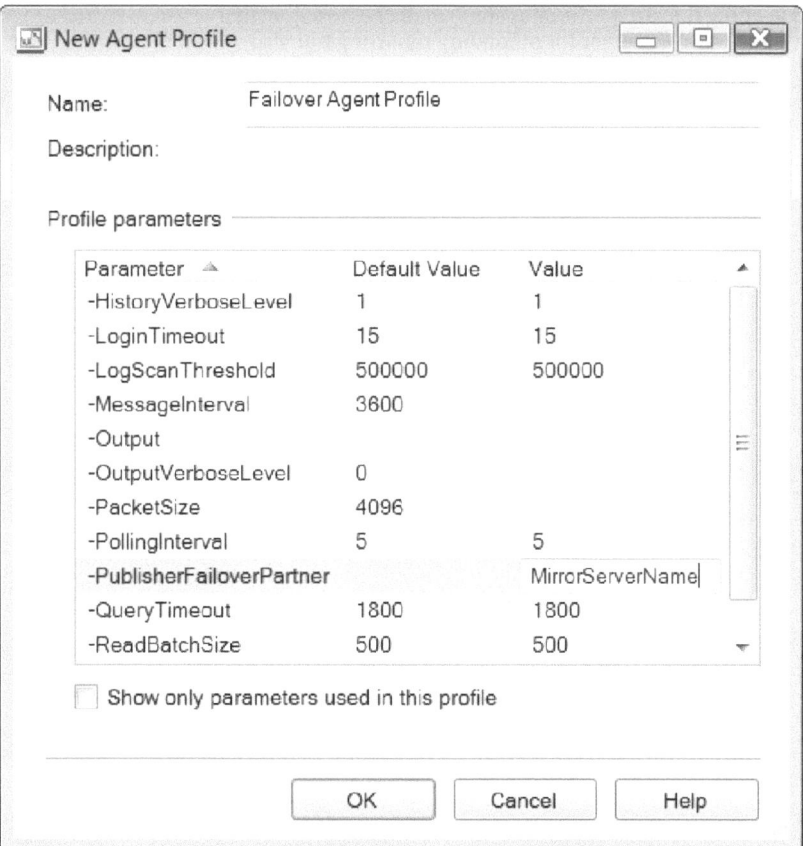

Figure 9-15. New Agent Profile dialog box for configuring parameters

Uncheck the "Show only parameters used in this profile" check box. Find the -PublisherFailoverPartner parameter, enter the mirror server name, and then click OK to return to the Agent Profiles dialog box in Figure 9-13. Select the new profile you just created and click Change Existing Agents. You will need to repeat this process for all of the other replication agents as well.

Summary

In this chapter, we discussed the different reporting options you can use when working with database mirroring. First, we covered how to use a database snapshot in order to query a point-in-time copy of the mirrored database, including a script that will allow you to create rolling snapshots. Next, we discussed how to configure log shipping to work with database mirroring that not only works as a reporting solution but also as another option for DR. Finally, we showed you how to implement replication with database mirroring, which works well when you need near-real-time reporting on a subset of tables.

There is no best solution when it comes to reporting; it all depends on your specific reporting needs. Database snapshots allow you to take advantage of the same hardware used by the mirror, but refreshing the data and keeping the size of the snapshot small can be somewhat of an awkward process. Log shipping offers not only a second server for offloading reporting but also another server that you can use for disasters as well. However, the need to have exclusive access to the database while restoring transaction logs doesn't provide the best reporting solution when you need relatively up-to-date data. While replication is a little more complex to configure than database snapshots and log shipping, it does provide the most up-to-date data with the least interference with the user. Luckily, all of these techniques all work well with database mirroring, and between the three, you should be able to implement the best solution for your environment.

CHAPTER 10

Planning for Failure

Planning for failure is one of the most important things you can do as a DBA. However, you should keep in mind that planning does little good unless you actually test your plans. This is true whether you are talking about backup and recovery, failover clustering, database mirroring, or any other techniques you are using to attain high availability. Having a DBA on staff is like having an insurance policy. Unfortunately, most of the time your phone rings, it's not a user telling you things are going great and to keep up the good work; they only call you when something goes wrong. A crisis or high-stress situation is not the time to realize that a process executes differently than what you originally expected. People will be asking you a lot of questions, and you will be much better off if you already know the answers. You should know what constitutes a failover, how long a failover will take, what happens in different failover scenarios, and what to expect after a failover has occurred. As long as you are well prepared, you will be able to remain calm and make the right decisions when a failure does arise.

Detecting Errors

The first thing you should know when planning for failure is how database mirroring detects and handles specific errors. Database mirroring can encounter two types of errors known as soft errors and hard errors. The amount of time that passes before database mirroring recognizes a failure varies not only between these two error types but also between the actual events that caused the error. You should also keep in mind that there are some errors that may occur that will not cause a failover at all. Once database mirroring recognizes a failure, the time it takes to fail over primarily depends on the amount of data in the redo queue on the mirror server. We will explain each of these errors and even show you how you can estimate the time it will take the mirror server to apply the remaining transactions in the redo queue.

Soft Errors

Soft errors are encountered due to database mirroring reaching a time-out threshold and declaring a failure. Soft errors are the only errors tracked by database mirroring, because soft errors may go undetected by components outside of SQL Server. The default time-out for a soft error is 10 seconds. Some causes of soft errors include:

- Unresponsive OS
- Unresponsive SQL Server instance
- Unresponsive database
- Network time-outs
- Over allocated OS resources (CPU, I/O, memory)

If SQL Server has not received a ping from a partner within the defined time-out threshold, a failover occurs. This is true even if the principal server is actively processing requests. Therefore, it is important to have the time-out set so that you do not encounter false failures due to slow performance. You cannot change the time-out value for high-performance mode; the default value should always be sufficient. However, you can change the time-out value for high-safety mode.

■ **Caution** You should not set the time-out value any lower than the default value of 10 seconds in order to avoid unnecessary failovers.

You can query the `sys.database_mirroring` catalog view to determine the current time-out value as shown in the following query. You can also add the `sys.databases` catalog view in order to get the name of the database and filter out the system databases.

```
SELECT d.name, mirroring_connection_timeout
FROM sys.database_mirroring AS m INNER JOIN
    sys.databases AS d
      ON m.database_id = d.database_id
WHERE m.database_id > 4
```

To change the time-out value, you can use the `ALTER DATABASE` command. For example, you can run the following command to set the time-out value to 20 seconds.

```
ALTER DATABASE [DatabaseName] SET PARTNER TIMEOUT 20
```

Hard Errors

Hard errors are encountered due to a component outside of SQL Server reporting a failure. The time it takes to detect a hard error varies by each component, because each component has different thresholds for reporting failures. Some hard errors cause a failure almost instantly, while others may take up to a minute. Some causes of hard errors include:

- OS failures
- Firewall issues
- Router issues
- Endpoint issues
- Faulty network interface card (NIC)
- Faulty network cables
- Faulty disk drives

An instance of SQL Server crashing is an example of an error that is detected almost instantly. Even though this may seem like a soft error, the OS will actually indicate that the port is closed before the soft error occurs. When SQL Server crashes

- The endpoint port closes.
- The network retry from the partner fails.
- The OS indicates that the port is closed.
- Failover usually begins within a second.

If SQL Server loses a log drive however, failover can take quite a bit longer to begin. When SQL Server loses a log drive

- Pending I/O's are queued for the log drive while the database mirroring pings continue to succeed.
- Twenty seconds later, SQL Server issues an I/O warning.

- It takes another 20 seconds before SQL Server issues an I/O error.
- Failover usually begins in around 40 seconds.

Non-Failover Errors

You should be aware that not every error causes a failover. Users may experience what seems like an outage or interruption of service while the database remains online. While users are experiencing errors, from a database mirroring perspective everything may look fine. For example in SQL Server Enterprise Edition, the database can remain online as long as the primary filegroup is available. You can lose an entire filegroup, and any time users request data from that filegroup they will encounter an error. Another example is corruption. If a user requests data from a corrupt page, they will receive an error. In the background, database mirroring will request the corrupt page from the partner, and the next time the user executes the query they should receive the requested data. However, if corruption causes the state of the database to become inconsistent, SQL Server will place the database in a SUSPECT status, and a failover will occur.

Failover Time

Once an error has been detected and failover begins, how long the failover takes depends mostly on the time it takes to process the remaining logs in the redo queue. This is true for both automatic and manual failovers. Several factors come into play when determining the failover time on the mirror server. For example, the hardware on the mirror server, the current workload on the mirror server, and the size of the redo queue all affect how long a failover will take. Another factor that may delay the failover time is the type of transactions that were in process on the principal server during the failover. For example, if a failover occurs while you are creating an index of a table and then altering that data, you will have to wait for the transaction to either complete or roll back. Database mirroring can also use single-threaded or parallel processing to apply the logs depending on the edition of SQL Server and the number of CPUs on the mirror server. With the Standard Edition of SQL Server, database mirroring always uses a single thread to redo the logs. With Enterprise Edition, database mirroring uses one thread per every four CPUs. For example, if you have five CPUs, database mirroring will use two threads to redo the logs. Generally, the redo phase takes less than a couple of seconds. Once the redo phase completes, the database goes through an undo phase rolling back any transactions that were uncommitted prior to the failover. However, the database is available during the undo phase. Therefore, from an end user perspective, the failover only takes the time it takes to detect an error and redo to logs on the mirror server.

Failure Scenarios

When you are using database mirroring, it is important to understand what happens in different failure scenarios so you are not surprised by unexpected behavior. This is especially true when using the automatic failover capabilities of high-safety mode. Depending on the location of your witness server, a simple network error could cause an automatic failover to the mirror server from a perfectly functioning principal server. In order to avoid unanticipated failovers and take the proper actions when a failover occurs, it is important to understand how a server failure, or network failure for that matter, affects the rest of the servers participating in a database mirroring session. Let's look at five different failure scenarios and discuss how each scenario affects the availability of the data.

■ **Note** No matter what mode of database mirroring you are using, you should test your failover strategies and feel comfortable that you can recover in the event of a failure.

Scenario 1: Principal Server Unavailable

Scenario 1 involves a failure on the principal server as shown in Figure 10-1. This is the most common scenario we all think of when we are configuring database mirroring with automatic failover.

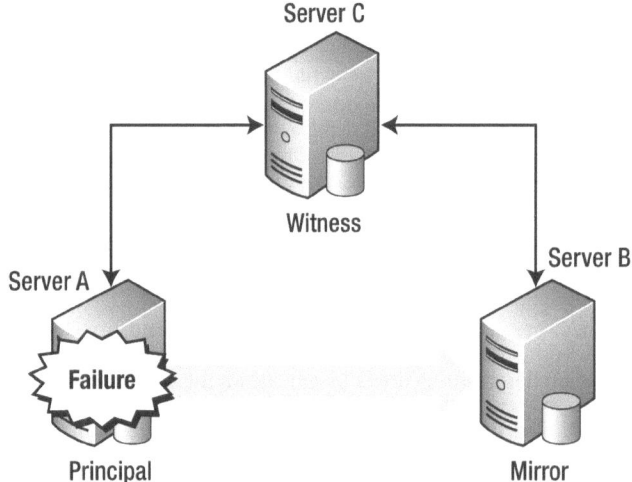

Figure 10-1. *Principal server unavailable*

When the principal server fails, the mirror server and the witness server still have a quorum. The witness server and the mirror server both agree that the principal server is down, and the failover process begins. Server B is now the new principal server. At this point database mirroring is said to be *running exposed* because if another failure occurs, there is no action that can be taken to allow the database to remain online. As long as Server A is down, transaction logs are building up on Server B. None of the transactions in the transaction log on Server B can be truncated as long as database mirroring is still configured. This situation could cause excessive transaction log growth and eventually lead to a failure on Server B, so if Server A is going to be offline for an extended period of time, you should remove database mirroring and set it up from scratch once Server A is available again. If Server A comes online before you remove database mirroring, Server A automatically takes on the role of the new mirror server and the partners begin to synchronize. However, the synchronization process may take quite a while depending on the size of the unsent log.

Scenario 2: Witness Server Unavailable

Scenario 2 involves a failure on the witness server as shown in Figure 10-2.

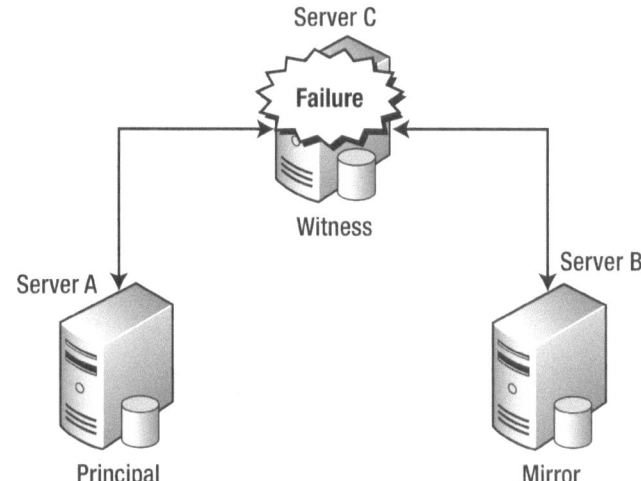

Figure 10-2. *Witness server unavailable*

In this scenario, database mirroring continues to work; you just lose the capabilities for automatic failover. However, if your witness server is going to be offline for an extended period of time, you should remove it from your database mirroring configuration and add it back once it becomes available. When you are running database mirroring with a witness, you need two servers in order to form a quorum, or SQL Server will suspend your database mirroring session to avoid what is known as *split brain*. If any other server fails, the remaining instance of SQL Server has no idea whether the two other servers have teamed up and started the failover process, so the safest thing to do is just stop accepting transactions to maintain data consistency. This is also true if you are using a witness server in high-performance mode. That is why you should not use a witness in high-performance mode; a witness server cannot provide automatic failover, and it can only hurt matters if server availability is lost.

Scenario 3: Mirror Server Unavailable

Scenario 3 involves a failure on the mirror server as shown in Figure 10-3.

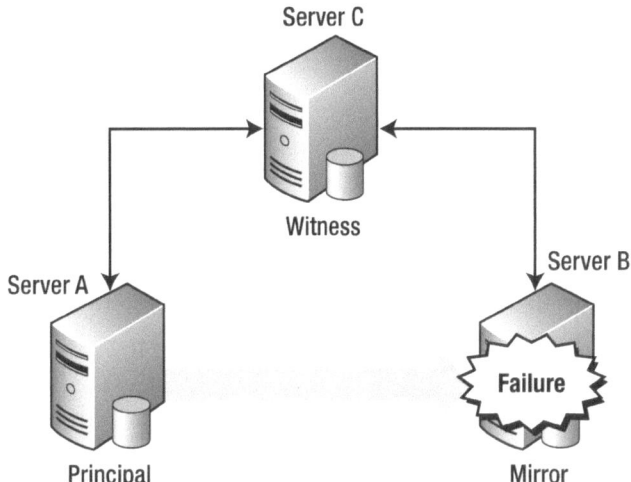

Figure 10-3. *Mirror server unavailable*

When the mirror server is unavailable, the principal server continues to accept transactions because it still has a quorum with the witness server. Now, database mirroring is running exposed until the mirror server is available again. Also, the transactions continue to build up on the principal server until they can be transferred to the mirror server. Just like Scenario 1, this log buildup can eventually cause the drive to fill up and the database to crash. Therefore, if the mirror server is going to be down for an extended period of time, you should break database mirroring and set it up once the mirror is available again. Also, a failure of the witness server at this point will cause the principal server to stop processing transactions to avoid a split-brain situation.

Let's take this scenario a bit further. You know that Server A has actively been processing requests since the loss of Server B. What happens if Server A crashes and then you bring Server B online? Because transactions have occurred on Server A since the failure on Server B, Server B will come online, take the role of the mirror server again, and wait for Server A to resume the role as principal. Database mirroring behaves this way to protect you from automatically losing the transactions that have occurred since the original failure of Server B.

Scenario 4: Mirror Server and Witness Server Unavailable

Scenario 4 involves a failure on the mirror server and the witness server as shown in Figure 10-4. Although it is unlikely that you will lose two servers at the same time, it is possible for the principal server to lose connectivity with both servers. For example, you may have your witness server and your mirror server in one data center and your principal server in another. If you lose connectivity between data centers, from the perspective of the principal server the witness server and the mirror server are unavailable.

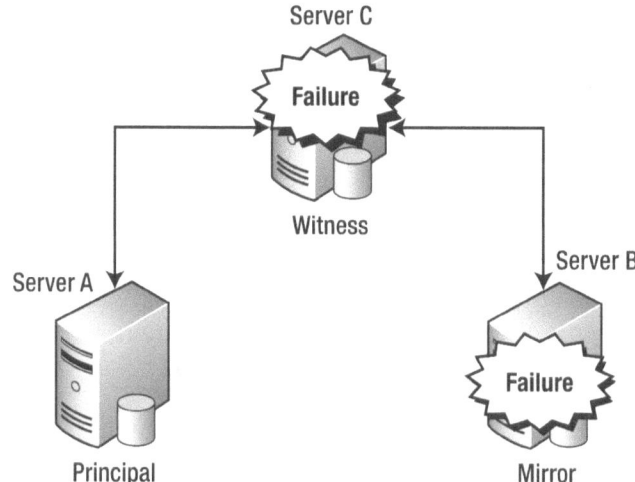

Figure 10-4. Mirror server and witness server unavailable

You may have guessed by now that if the principal server cannot communicate with the mirror server or the witness server, it will stop processing transactions. This is where the placement of the witness server becomes very critical. Do you really want to cause a failover because of a connection issue between data centers? If your witness server and your mirror server lose connectivity with the principal server and can still communicate with each other, they will form a quorum and fail over (even if all three servers are still properly functioning). If possible, you should place your witness server at a third location. If a third location is out of the question, you should place your witness server in the same location as your principal server.

Scenario 5: Principal Server and Witness Server Unavailable

Scenario 5 involves a failure on the principal server and the witness server as shown in Figure 10-5. Just as with Scenario 4, it is unlikely that you will have two server failures at once, but again, a network or connectivity issue between the servers would most likely cause Scenario 5.

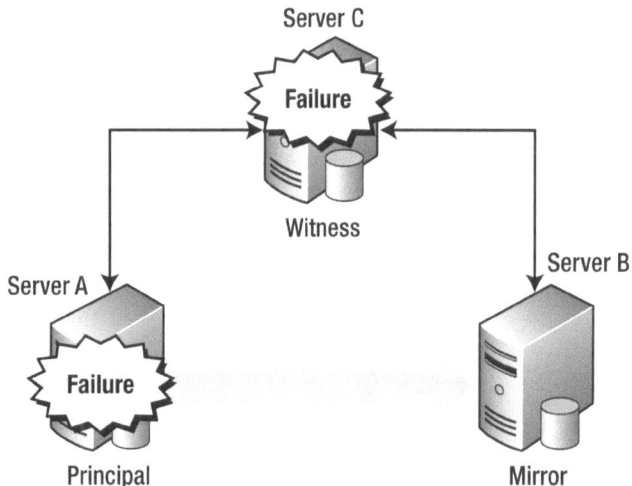

Figure 10-5. *Principal server and witness server unavailable*

If both the principal server and the witness server are unavailable, the mirror server cannot from a quorum, so no automatic failover occurs and the database is down. However, this scenario assumes that the witness server fails followed by the principal server; otherwise, the mirror server would have probably had time to form a quorum with the witness server and a failover would have occurred. At this point, if the witness server is brought back online Server B will not assume the role of the principal server because it cannot guarantee that no transactions have occurred on Server A since they last communicated. As soon as you bring up Server A and Server C, database mirroring will resume normal operations. If you have completely lost Server A, you will have to bring the database on Server B online manually with the understanding that you could potentially lose data by running the following commands.

```
ALTER DATABASE [DatabaseName] SET PARTNER OFF
RESTORE DATABASE [DatabaseName] WITH RECOVERY
```

Procedure to Drop Mirroring Sessions

You have seen in several of the preceding failure scenarios that if the mirroring partner does not come back online within an acceptable amount of time, you may need to drop the mirroring sessions to prevent excessive log growth. You can use the following procedure called dba_DropMirroring to drop mirroring sessions for mirrored databases. You can execute the procedure on either the mirror or the principal server, and you can drop mirroring for either a single database or all databases. You only need to provide a single input for this procedure that tells the procedure which mirroring sessions to drop. You have to provide a hard value of "drop all" in order to drop the mirroring sessions for all mirrored databases or a single database name to drop the mirroring session for that database. If you do not provide a value for the @DBName parameter, the procedure will return help information. Following is the code for the procedure:

```
CREATE PROCEDURE dbo.dba_DropMirroring
        @DBName sysname = NULL -- NULL returns help text
AS
DECLARE @SQL NVARCHAR(1000),
        @MaxID INT,
        @CurrID INT,
        @PartnerServer sysname

DECLARE @Databases TABLE (DatabaseID INT IDENTITY(1, 1) NOT NULL PRIMARY KEY,
                                              DBName sysname NOT NULL)


SET NOCOUNT ON

-- Returns help info if no value entered
IF @DBName IS NULL
  GOTO PrintHelp

IF @DBName <> 'drop all'
  BEGIN
    -- Check to see if database is mirrored
    IF EXISTS (SELECT 1
                       FROM sys.database_mirroring WITH(nolock)
                       WHERE database_id = DB_ID(@DBName) AND
                                         mirroring_role IS NULL)-- NULL = not
mirrored
      BEGIN
        RAISERROR('%s is either not mirrored or is not currently in the principal
role.',
                              1, 1, @DBName)
          GOTO Failed
      END

      IF EXISTS (SELECT 1
                       FROM sys.database_mirroring WITH(nolock)
                       WHERE database_id = DB_ID(@DBName) AND
                                        mirroring_role IS NOT NULL)
        BEGIN
          SET @SQL = 'Alter Database ' + QUOTENAME(@DBName) +
                                  ' Set Partner Off;'
```

```
            EXEC sp_executesql @SQL
          END
  END
ELSE
  BEGIN
    INSERT INTO @Databases (DBName)
    SELECT DB_NAME(D.database_id)
    FROM sys.databases D INNER JOIN
                 sys.database_mirroring DM
                  ON DM.database_id = D.database_id
    WHERE D.state = 0 -- online AND
                    DM.mirroring_state IN (2, 4) AND-- Synchronizing, Synchronized
                    DM.mirroring_role IS NOT NULL

    SELECT @MaxID = MAX(DatabaseID),
                    @CurrID = 1
    FROM @Databases

    /* Turn of Partner Instance */
    WHILE @CurrID <= @MaxID
      BEGIN
        SELECT @DBName = DBName
        FROM @Databases
        WHERE DatabaseID = @CurrID

        SET @SQL = 'Alter Database ' + QUOTENAME(@DBName) +
                              ' Set Partner Off;'

        EXEC sp_executesql @SQL

        SET @CurrID = @CurrID + 1
      END
  END

GOTO Completed
Failed:
PrintHelp:
  PRINT 'Procedure: dbo.dba_DropMirroring'
  PRINT 'Parameters: @DBName sysname, default = Null'
  PRINT CHAR(9) + CHAR(9) +
```

```
'When Null, procedure returns help information about the procedure.'
PRINT CHAR(9) + CHAR(9) +
'When set to name of a mirrored database, '  +

' drops mirroring for that database only.'
PRINT CHAR(9) + CHAR(9) +
'When set to "drop all", drops mirroring for all mirrored databases.'
PRINT CHAR(9) + CHAR(9) +
'When set to name of a non-mirrored database, returns a warning.'
PRINT 'Purpose: Drops mirroring for the selected database or for all databases.'
PRINT 'Examples: Exec dbo.dba_DropMirroring @DBName = ''MirrorTest'''
PRINT CHAR(9) + CHAR(9) +
'Exec OpsDB.dbo.ops_DropMirroring @DBName = ''drop all'''
PRINT CHAR(9) + CHAR(9) +
'Exec OpsDB.dbo.ops_DropMirroring'
PRINT 'Tasks performed:'
PRINT CHAR(9) +
'1. If a single database name is supplied:'
PRINT CHAR(9) + CHAR(9) +
'a. Verifies that the database is mirrored.'
PRINT CHAR(9) + CHAR(9) +
'b. Drops database mirroring for the specified database.'
PRINT CHAR(9) + CHAR(9) +
'c. Leaves the mirrored database in a restoring mode.'
PRINT CHAR(9) +
'2. If "drop all" is supplied:'
PRINT CHAR(9) + CHAR(9) +
'a. Drops all database mirroring sessions on the server.'
PRINT CHAR(9) + CHAR(9) +
'b. Leaves all mirrored databases in a restoring mode.'
PRINT CHAR(9) +
'3. Else:'
PRINT CHAR(9) + CHAR(9) +
'a. Returns a warning and/or help information'
Completed:
PRINT ''
```

Failover Considerations

One of the things you should take into consideration is that you cannot mirror system databases such as master and msdb. The master database is where logins are stored, and the msdb database contains all of your jobs for SQL Server Agent. If you do not maintain the same user logins on your mirror server, users will not be able to login after a failover, and you will have to manually fix those users. Also, if you need any jobs to run on your mirror server after a failover, you should make sure you have them on the mirror server as well. These considerations do not stop with logins and jobs. Anything you rely on outside the mirrored database should be available on the mirror server, even at the OS level. Following are some things you should take into consideration that may impact a seamless failover to the mirror server.

- SQL Server logins
- SQL Server Agent jobs
- Interdependencies between databases
- Windows Scheduled Tasks
- SSIS/DTS packages
- Linked servers
- User-defined error messages
- Database encryption
- Startup procedures
- Extended stored procedures
- Instance-level settings such as enabling Common Language Runtime (CLR), Database Mail, or xp_cmdshell
- OS files and folder structures
- OS-level permissions such as server logins and shared folders

One or all of these objects outside the mirror database may affect you; however, it only takes one missing piece to cause a disruption to the user during a failover. There are two particularly helpful articles in SQL Server Books Online that you can use to help you make sure you are prepared in the event of a failover. You can use "Managing Logins and Jobs After Role Switching" located at http://go.microsoft.com/fwlink/?LinkId=93761&clcid=0x409 for help specifically pertaining to logins and jobs. You can use "Managing Metadata When Making a Database Available on Another Server Instance" located at http://msdn.microsoft.com/en-us/library/ms187580.aspx that will help you with many of the other objects you should be concerned with during a failover.

Procedure to Copy Logins and Roles

Many of the failover considerations are specific to your environment; however, it is pretty safe to say that you should set up a job to copy logins and roles to the mirror server. If you create a job to copy the logins and roles to the mirror server, you will not have to remember to do manually do it every time you add one to the principal server. You can use the following procedure called dba_CopyLogins to automatically copy the logins and roles from the principal server to the mirror server. You should schedule this procedure to run at least once a day. You can also use the procedure to keep the logins and roles in sync while you are preparing your servers for database mirroring. The only parameter you need to pass the dba_CopyLogins procedure is the name of the partner server where you would like to copy the logins and roles. Following is the code for the procedure:

```
CREATE PROCEDURE dbo.dba_CopyLogins
        @PartnerServer sysname

AS
```

```
DECLARE @MaxID INT,
        @CurrID INT,
        @SQL NVARCHAR(MAX),
        @LoginName sysname,
        @RoleName sysname,
        @Machine sysname

DECLARE @Logins TABLE (LoginID INT IDENTITY(1, 1) NOT NULL PRIMARY KEY,
                                        [Name] sysname NOT NULL,
                                        [SID] varbinary(85) NOT NULL,
                                        IsDisabled INT NOT NULL)

DECLARE @Roles TABLE (RoleID INT IDENTITY(1, 1) NOT NULL PRIMARY KEY,
                                        RoleName sysname NOT NULL,
                                        LoginName sysname NOT NULL)

SET NOCOUNT ON

IF CHARINDEX('\', @PartnerServer) > 0
  BEGIN
    SET @Machine = LEFT(@PartnerServer, CHARINDEX('\', @PartnerServer) - 1)
  END
ELSE
  BEGIN
    SET @Machine = @PartnerServer
  END

-- Get all Windows logins from principal server
SET @SQL = 'Select name, sid, is_disabled' + CHAR(10) +
        'From ' + QUOTENAME(@PartnerServer) + '.master.sys.server_principals' +
        CHAR(10) + 'Where type In (''U'', ''G'')' + CHAR(10) +
        'And CharIndex('''' + @Machine + '''', name) = 0';

INSERT INTO @Logins (Name, SID, IsDisabled)
EXEC sp_executesql @SQL;

-- Get all roles from principal server
SET @SQL = 'Select RoleP.name, LoginP.name' + CHAR(10) + 'From ' +
        QUOTENAME(@PartnerServer) + '.master.sys.server_role_members RM' +
        CHAR(10) + 'Inner Join ' +
```

```
                QUOTENAME(@PartnerServer) + '.master.sys.server_principals RoleP' +
                CHAR(10) + CHAR(9) + 'On RoleP.principal_id = RM.role_principal_id' +
                CHAR(10) + 'Inner Join ' +
                QUOTENAME(@PartnerServer) + '.master.sys.server_principals LoginP' +
                CHAR(10) + CHAR(9) + 'On LoginP.principal_id = RM.member_principal_id' +
                CHAR(10) + 'Where LoginP.type In (''U'', ''G'')' + CHAR(10) +
                'And RoleP.type = ''R''' + CHAR(10) +
                'And CharIndex(''' + @Machine + ''', LoginP.name) = 0';

INSERT INTO @Roles (RoleName, LoginName)
EXEC sp_executesql @SQL;

SELECT @MaxID = MAX(LoginID), @CurrID = 1
FROM @Logins

WHILE @CurrID <= @MaxID
  BEGIN
    SELECT @SQL = 'If Not Exists (Select 1' + CHAR(10) + CHAR(9) +
                  'From sys.server_principals' + CHAR(10) + CHAR(9) +
                  'Where name = ''' + Name + ''')' + CHAR(10) + CHAR(9) +
                  'Create Login ' + QUOTENAME(Name) + ' From Windows;' +
                  CASE IsDisabled WHEN 1 THEN CHAR(10) + CHAR(9) +
                  ' Alter Login ' + QUOTENAME(Name) + ' Disable;'
                  ELSE '' END
    FROM @Logins
    WHERE LoginID = @CurrID

    EXEC sp_executesql @SQL

    SET @CurrID = @CurrID + 1
  END

SELECT @MaxID = MAX(RoleID), @CurrID = 1
FROM @Roles

WHILE @CurrID <= @MaxID
  BEGIN
    SELECT @LoginName = LoginName,
                  @RoleName = RoleName
    FROM @Roles
```

```
    WHERE RoleID = @CurrID

    IF NOT EXISTS (SELECT 1
                        FROM sys.server_role_members RM INNER JOIN
                              sys.server_principals RoleP
                            ON RoleP.principal_id = RM.role_principal_id
                          INNER JOIN sys.server_principals LoginP
                        ON LoginP.principal_id = RM.member_principal_id↵
                    WHERE LoginP.type IN ('U', 'G') AND
                              RoleP.type = 'R' AND
                              RoleP.name = @RoleName AND
                              LoginP.name = @LoginName)
      BEGIN
        EXEC sp_addsrvrolemember @rolename = @RoleName,
                                            @loginame = @LoginName;

      END

      SET @CurrID = @CurrID + 1
  END
```

Planning and Research

Configuring and maintaining a highly available database environment takes a lot of planning and research. Luckily, there is no shortage of information. There are several resources available such as web sites, white papers, webcasts, podcasts, and even free training events. You should definitely take advantage of the knowledge and experience offered by others to help you enhance your environment. If you have a question or an issue, chances are that you are not the first and that there is already a well-documented solution on the Internet; you just need to know where to find it. The next few sections contain several links that will help you with your planning and research, along with finding the answers to any question or issues you may encounter along the way.

SQL Server Web Sites

There is a forum completely dedicated to database mirroring located at http://social.msdn.microsoft.com/Forums/en-US/sqldatabasemirroring. Following are a few other web sites that you may find useful. Not only do these web sites offer several useful scripts and articles, there are also plenty of people who frequent these web sites and who are willing to answer any questions you may have.

- Professional Association for SQL Server (www.sqlpass.org)
- SQL Server Central (www.sqlservercentral.com)
- Simple-Talk (www.simple-talk.com/sql)
- SQLServerPedia (www.sqlserverpedia.com)
- MSSQLTips.com (www.mssqltips.com)
- SQLTeam.com (www.sqlteam.com)

- SQL Server Performance (`www.sql-server-performance.com`)
- SQL Server Community (`www.sqlcommunity.com`)

White Papers

White papers offer an in-depth look into a specific topic within SQL Server, and there are several good white papers on database mirroring. Even though some of the following white papers were written specifically for SQL Server 2005, the information is still relevant for SQL Server 2008 as well.

- SQL Server Replication: Providing High Availability Using Database Mirroring (`http://download.microsoft.com/download/d/9/4/d948f981-926e-40fa-a026-5bfcf076d9b9/ReplicationAndDBM.docx`)
- Database Mirroring and Log Shipping Working Together (`http://download.microsoft.com/download/d/9/4/d948f981-926e-40fa-a026-5bfcf076d9b9/DBMandLogShipping.docx`)
- Implementing Application Failover with Database Mirroring (`www.microsoft.com/technet/prodtechnol/sql/bestpractice/implappfailover.mspx`)
- Database Mirroring Best Practices and Performance Considerations (`http://technet.microsoft.com/library/cc917681`)
- Database Mirroring in SQL Server 2005 (`http://technet.microsoft.com/en-us/library/cc917680.aspx`)
- Database Mirroring FAQ (`http://technet.microsoft.com/en-us/cc984166.aspx`)
- Using SQL Server Database Mirroring with Office SharePoint Server and Windows SharePoint Services (`http://go.microsoft.com/fwlink/?LinkId=83725&clcid=0x409`)

Webcasts

Microsoft occasionally hosts webcasts on database mirroring that tend to last about an hour. Webcasts usually go pretty deep into a specific topic, even going into demonstrations and code samples. You can visit the Microsoft Events home page at `http://msevents.microsoft.com` to search for prerecorded or upcoming webcasts as well as many other events. Following is a list of prerecorded webcasts specifically covering database mirroring:

- Implementing Database Mirroring in SQL Server 2005 (Part 1 of 2) (`http://msevents.microsoft.com/cui/WebCastEventDetails.aspx?culture=en-US&EventID=1032290576&CountryCode=US`)
- Implementing Database Mirroring in SQL Server 2005 (Part 2 of 2) (`http://msevents.microsoft.com/cui/WebCastEventDetails.aspx?EventID=1032290565&EventCategory=5&culture=en-US&CountryCode=US`)
- How to Increase Availability Using Database Mirroring in SQL Server 2005 (`http://msevents.microsoft.com/cui/WebCastEventDetails.aspx?EventID=1032282290&EventCategory=5&culture=en-US&CountryCode=US`)
- Level Database Mirroring: Why, When and How? (`http://msevents.microsoft.com/CUI/WebCastEventDetails.aspx?culture=en-US&EventID=1032282668&CountryCode=US`)

Podcasts

Podcasts are another resource that many people often overlook. Podcasts are a great way to learn things while you are on the go. One good thing about the Microsoft webcasts is that you can download them in both audio and video formats. However, we have downloaded the audio versions and didn't find a lot of value in listening to a demo; you really need to see what's going on. Several free podcasts are available for download. Some of the available podcasts include

- The Voice of the DBA (http://sqlservercentral.mevio.com)
- SSWUG.org (www.sswug.org/media)
- SQL Down Under (www.sqldownunder.com)
- Microsoft Events (www.microsoft.com/events/podcasts)
- SQLServerPedia (http://sqlserverpedia.com/wiki/SQL_Server_Tutorials)

Free Training Events

Always be on the lookout for free training events in your area. Many times Microsoft will come near your area with a road show to present some of the latest technology. SQL Saturday is another way to get free training. SQL Saturday is a one-day training event packed full of sessions dealing with all aspects of SQL Server. Finally, find a local users group and get involved. Local users groups generally have monthly meetings with a one-hour session that covers various topics within SQL Server. A local users group is a good way to network with other SQL Server professionals in your area and learn something new in the process. You can find more information at the following links.

- www.msdnevents.com
- www.sqlsaturday.com
- www.sqlpass.org/PASSChapters.aspx

Microsoft Support Options

When all else fails, Microsoft offers several support options to help you with anything from researching implementation to assisting you in the event of a disaster. You can choose something as basic as per-incident support to an all-out enterprise support agreement. You can find the option that meets your needs on the Microsoft Help and Support web site located at http://support.microsoft.com/default.aspx?scid=fh;EN-US;OfferProPhone. The following table shows the Problem Resolution Services support options at the time of this writing. Business hours are Monday through Friday from 6:00 a.m. to 6:00 p.m. Pacific Time.

Table 10-1. Microsoft Problem Resolution Services Support Options

Support Option	Price
E-mail only support	$99 (one incident)
Business hours telephone support	$259 (one incident)
Business hours telephone support	$1,289 (five-pack of incidents)
Business-critical after hours telephone support	$515 (one incident)

The next level of support is Microsoft Advisory Services. Contacting Microsoft Advisory Services is like hiring an offsite consultant for a rate of $210 per hour. Microsoft Advisory Services consist of a short-term agreement that allows you to work with the same technician. This provides a higher level of support, offering analysis and recommendations that go beyond the scope of Problem Resolution Services. You can read more about Advisory Services by visiting their web site located at `http://support.microsoft.com/gp/advisoryservice`. Finally, if you have enterprise support needs that go beyond Microsoft Services, you can visit the Enterprise Support web site located at `www.microsoft.com/services/microsoftservices/srv_enterprise.mspx`.

Summary

In this chapter, we discussed the different types of errors, including how they impact failover time. We then discussed many of the failover scenarios you may encounter with database mirroring so you will be more prepared to handle each one. Next, we covered the many failover considerations you need to prepare for in order to have a seamless failover. Finally, we emphasized the importance of proper planning and research along with knowing what support options are available to you in the event of a disaster.

Don't sit around and think you are covered just because you have certain measures in place for high availability and disaster recovery. Bad things happen; it's just a fact of life. Backups get corrupt, network connections fail, servers crash, and sometimes people just make mistakes. It's your job to correct those errors as fast as possible and have the confidence to make the right decisions during the process. Having a good understanding of what causes a failure will also help you to avoid accidental failures due to lack of knowledge. Database mirroring acts differently depending on the location and availability of each server. As long as you know the different behaviors for your database mirroring configuration, you should be able to quickly resolve any issues that may arise as well as maintain a dependable environment for your users.

Index

You Need the Companion eBook

Your purchase of this book entitles you to buy the companion PDF-version eBook for only $10. Take the weightless companion with you anywhere.

We believe this Apress title will prove so indispensable that you'll want to carry it with you everywhere, which is why we are offering the companion eBook (in PDF format) for $10 to customers who purchase this book now. Convenient and fully searchable, the PDF version of any content-rich, page-heavy Apress book makes a valuable addition to your programming library. You can easily find and copy code—or perform examples by quickly toggling between instructions and the application. Even simultaneously tackling a donut, diet soda, and complex code becomes simplified with hands-free eBooks!

Once you purchase your book, getting the $10 companion eBook is simple:

❶ Visit **www.apress.com/promo/tendollars/**.

❷ Complete a basic registration form to receive a randomly generated question about this title.

❸ Answer the question correctly in 60 seconds, and you will receive a promotional code to redeem for the $10.00 eBook.

Apress®
THE EXPERT'S VOICE™

233 Spring Street, New York, NY 10013

Offer valid through 4/10.